SOUVENIRS: THE MATERIAL CULTURE OF TOURISM

Souvenirs: The Material Culture of Tourism

Edited by
MICHAEL HITCHCOCK
KEN TEAGUE

ASHGATE

© Michael Hitchcock and Ken Teague 2000

Published by
Ashgate Publishing Ltd
Gower House
Croft Road
Aldershot
Hants GU11 3HR
England

Ashgate Publishing Company
Suite 420
101 Cherry Street
Burlington, VT 05401-4405
USA

Ashgate website: http://www.ashgate.com

British Library Cataloguing in Publication Data
Souvenirs : the material culture of tourism. - (University
    of North London voices in development management)
    1. Souvenirs (Keepsakes) 2. Tourist trade - Social aspects
    3. Material culture 4. Tourist trade and art
    I. Hitchcock, Michael II. Teague, Ken
    306.4'89

Library of Congress Control Number: 00-132794

ISBN 0 7546 1055 1

Reprinted 2004

Printed in Great Britain by Biddles Limited, King's Lynn.

Contents

List of Figures

Foreword

NELSON H. H. GRABURN

Souvenirs, broadly conceived, are generally thought to be the material counterpart of travels, events, relationships and memories of all kinds. The material items classed as souvenirs discussed in this book have memorial functions, usually connected with the owner's travels. But not all of the items are souvenirs of tourism; they are also souvenirs of *other past* phenomena, such as political events (Suffragettes, chapter 7), colonial history (India), former artistic pre-eminence (Awaji Ningyo puppetry, chapter 12), or former ways of life (South American ceramic archaisms (chapter 15), New Guinea story boards (chapter 16), contemporary Ainu crafts (chapter 11)).

The authors do not necessarily focus on material souvenirs in their memorial function as *souvenirs*, i.e. prompters of memory. They also use their case studies as starting points for the discussion of many interesting *contemporary* phenomena, such as cottage industries for economic development (Mexico, Kyrgyz, Ainu), as devices to invigorate or maintain artistic practices (Inuit art, Kente cloth), as emblems of cultural nonconformity (Surrealists), or as symbolic weapons in national and international political arguments (the Swedish horse, chapter 19). Indeed, many of these phenomena have multiple functions.

A key focus of many of these chapters, indeed of any discussion of souvenirs, is the question of *meaning*: *what* is the meaning of any particular souvenir or collection, and *for whom* does it bear that meaning? Many of the chapters are not snapshots in time but tell us about souvenirs over longer or shorter periods of history (Santiago, Turkey, Nepal). Cohen (1999) shows in detail how souvenirs from the mountains and plains of rural Thailand have changed their forms in response to commercialization. In the temporally extended cases in this volume, not only may the material forms of the souvenirs change but, more importantly, the ownership of the objects changes, and hence their meanings too. From these historical cases we can see that souvenirs whose function is to store or stimulate memories must represent different memories to different people over time. Indeed, the meanings of any object may be cumulative and multiple.

For the individual owner, the importance of a souvenir is the memorial link with some occasion, usually an occasion centring on a person or place. The meaning of a souvenir object may be more than just its souvenir function. The owner may value it for some other reason, e.g. home decor, monetary value, or class or status marker. Thus souvenirs are not just specific objects *per se*, but are material items with a relationship to someone or something else, usually in the past. That is to say, they have a memorial meaning or, from the manufacturer's or seller's point of view, are intended to function by having that kind of meaning for the acquirer or purchaser. The variety of the case studies illustrate that the production of souvenirs is not only subject to limitations of size and weight, but to the expectations that travellers have about the salient characteristics of the place or people visited (Bunn on Kyrgyz; Graburn, 1976; Teague on Nepal; Thurner, 1997; Wilkinson on Ainu). Much of this is wrapped up in the concept of 'authenticity' (MacCannell, 1976; Horner, 1994) as discussed in this book by Hitchcock (Introduction) and in many of the case studies. Many of these studies show that the tourist public's understanding of the people they visit is subject to stereotyping and therefore souvenirs consist of condensed or simplified visions of their lives (Lombok women's pottery, New Guinea storyboards), and especially the one play performed over and over by the Awaji Ningyo puppeteers in Japan. Paula Ben-Amos (1977) has demonstrated how these tourist arts must be simplified to their basic or stereotypic forms in order to have meaning for foreigners just as pidgin languages are simple mechanisms of communication between people who do not speak each other's languages.

A further set of critical factors in the nature of souvenirs involves the culture and expectations of the tourists or collectors. Matters of class, gender and taste (Lee, 1998) are central to the discussions of Blackpool pottery souvenirs, Nepali crafts and Kente cloth. In addition, the religion and other subcultural characteristics are crucial for pilgrims to Santiago (Houlihan, chapter 2; Frey, 1998), or artistic specialists such as Philla Davis (West, chapter 9) and the Surrealists (Tythacott, chapter 6). In general it has been suggested that the more educated or more status-conscious the traveller, the more they are concerned that their souvenirs are 'authentic' by the standards that have authority in their home country (Cohen, 1988). Also, the people who make the souvenirs understand this and have a stake in presenting themselves as ethnically distinctive; thus there is often a *collusion*, willing or otherwise, between the Native peoples and the collectors to practice a kind of 'ethnic cleansing' in upholding an image of 'traditional purity', as in the avoidance of imported materials in Inuit-Aleut objects in Scottish museums (cf. Graburn,

1996), or the strict portrayal of non-modernity in Sepik storyboards, or even in the so-called 'traditional' clothing of waiters in Indian exhibition pavilions and restaurants. One common theme in many of these cases is that souvenirs, such as those being made in India, Nepal and Kyrgyzstan, are made to look ancient, and others, particularly ceramics from South and Central America, are copies of prehistoric, i.e. archaeological, forms. In the latter case, such arts appear 'pre-Columbian', hence really authentic and rare, and are no longer legally allowed out of their countries of origin; a similar story is told by Bankes where pre-modern artifacts are also banned from export, and thus may be sold at high prices from the back rooms of shops or, more likely, faked but sold to the tourists as rare traditional objects.

Stanley, in discussing South Pacific island souvenirs, makes the important observation that 'Dealers and auction houses turn private souvenirs into public exhibitions'. This reminds us that the complex meanings of souvenirs have to include a consideration of whether their meanings rest in the mind of a particular individual or small primary group (*private*) or are shared by a defined cultural group (*public*). Many of the case studies describe the passage of the souvenir out of the hands of the original collector or purchaser; for them the object had meanings that must have included the occasion, particularly the place and the personnel involved in the transaction, within, for instance, a trip to a resort town (Mars and Mars on Blackpool, chapter 8), a foreign tour or pilgrimage (Scarce on Turkey; Houlihan on Santiago), or a collecting expedition (Crozier on Inuit artifacts, chapter 5). Though the 'meanings' of souvenir objects may be culturally shared and subject to authoritative assertion – e.g. is it an 'authentic' example of the art of X or the history of Y? – more personal and possibly dominant meanings are always attached too. Horner (1994) has analysed how 'personally negotiated authenticities' are additional meanings created by individual tourists, out of their particular travel experiences in relation to their personal backgrounds. However, as Stanley suggests, when the object passes into the hands of others, its meaning or set of meanings changes.

If an object is inherited or given to a friend or relative, its private meaning for the recipient would again include the occasion, particularly the person and the place involved in the transaction, perhaps as a material memento for a deceased relative or friend, or an heirloom. A traveller may acquire souvenirs (or take photographs) to keep back at home as mementos of their journey or some private aspect of it; they may of course be displayed in the home to inform others of their travels or as mnemonic devices around which to tell stories. Mars and Mars make the point that many souvenirs are also purchased as gifts, and that is a second function: they acquire something specifically to give away later to a friend or relative. Of course, *all gifts* are souvenirs in the sense that they remind the recipient of the donor (and the occasion) and that is the purpose of many gifts, but the souvenir-gift related to travel is also a near universal category. Travelling Japanese, for instance, always buy gifts *omiyage,* objects typical of the area visited, for specific acquaintances and kin left at home, in exchange for the *senbetsu,* the parting gifts of (money, travel equipment, camera, etc.) that they received (Befu, 1977; Graburn, 1987). Thus *omiyage* carry strong meanings maintaining relational bonds during and after the trip.

Many of the case studies are concerned with the passage of objects from personal to institutional possession, particularly to museums, and related to them, exhibitions and commercial displays. We can learn a lot about materials and changing meanings from these instances. The problems of the late Philla Davis's collection of baskets and textiles are most illuminating, because the recipients were not personal heirs but were the museum curators. They did not receive any 'stories' along with the objects, indeed they did not usually know whether she had purchased them from their makers in foreign countries or from junk shops in the UK. Hence they did not know what story to attach in creating their new public souvenir function. For the museum-going public who did not know Ms Davis personally, were the objects to carry the memory of a relatively unknown British eccentric, of her travels in various parts of the world in the mid-twentieth century, or of crafts techniques and peoples which may now be rare or extinct? As Levell (chapter 4) points out in her chapter on India 'A souvenir is predicated on the tale that can be told'. And in his chapter on Nepal, he shows that tourist souvenirs which 'lack documentation', i.e. without an accompanying tale, lose their 'educational value' presumably because we cannot be sure of the authenticity of any story that is exhibited with them.

The institutional possession of formerly private souvenir possessions illustrates the creation of public culture. Museum curators, writers and exhibition designers are all concerned with promulgating sets of meanings which will enter in the general accepted culture of the public. There are many examples in our case studies. Exhibitions of colonial India taught the British at home an 'Oriental version' of what India was and how it was ruled. The Inuit-Aleut crafts in Scottish museums tell us of the great ages and prowess of Scottish explorers, as well as about the earlier cultures of the Natives of the American North. The unusual purchases, usually not souvenirs, of the artists in the Surrealist movement give us a good example of how collections of the banal debris of the lives of others can become famous and valuable in the hands of perceptive and well-connected people. Similarly, Mars and Mars wonder if the Blackpool *kitsch* which they describe will turn into 'valuable antiques' and, as they cite Thompson's *Rubbish Theory* (1979) which explains such transformations, they should know that their scholarly chapter will aid the process!

The publicly shared material souvenirs of memories and history take us into another realm. As MacCannell (1976) has shown, the relationship between private souvenirs collected by individuals and publicly approved tourist *sights* 'collected' by entire societies, the transformation of private markers of experience into publicly accepted memorials, illustrates a parallel process. In this process, illustrated by some of our case studies (e.g. Houlihan, Teague on India, Crozier, Bradley (chapter 7), Dougoud (chapter 16) and Hanefors and Selwyn), public meanings are created which circulate in textual and media forms, subject to manipulation for chauvinist and political purposes. Indeed, the creation of *public* memorabilia or *lieux de memoire* (Nora, 1983) out of private souvenirs eliminates experiential memory and replaces it with an ideological narrative. This would lead us away from the more personal topic of souvenirs into the broader subject of public memory, monuments and the creation of heritage.

References

Befu, H. (1977), 'Social exchange', *Annual Review of Anthropology*, 6, pp. 255–81.

Ben-Amos, P. (1977), 'Pidgin languages and tourist arts', *Studies in Visual Communication*, 4 (2), pp. 128–39.

Cohen, E. (1988), 'Authenticity and commoditization in tourism', *Annals of Tourism Research*, 15, pp. 370–86.

Cohen, E. (1999), *The Commercialized Arts of Thailand*, London: Curzon Press.

Frey, N.L. (1998), *Pilgrim Stories: On and Off the Road to Santiago*, Berkeley: University of California Press.

Graburn, N.H.H. (1987), 'Material Symbols in Japanese Domestic Tourism', in D. Ingersoll and G. Bronistky (eds), *Mirror and Metaphor: Material and Social Constructions of Reality*, Lanham, Maryland: University Press of America.

Graburn, N.H.H. (1996) 'Introduction', in N. Graburn, M. Lee and J-L. Rousselot (eds), *Catalogue Raisonne of the Alaska Commercial Company: Phoebe Hearst Museum of Anthropology*, Berkeley: University of California Press.

Horner, A.E. (1994), 'Personally Negotiated Authenticities', paper presented at the Conference 'New Directions in Tourism Research', National Museum of Ethnology: Osaka.

Lee, M.C. (1998), 'Tourists and Taste Cultures: Collecting Native Art in Alaska at the Turn of the Twentieth Century', in R.P. Phillips and C. Steiner (eds), *Unpacking Culture: Art and*

Commodity in the Colonial and Postcolonial Worlds, Berkeley: University of California Press.

MacCannell, D. (1976), *The Tourist: a New Theory of the Leisure Class*, New York: Schocken (3rd edn, 1999, Berkeley: University of California Press).

Nora, P. (1983), *Les Lieux de Memoire*, Paris: Gallimard.

Thompson, M. (1979), *Rubbish Theory: The Creation and Destruction of Capital*, Oxford: Oxford University Press.

Thurner, V.I. (1997), 'Kunst fur Touristen: Die Welt der Reisenden im Souvenir', *Sociologus*, (Berlin), 44 (1), pp. 1–21.

1 Introduction

MICHAEL HITCHCOCK

Souvenirs are mementos of places and occasions and, though often regarded as ephemeral, may be counted among the most valued items acquired by international tourists during a vacation (Littrell, 1990, p. 229). Items purchased on holiday are meaningful and are often more than simple mementos of time and place. Souvenirs acquired during a holiday are associated with the travel experience, but are also linked to a generalized image of a culture, or even a specific town or village. Many tourists read around the subject to find out more about their purchases, and some become specialist collectors and experts. Specialist tours involving handicrafts form a small but increasingly important niche market. Other tourists are oriented towards clothing and ready to wear jewellery as expressions of taste and identity.

The essays in this volume suggest that souvenirs, though often difficult for museums to categorize, are not simply 'messengers of the extraordinary' (Gordon, 1986). It is as significant to know what a souvenir is as to appreciate how it is perceived. It is as important to know how authenticity is constructed as it is to enquire whether or not a souvenir is genuine. Different social worlds are connected through the production, sale and purchase of souvenirs and at each point of interaction meanings and identities may be negotiated. The evolution of souvenir arts is not a simple unilinear process, either as degeneration of traditional art form on one hand or as transformation to a modern art on the other (Cohen, 1993a, p. 2).

Historically, handicrafts satisfied the functional and ceremonial needs of societies that were not closely integrated into market economies. Improved transportation and distribution systems have enabled mass produced goods to penetrate these societies. Changes in buying patterns have lead to a loss of income among craftsmen and women in the developing world, and economic necessity has forced many of them to search for alternative markets (Popelka and Littrell, 1991, p. 393). Tourism is clearly important in this context since the developing world's share of receipts from tourism may be as high as 26 per cent (Sinclair and Asrat, 1990, p. 496). There are, however, difficulties associated with modifying traditional goods and developing new ones for customers such as tourists. Producers understand the needs and preferences

1

of their own societies, but these criteria cannot invariably be applied to customers from other cultures (Graburn, 1982).

The body of literature concerning souvenirs is diverse and it would be reasonable to suggest that all the major disciplines in the humanities and social science have at some point considered this topic. An overarching cross-disciplinary analysis, though undoubtedly worthwhile, lies beyond the confines of this volume and it is the intention of this chapter to concentrate on the related subject fields of sociology, anthropology and museum ethnography. Even within these cognate disciplines discussions concerning souvenirs are highly eclectic, but what is significant about this volume is that many of the papers take as their starting point the edited volume entitled *Ethnic and Tourist Arts* (Graburn, 1976). Before the appearance of this volume many commentators tended to disparage the study of tourist arts as a legitimate field of anthropological and sociological investigation (Cohen, 1993a, p. 1). The publication of Graburn's book marks the start of more objective and substantive research as is confirmed by the growing number of books and articles devoted to this field of enquiry.

Given the orientation of much of this volume, the purpose of this introduction is to help contextualize Graburn's own work and the papers that engage with him. In a chapter which appears in the Ashgate volume that precedes this one, *Building on Batik*, Graburn provides some observations that can serve as a opening for this collection of papers. Drawing on his work among the Inuit, he describes how the indigenous people of the Canadian and American Arctic were drawn into the world system as trappers; only later did tourism become important. They produce souvenirs to satisfy the following quite different demands. First, they provide buyers with attractive arts and crafts. Second, they strive to control the outside world's image of themselves. Third, they aim to be commercially viable in an increasingly competitive world. Running through these observations are a number of related questions which, for the sake of convenience, can be divided into four themes that help to orientate this book: authenticity, identity, consumption and commodification, and development.

Authenticity

Souvenirs are signs of the tourist's travels and are thus often taken as tangible proof of where he or she has been. In these contexts it is perhaps not surprising that many of questions that have been asked about souvenirs should concern authenticity. Some authors take as a starting point a paper by Dean MacCannell which attracted attention when it was published in 1973. The article was later developed into a much cited book, *The Tourist: A New Theory of the Leisure Class* (1976). These publications may partly be understood as a reaction to Boorstin's (1964) cautionary perspective that just as the mass media create and maintain celebrities for mass consumption, tourism provides pseudo events and inauthentic attractions and destinations for credulous consumers. MacCannell agrees with Boorstin concerning the pervasive inauthenticity of contemporary life and attendant alienation, but disagrees with regard to the motives of the tourist in this context. In contrast MacCannell argues that the tourist is in search of the authentic, but is forced to seek it in other times and places, in a manner that resembles the pre-modern quest for the sacred. Thus the tourist may be characterized as a kind of pilgrim paying his respects to the numerous attractions of the secular world. The tourist industry, according to MacCannell, impedes this sacred quest by creating a tourist space from which there is no escape.

The sacred journey idea was developed further by Nelson Graburn who argues that tourism comprised 'structurally necessary' ritual breaks to the routine that characterizes ordinary experience (1977). Tourism functions outside ordinary time as the secular equivalent of religion. Leaving behind the mundane, the tourist passes through a series of rites of passage, crossing the threshold of the sacred, eventually returning home anew. The journey may be likened to the spiritual death and rebirth that characterizes baptism and pilgrimage. The related perspectives of MacCannell and Graburn are not without their critics, not least of the slightly strange notions that tourism supplies the symbols which makes modern life meaningful on one hand and that tourists search for authenticity in order to engage more closely with society on the other.

Questions concerning authenticity have been the subject of a number of celebrated essays in the social sciences, not all of which directly concern tourism and souvenirs. One of the most frequently cited authors is Baudrillard, especially with regard to his writings on simulation, simulacres and Disneyland (1981). Put simply, his main thesis is that simulacra and simulations replace the real thing. Disneyland is deliberately presented as imaginary in an attempt to persuade us to accept Los Angeles and the surrounding state of America as real. This is necessary, according to Baudrillard, because the surrounding America is itself no longer real, and has instead become hyperreal. A similar stance has been adopted by Umberto Eco in a series of papers that are known as *Travels in Hyperreality* (1986). Eco advances the controversial view when referring to copies of Old Masters and reconstructions of historic scenes that the fake is so good that the consumer no longer feels the need for the original. This is essentially a critique of the American use of technology in simulation, but as Graburn has suggested, it is absurd for Eco and Baudrillard to find hyperreality only in the USA when their countries of origin are replete with substantial and realistic images of religious and mythological origin – just like Disney.

It is not the intention here to document the cut and thrust of this debate, but to draw attention to the what light these perspectives may shed upon the study of souvenirs. In order to illustrate how best to proceed, it is useful to make two opening remarks. First, souvenirs are intimately connected with the idea of pilgrimage and this applies as much to Western religions such as Christianity as to eastern ones such as Buddhism (see Teague, 1997, p. 183). As the chapters by Houlihan and Scarce show, pilgrimage and tourism in the late twentieth century can easily coexist alongside one another. Second, the tourism industry does provide consumables such as souvenirs, but whether or not gullible tourists assume that they are authentic remains a moot point. Souvenirs are mementos of the out of ordinary experience of the holiday and as such may be likened to holiday photographs, but they are also a great deal more besides.

In the absence of sustained and comparative research on an international scale the response of tourists to souvenirs is difficult to gauge accurately, though some recurring themes may be identified. Littrell, Anderson and Brown, for example, argue that authenticity is usually defined by the tourists who often places emphasis on the handmade, particularly with regard to quality and the time invested in its manufacture (1993, p. 205). These purchases not only evoke memories of the special people encountered on a holiday, but may also be considered to be objects that stand as generalized symbols of the developing world. For one of Littrell's respondents study, the souvenir was not so much valued for its authenticity, but because of its strong empathetic response to the artisan as a representative of the poorer people of the world (1990, p. 238). A similar theme is addressed by Graburn, who argues that many tourist arts depend for their appeal of a definable ethnicity, an expression of the perceived cultural difference between the tourist and the person living in the tourist destination, the touree (1987, p. 396).

As Dougoud argues in this volume, what many tourists appear to be seeking in New Guinea is a set of qualities that correspond to their idea of a traditional primitive life. Tourists seem to ignore evidence of encounters with modernity, but tourees know this and thus make their objects more authentically primitive, according to the codes of this interaction, in order to convey these messages. The resuscitation of ancient crafts, particularly around important archaeological sites, is also a feature of souvenir production. The artisans may have little historical connection with the ancient culture which produced the prototypes that they copy. The goods that they learn to produce are often sold as antiques and, indeed, 'antiquing' has become a style of manufacture (Cohen, 1993a, p. 3).

The authenticity of the artefact is linked by purchasers to the perceived authenticity of the experience. The purchase of the souvenir, as is noted by Evans, often represents the only interaction between the tourist and the touree beyond the confines of the hospitality industry.

The person with whom the tourist interacts in the marketplace is often assumed to have a close cultural link to the items being sold, but this is not necessarily the case. Souvenirs move along the hub and spoke distribution systems of market economies and may involve quite different producers and retailers. Goods drawn from the length and breadth of the vast Indonesian archipelago may, for example, be purchased in Kuta Beach, Bali, often without any information whence they came. Production may also be delegated to a client group such as the Zapotec/Mixtec who work in the style of the Dineh (Navaho). Sometimes ethnic groups become so closely associated with particular kinds of goods and services that others cash in on their reputation. Much of the trade in Sumba textiles has little to do with the island of that name and originates in factories in Java where cheap copies are mass produced.

Deirdre Evans Pritchard adds, moreover, that the items bought by tourists are often judged by the yardstick of what is in museums or private collections (1989). This is a problematic issue as far as this volume is concerned since many items of great aesthetic and ethnographic value in Western museums were originally collected as souvenirs. It is not only the tourists who orientate themselves by museum collections, but also many producers. As Wilkinson notes, museum objects are used by many Ainu as points of reference and other indigenous peoples elsewhere doubtless do the same. As the contributors to this volume acknowledge, the existence of such objects in museums is problematic. Within many museums no sharp line is drawn between archaeology and anthropology, and many place material from contemporary cultures in what is now referred to as the 'developing world' alongside ancient cultures. Many of these artefacts were collected by travellers and tourists and have at least a partial history as souvenirs. Some are nothing but souvenirs.

Fascination with ancient artefacts and curios of the kind seen in museums and historic sites is stimulated by emotional responses to the past and the attendant social attitudes (Evans Pritchard, 1993, p. 14). The relationship between tourism and the collection of antiquities is not solely a twentieth century phenomenon. Marketing the past has long been well established in tourism, especially with regard to the Grand Tour. The authenticity of religious relics came under attack in the seventeenth and eighteenth centuries in Europe, and the void was filled by a demand for antiquities (ibid., p. 15). The collection of arts and curiosities is not simply a Western phenomenon, but the pervasive attitudes towards the past that influence modern tourism have European and American origins. The commodification of the past through the antiquities market for tourists and collectors has helped to shape the growing heritage industry (Cohen, 1993, p. 6).

Identity

Tourism does not invariably bring different peoples into contact with one another, though it is often assumed that tourists are attracted to exotically different societies (Wood, 1997, p. 19). The idea that tourism does do this remains, however, a dominant feature of the modern global industry. Many tourists, even when visiting a foreign land, may not stray much beyond the boundaries of the hospitality sector, but if they do so, it may often be in context of buying souvenirs. There is also a demand within global tourism for access to what are perceived as ethnically distinct cultures which van den Berghe has characterized as the 'search for the other', the quest for the 'ethnically exotic, in as untouched, pristine, authentic form' as can be found (1994, p. 8). Destination activities for tourists interested in these kinds of cultural attractions may include '... visits to native homes and villages, observation of dances and ceremonies, shopping for primitive wares and curios ...'(Smith, 1989, p. 4). For some this may be the main purpose of the holiday, whereas for others it comprises a minor part of a wider itinerary.

In his two major works MacCannell argues that modern tourists commonly assume that the 'Other' of the holiday destination belongs to a world which is in many ways more complete, structured and real than the one lived in by the tourist for the remainder of the year. The ethnic attributes, of what are often pre-modern 'Others', are preserved and maintained for entertainment within what MacCannell claims is a White cultural frame; lacking specificity, the message is diffuse (1992, p. 168). These new reconstructed forms appear almost automatically as these groups enter into global commercial transactions (ibid.). These global-local articulations of ethnicity may be seen as forms of rhetoric, as symbolic expressions of exchange values. This is not simply a division along ethnic lines, but an intersection of different value systems, an attempt to universalize the Western sense of exchange value (ibid., pp. 168–9). In a similar manner, Gabriel argues that the packaging of identity in the Third World resembles the way heritage is commercialized in the West (1994, p. 148).

MacCannell's thesis has been subjected to various kinds of critical scrutiny, two of which are relevant to this discussion. First, Cohen (1988) objects to the view that there is such a person as the tourist and remains unconvinced that all tourists seek mythological structures, arguing that there are many kinds of tourists, some of whom are seeking no more than mere relaxation. Second, Cohen, Crick (1989, p. 333) and others have cast doubt upon the notion that tourists seek authenticity, pointing out that this perspective is based on a series of outdated assumptions about alienation. Despite these reservations, MacCannell's views about the intersection of different exchange values and the appearance of reconstructed markers of identity are helpful when considering the material culture of tourism.

The World of Goods draws attention to the metaphorical use of goods as indicators of cultural categories (Douglas and Isherwood, 1979). As part of the information system, material culture helps to make and maintain social relationships. Those who understand the codes of the information system share agreed values concerning goods as category markers. Goods are particularly sought after if there is ambiguity in the social hierarchy (Miller, 1987, p. 136). Through the acquisition and display of goods associated with higher status, low ranking people strive to emulate those above them. Fashion is part of a rapidly changing information system and may include and exclude on the basis of knowledge and understanding. More recent studies discuss the consumption of 'tourist myths' (Selwyn, 1996) and the transcendent and identity related experiences of shopping (Miller, 1998).

These themes emerge at various points throughout this volume, and it is the intention here to highlight a few examples. Crozier, for example, discusses individualized souvenirs, especially those made directly for purchasers, whereas Tythacott explores the aesthetic preferences and personalities behind the creation of cabinets of curiosities. Implicit in West's account of Philla Davis' travels and collections is the idea that identity may be in some ways created and mediated with the aid of souvenirs. Philla Davis' motorbike, festooned with the tools of her trade, conjures up an image of an adventurous and self-reliant woman, whose social capital was enhanced through travel. Mars and Mars focus on the symbolic qualities of gifts bought for people in different kinds of relationships with the purchasers. Their rich ethnography of the material culture of the Wake's Week holiday maker reveals much about the inter-connectedness of identities in working class Lancashire. Souvenirs reveal as much about who one is as with whom one wishes to be identified, as is particularly the case with political memorabilia. Historians, like tourists, may seek out objects because of their associations, often eschewing the material culture associated with unpopular causes. Thus, as Bradley notes, successful movements such as the Suffragettes are over-represented in the material record.

The Suffragette souvenirs may be regarded as a forerunner of what has become known in the international crafts trade as the 'solidarity market'. These goods are sold cheaply for charity as symbols of association to promote various causes. The purchaser does not necessarily have high expectations and may not even like the product: quality is secondary, it is the message that counts. Solidarity souvenirs arrive on the international market from time to time, some of the most striking being from Mexico. Dolls in Indian dress wearing sinister masks and bandoliers appeared during the Chiapas insurgency of the mid-1990s, though it remained unclear whether the profits from their sale went to *Zapatanista* causes. Assertions of indigenous identity, though often denigrated by elites, may paradoxically stimulate the interest of tourists.

The *Kente* cloths described by Grieco may also be partly understood in terms of solidarity. Adopted by Black Americans as generalized symbols of African pride and affinity, textiles from Ghana are traded in both the tourist and international craft markets. In *Building on Batik* Graburn likens *Kente* to other kinds of what he refers to as 'pride' cloths, such as batik cloth from Indonesia, Maori cloaks, Fijian *tapa* and Navaho blankets. Similar observations may be made to the storyboards of Papua New Guinea discussed by Dougoud in this volume. Likewise, Butler has drawn attention to the reinterpretation of Scotland's identity with regard to tartan, tourism and national consciousness.

Souvenirs and national emblems have similar properties, but as is indicated by a chapter in *The Invention of Tradition* (Morgan, 1983), they may become entangled almost accidentally. In that paper the author argues that visitors to Wales, who often recorded their impressions of the upland peasantry, were struck by the cloaks and high crowned hats worn by Welsh women. It would appear that what had been fashionable in lowland England in the 1620s had survived among the poor in Wales. The Welsh woman's attire, though not in any sense a national costume, had by the 1830s been turned into a caricature of Wales, becoming part of the illusion of Welshness reproduced on Victorian postcards and dolls (Morgan, 1983, pp. 79–85). The processes by which a local folk art may become a national iconic souvenir are documented in this volume by Hanefors and Selwyn with regard to the Dalecarlian horse of Sweden. Adding an unusual twist, however, the authors show how the globally overexposed Swedish tourist has come to eschew souvenirs of other cultures in favour of more home-grown fare like the horse.

Consumption and Commodification

The production and consumption of souvenirs involves a pattern of exchange that intersects diverse groups of producers and consumers. These transactions often involve middlemen as interpreters, ranging from street hawkers to sophisticated gallery owners. The discourse between the purchaser and vendor provides opportunities to negotiate the meanings associated with the souvenir. As Shenhav-Keller argues, Jewish tourists visiting Israel often come with a set of expectations reflecting individual concerns about identity (1995, p. 152). The way tourists respond to souvenirs is partly dependent on their reaction to specific symbolic codes. The Jewish tourist does not simply buy souvenirs as evidence of travel, but as a component of the construction of identity (ibid., p. 149).

Shops selling souvenirs are a vital ingredient in the social creation of reality and may be organized in particular ways that enhance the authenticity of the goods being sold (ibid., p. 146). The sale of souvenirs also takes place in special zones and, following Berger, it is useful to consider Goffman's celebrated distinction between 'backstage' and 'frontstage'. Tourists may be permitted to pass beyond the front region and visit the society that allegedly lies behind, though a firm distinction cannot always be readily drawn between these areas since there are, what Maccannell (1976, p. 95) has called, 'false fronts'.[1] When the staging becomes too obvious, the attraction becomes less authentic (Brown, 1996, p. 37).

Another frequently cited perspective is Graburn's contention that goods destined for tourists may be regarded as those which are 'outwardly' directed, in contrast to those used that are 'inwardly' directed and are retained for traditional purposes (1976, pp. 4–5). In some contexts, especially where there is a long experience of international trade, it may be difficult to distinguish between a 'touristic' and 'traditional' artefact. Goods are often made for a domestic artefact in which tourists may share a similar background to the makers. Attitudes to goods may change over time and, as Hill (Hitchcock et al., 1993, p. 11), has shown that goods made for tourists in one period may be appreciated by the culture that made them in another. There are, for instance, examples of Balinese *kris* from the early days of tourism being valued on account of the quality of workmanship invested in their production. It may be useful to regard Graburn's distinction as a kind of continuum which is more sharply marked in the developing world where the backgrounds of producers and consumers differ markedly.

The tension between material culture as either a commodity or sacred artefact is a recurring theme. Several authors in this volume (e.g. Punnett, Wilkinson) liken the debates about material culture to those concerning the performing arts, and it is useful at this juncture to consider briefly one of the most widely cited analyses on the adverse impacts of commodification on traditional festivals. Under the alarming title 'Culture by the Pound', Greenwood describes how the Alarde festival of the Basque town of Fuenterrabia in Spain, a potent symbol of local identity and community, became severely compromised when the municipal authorities attempted to make the celebration more accessible to tourists by holding two performances on the same day. This policy was never fully implemented, but the impact was catastrophic, and what '... was a vital and exciting ritual became an obligation to be avoided' (Greenwood, 1977, p. 135). Greenwood's bleak conclusion is that tourism turns culture into a commodity, which is then packaged for tourists and '... made meaningless to the people who once believed in it' (ibid., p. 131).

Greenwood's paper, however, suffers from being a 'one-off', a snapshot of a particular point in time, which has become fixed in the literature, neither confirmed nor balanced by additional research (Wilson, 1993, pp. 36–7). Young's re-examination of this paper, under Wilson's supervision, indicates that the festival, instead of being an onerous duty, remains a vibrant and exciting ritual. The government at the time of Greenwood's study was seen as a corrupt and undemocratic Spanish bureaucracy with little interest in Basque culture and thus tourism *per se* had little do with the festival's apparent decline (ibid., 37). The festival, moreover, owes its ongoing vitality to its association with Basque identity, which Greenwood appears to acknowledge in an epilogue to the re-republication of his paper (1989, p. 181).

Debates about tradition versus modernity, however, have been around a long time and what many authors in this volume suggest is that it is not particularly helpful in the case of souvenirs to argue that one necessarily negates the other. 'Traditional' artefacts are continuing to be turned into commodities and new designs go on being created to satisfy new markets. Not only are the designs affected by these changes, but so are the social relations of production. Occupational roles associated with a particular gender, for example, may be disrupted during the process of commodification.

The sheer diversity of the audience rules out a single set of aesthetics based on universal standards, though some trends are noted in this volume. In New Guinea, for example, stroryboards have undergone conceptual changes and have become more narrative. New elements, often to do with daily life, are introduced to make the storyboards more accessible by reducing the need for previous knowledge and thereby bridging the cultural gap. Purchasers of souvenirs are often able to identify standardized styles and genres, such as idyllic landscapes and picturesque representations of indigenous peoples. By working within these widely accepted genres, the makers of souvenirs modify their work, often adopting a set of symbols that are assumed to be meaningful to tourists. Benin ebony carvers in West Africa distinguish between commercial works, such as European articles like salad bowls and Fulani girls' heads, which are turned out quickly for sale, and 'traditional' carvings of Obas, chiefs and warriors, which they value most (Ben-Amos, 1976, pp. 326–7). Souvenirs are, therefore, not characterized by the holistic system of signs that is often a feature of 'inwardly' directed goods.

Commodification transforms the original meaning of an object and its attendant symbolic codes. In order to identify specific genres and interpret what are perceived to be artistic codes, the purchaser must understand the some of the intentions of the producer. The exchange is often characterized by ambiguity, since the maker's original intentions and the buyer's response often diverge. These rules are perceived by those involved in the artistic exchange, though the rules operate at many levels and are often modified and broken. Souvenirs do not comprise a unified set of objects and cultural meanings, though they often hint at the experience sought by tourists.

Development

Tourism as one of the forces of globalization undoubtedly contributes to this process of cultural adaptation and many authors grapple with the apparent contradiction of the need to earn income on one hand and the desire to protect the dignity of traditional cultures on the other. Of concern here is the evolution of a division of labour which connects ever increasing circles of people in commodity production and exchange (Hart, 1982, p. 38). Craft tours can also take tourism to areas that want the revenue from visitors but are not directly linked to international tourism. Poor areas also have to face stark choices concerning employment, but Crippen notes in *Building on Batik* the value of handicrafts in raising self esteem among rural women in India. In Chiang Mai in Thailand a weaving career may provide an alternative to employment in sex tourism.

The production of souvenirs in the lesser developed countries often involves changes in the social relations of production, particularly with regard to the use of standardized components and mass production methods. As is noted by Bunn an attendant feature of productive change is the introduction of new materials leading to a kind of mix and match approach to the creation of souvenirs. The changes may boost output, but are often accompanied by a reduction in skill. The Hmong of North Thailand, for example make crossbows for tourists of questionable quality, but since they will rarely be fired this is less important than the cheap sales price arising from high productivity. Output may be raised, but because so many shops sell the same product, the individual maker has to operate on slim profit margins (Cooper ,1984). Teague, however, take a different view with regard to his research in Nepal where there is a long established souvenir craft industry which grew out of the even older pilgrim trade. He argues that, although producers specialize in order to speed up production, all the craftsmen possess a range of skills; generalist skills have not been discarded.

What is significant about these developmental processes is that newer methods do not invariably oust older ones. Production methods may remain virtually unaltered while the products themselves undergo extensive diversification (Cohen, 1993a, p. 2). The reasons are not clear cut and may be linked to the presentation of crafts within the context of tourism. Access to 'backstage' production areas, in which emphasis is often placed on the 'traditional' qualities of the goods being made is an important factor. Tourists also value the opportunity to try out unfamiliar skills and technologies for themselves, and there is growing educational element in the holiday experience. In Yogyakarta in Java, for example, one can not only purchase batik and see how it is made, but can also learn how to make it for one's self on locally organized courses. Outside the specialist tours, however, one should not overestimate the importance of handicrafts. Souvenirs alone do not necessarily act as a draw, though they may contribute to the generalized image of a destination.

Another point to consider is the cost effectiveness of the basic technology. Tourism is often seasonal and overheads have to be kept low by using inexpensive tools and machines that can be brought into use rapidly as and when required. The value added is thus linked to the skill of the maker and, unless the product can command a high value in the marketplace, the margins may be minimal. It remains uncertain, however, whether or not tourists are prepared to pay well for quality products with which they are unfamiliar. The development of an international craft market, which often depends on the trade and transport facilities provided by tourism, renders the label 'tourist art' inadequate. Handicrafts of the kind found on roadside stalls in Bali are, for example, readily available in shops and markets in Europe and North America. Crafts serve both the tourist and export markets and it remains unclear whether or not the availability of similar crafts in the tourists' home countries will deter spending during the vacation.

Souvenirs, though often based on traditional art forms, are often miniaturized to suit the needs of long distance, especially airborne, travellers. Sometimes a similar purpose is served by substituting lightweight materials for heavier traditional ones. But there is also a counter trend to what Cohen refers to as 'gigantism' in which ordinary-sized functional items (e.g. combs, spoons, knives) are enlarged (Bascom, 1976, p. 314; Cohen, 1993a, p. 5). These items might otherwise be insufficiently attractive in their normal state to spark the interest of potential customers and 'gigantism' might be regarded as a crude kind of value-added.

Grieco stresses the importance of the Internet in stimulating demand, raising consciousness and avoiding export bottlenecks. The Internet provides a wide range of services for craftspeople and enhances customized production. Consumer protection laws are a potential hazard with regard to the marketing crafts, since purchasers used to consuming industrial products often expect standardized goods. Standardization can, however, pose shipment problems, since transporters in the developing world often take advantage of the diversity of sizes to slot goods into one another to save space. According to Wilkinson, the interpretation of crafts that are not likely to be well understood by visitors should also include videos, well trained guides and informative guidebooks.

A common problem with the use of handicrafts in tourism and international trade is product recognition. Many aesthetically satisfying traditional goods are simply too plain to arose the interest of tourists. Surface decoration may be applied to please the customer and add provenance, as well as raise the value-added. These changes may affect the social relations of production, particularly with regard to gender, as is noted by Herald (personal communication) with regard to Lombok. Traditionally, women are the potters on this Indonesian island, but it is the men who add the decorative flourishes, thereby becoming 'artists'. A similar kind of transformation is reported by Bankes in Peru, where the producers of pots for tourists sign upmarket vessels, but leave cheaper versions unsigned. Peoples remote from markets may also produce a product that is given a finish by another group that has greater access to the needs of customers. Sometimes these 'finishers' are members of the urban majority population (ibid., p. 2).

The process of adapting goods to suit the tastes of tourists is highly variable and products do not necessarily change along identical lines. The new designs may be unrelated to the culture of the producers, but sometimes traditionalist and even archaic trends emerge. In order to enhance product recognition and overcome the ignorance of purchasers, traditional abstract styles may be replaced by more naturalistic ones. The opposite can also occur as producers move towards more abstraction, sometimes imitating modern Western styles (Cohen, 1993a, p. 5). Contrary trends may also be present within the same culture.

The highest value-added is often associated with the self-sustaining and economically successful arts that are sometimes called para-tourist arts (Wollen, 1993). These arts become established in areas that have a great appeal to international tourists, particularly if associated with a well publicized and widely acknowledged ancient heritage. Of particular relevance in this context was the role of colonial 'animateurs' in developing craft production for external markets in West Africa in the interwar years (Horner, 1993; Cohen, 1993a). A great deal has also been written about the aesthetic legacy of Western artists in the Dutch East Indies colony of Bali in the same period. After the bloody campaigns of 1906–8 and the subjugation of the last independent Balinese kingdoms, the Dutch introduced tourism as means of salvaging their reputation as enlightened colonists. They introduced a controversial policy known as *Balisering*, Balinization, that was designed to conserve the island's precious heritage (Picard, 1993, p. 74).

A regular steam packet service from Surabaya was introduced in 1924 and the island rapidly became a kind of elite tourist destination that proved very attractive to Western artists. Three of them – Walter Spies, Rudolf Bonnet and Miguel Covarrubias – exerted a decisive influence on Balinese arts, encouraging the production of arts for tourists in the belief that, deprived of royal sponsorship, the crafts would wither away. The Balinese who watched Spies at work, or who were supervised by Spies' friend, the Dutch artist Rudolf Bonnet, went on to develop a new style of painting that became very popular with upmarket tourists. Scenes from everyday life, new compositions and experiments with perspective were added to the existing repertoire of gods and heroes and scenes from the great epics. As is noted by Stanley in this volume, similar processes are at work at the close of the twentieth century with many aid agencies employing design consultants.

Note

1 Cohen (1989, p. 372) later discusses 'false backs'.

References

Bascom, W. (1976), 'Changing African Art', in N.H.H. Graburn (ed.), *Ethnic and Tourist Arts: Cultural Expressions from the Fourth World*, Berkeley: University of California Press.

Ben-Amos, P. (1976), '"A la recherche du temps perdu": on being an ebony carver in Benin', in N.H.H. Graburn (ed.), *Ethnic and Tourist Arts: Cultural Expressions from the Fourth World*, Berkeley: University of California Press.

Berger, B.M. (1986), 'Foreword', in E. Goffman, *Frame Analysis: An Essay on the Organization of Experience*, Boston: Northeastern University Press.

Boissevain, J. (1996), 'Introduction', *Coping With Tourists: European Reactions to Mass Tourism*, Providence: Bergham Books.

Boorstin, D.J. (1961), *The Image: a Guide to Pseudo-events in America*, New York: Harper and Row.

Brown, D. (1996) 'Genuine Fakes', in T. Selwyn (ed.), *The Tourist Image: Myths and Myth Making in Tourism*, Chichester: Wiley.

Cohen, E. (1988), 'Authenticity and commoditization in tourism', *Annals of Tourism Research* Vol. 15, pp. 370–86.

Cohen, E. (1992), 'Tourist Arts', in C.P. Cooper and A. Lockwood (eds), *Progress in Tourism, Recreation and Hospitality Management*, Vol. 4, London: Belhaven, pp. 3–32.

Cohen, E. (1993a) 'Introduction: Investigating Tourist Arts', *Annals of Tourism Research*, Vol. 20, pp. 1–8.

Cohen, E. (1993b), 'The study of touristic images of native people: mitigating the stereotype of a stereotype', in R. Butler and D. Pearce (eds), *Tourism Research: Critiques and Challenges*, London: Routledge.

Cooper, R. (1984), *Resource Scarcity and the Hmong Response: Patterns of Settlement and Economy*, Singapore: Singapore University Press.

Crick, M. (1989), 'Representations of international tourism in the social sciences: sun, sex, sights, savings, and servility', *Annual Review of Anthropology*, 18, pp. 307–44.

Douglas, M. and Isherwood, B. (1979), *The World of Goods: Towards an Anthropology of Consumption*, New York: Basic Books.

Eco, U. (1986), *Faith in Fakes: Travels in Hyperreality*, London: Minerva.

Errington, S. (1994), 'What became authentic primitive art?', *Cultural Anthropology*, 9, 2, pp. 201–26.

Esman, M.R. (1984), 'Tourism as ethnic preservation: the Cajuns of Louisiana', *Annals of Tourism Research*, Vol. 11, No. 3, pp. 451–67.

Evans Pritchard, D. (1989), 'How they see us: Native American images of tourism', *Annals of Tourism Research*, Vol. 16, No. 1, pp. 89–105.

Evans Pritchard, D. (1993) 'Ancient art in modern context', *Annals of Tourism Research*, Vol. 20, pp. 9–31.

Gabriel, J. (1994), *Racism, Culture, Markets*, London and New York: Routledge.

16 *Souvenirs: The Material Culture of Tourism*

Goffman, E. (1959), *The Presentation of Self in Everyday Life*, Garden City, New York: Doubleday.

Gordon, B. (1986), 'The souvenir: messenger of the extraordinary', *Journal of Popular Culture*, 20, pp. 135–46.

Graburn, N.H.H. (1976), 'Introduction: Arts of the Fourth World', in N.H.H. Graburn (ed.), *Ethnic and Tourist Arts: Cultural Expressions from the Fourth World*, Berkeley: University of California Press, pp. 1–32.

Graburn, N.H.H. (1977), 'Tourism: The Sacred Journey', in V.L. Smith (ed.), *Hosts and Guests: The Anthropology of Tourism*, Philadelphia: University of Philadelphia Press, pp. 17–32.

Graburn, N.H.H. (1982), 'The Dynamics of Change in Tourist Arts', *Cultural Survival Quarterly*, 6, 4, pp. 7–11.

Graburn, N.H.H. (1987), 'The evolution of tourist arts', *Annals of Tourism Research*, Vol. 11, No. 3, pp. 393–420.

Graburn, N.H.H. (1997), 'Tourism and cultural development in east Asia and Oceania', in S. Yamashita, K.H. Din and J.S. Eades (eds), *Tourism and Cultural Development in Asia and Oceania*, Bangi: Penerbit Universiti Kebangsaan Malaysia, pp. 194–212.

Greenwood, D.J. (1989), 'Culture by the Pound: an anthropological perspective on tourism as cultural commoditization', in V. Smith (ed.), *Hosts and Guests: The Anthropology of Tourism*, 2nd edn, Philadelphia: University of Pennsylvania Press.

Hart, K. (1982), 'On commoditization', in E.N. Goody (ed.), *From Craft to Industry: The Ethnography of Proto- Industrial Cloth Production*, Cambridge: Cambridge University Press.

Hitchcock, M., King, V.T. and Parnwell, M.J.G. (eds) (1993), 'Introduction', in *Tourism in South-East Asia*, London: Routledge.

Horner, A.E. (1993), 'Tourist arts in Africa before tourism', *Annales of Tourism Research*, Vol. 20, No. 1, pp. 52–63.

Littrell, M.A. (1990), 'Symbolic Significance of Textile Crafts for Tourists', *Annals of Tourism Research*, Vol. 12, pp. 228–45.

Littrell, M.A., Anderson, L.F. and Brown, P.J. (1993), 'What makes a craft souvenir authentic?' *Annals of Tourism Research*, Vol. 20, No. 1, pp. 197–215.

MacCannell, D. (1976), *The Tourist: a New Theory of the Leisure Class*, New York: Schoken.

MacCannell, D. (1992), *Empty Meeting Grounds: The Tourist Papers*, London: Routledge.

Miller, D. (1987), *Material Culture and Mass Consumption*, Oxford: Basil Blackwell.

Miller, D. (1998), *A Theory of Shopping*, Cambridge: Polity.

Morgan, P. (1983), 'From a death to a view: the hunt for the Welsh past in the Romantic Period', in E. Hobsbawm and T. Ranger (eds), *The Invention of Tradition*, Cambridge: Cambridge University Press.

Picard, M. (1993), 'Cultural tourism in Bali: national integration and regional differentiation', in M. Hitchcock et al. (eds), *Tourism in South-East Asia*, London: Routledge.

Popelka, C.A. and Littrell, M.A. (1991), 'Influence of Tourism on Handicraft Evolution', *Annals of Tourism Research*, Vol. 18, No. 3, pp. 392–413.

Selwyn, T. (1996), 'Introduction', in T. Selwyn (ed.), *The Tourist Image: Myths and Myth Making in Tourism*, Chichester: Wiley.

Shenhav-Keller, S. (1995), 'The Jewish Pilgrim and the Purchase of a Souvenir in Israel', in M-F. Lanfont (ed.), *International Tourism: Identity and Change*, London: Sage.

Sinclair, M.T. and Tsegaye, A. (1990), 'International tourism and export instability', *Journal of Development Studies*, 26, 3, pp. 487–505.

Smith, V. (1989), 'Introduction', in *Hosts and Guests: The Anthropology of Tourism*, 2nd edn (1st edn, 1977), Philadelphia: University of Pennsylvania Press.

Teague, K. (1997), 'Representations of Nepal', in S. Abram, J.D. Waldren and D.V.L. Macleod (eds), *Tourism and Tourists: Identifying with People and Places*, Oxford: Berg.

van den Berghe, P.L. (1994), *The Quest for the Other: Ethnic Tourism in San Cristobal, Mexico*, Seattle and London: University of Washington Press.

van den Berghe, P.L. (1995), 'Marketing Mayas: ethnic tourism promotion in Mexico', *Annals of Tourism Research*, Vol. 22, No. 3, pp. 568–88.

van den Berghe, P.L. and Keyes, C.F. (1984), 'Introduction: tourism and re-created ethnicity', *Annals of Tourism Research*, Vol. 11, No. 3, pp. 342–52.

Wilson, D. (1993), 'Time and tides in the anthropology of tourism', in M. Hitchcock, V.T. King and M.J.G. Parnwell (eds), *Tourism in South-East Asia*, London: Routledge.

Wollen, P. (1993), *Raiding the Icebox, Reflections on Twentieth-Century Culture*, London: Verso.

Wood, R. (1984), 'Ethnic tourism, the state, and cultural change in Southeast Asia', *Annals of Tourism Research*, Vol. 11, pp. 353–74.

Wood, R. (1997), 'Tourism and the state: ethnic options and constructions of otherness', in M. Picard and R. Wood (eds), *Tourism, Ethnicity and the State in Asian and Pacific Societies*, Honolulu: University of Hawaii Press.

2 Souvenirs with Soul: 800 Years of Pilgrimage to Santiago de Compostela

MICHAEL HOULIHAN

For this chapter, I have taken a very broad definition of souvenir. I have tended to use the word in the Spenserian idiom of memory, remembrance and of being in touch with the past. Anyone visiting the French battlefields of the First World War will see it used frequently in this way, usually as 'Route de Souvenir'.

For over 30 years Spain, and particularly its Costas, has been synonymous with that product of intensive, factory tourism, the 'package holiday'. A two-week diaspora for the pallid population of northern Europe seeking liberation from their daily, grey grind in a paradise of sun, sea, sand and sangria. However, Spain is no newcomer to either paradise or tourism on the grand scale. For almost 1,000 years, millions of men and women have made their way to the shrine and, so legend has it, the tomb of St James at Santiago de Compostela in Galicia. It has been estimated that during the Middle Ages, half a million people each year, and even more in Holy Years, thronged the network of Roman-built roads which took them across France, over the principal Pyrenean passes and onward and westward into northern Spain to the remote town of Santiago. After Rome and Jerusalem, it was one of the three great pilgrimages of medieval Christendom. Pilgrims travelled along the 'Way of St James' stopping at purpose-built hostels, visiting the churches and other shrines along the route. Over the centuries a 'cultural highway' emerged which has left an indelible mark on the artistic, religious and social map of Europe.

It is probably no coincidence that the shrine of St James is situated on the very edge of Europe, a place known to the ancients as *Finis Terrae*. As with other Christian pilgrimages, it is postulated that the one to Santiago superseded some pagan cult which, perhaps, drew its devotees, guided by the *Milky Way*, to the boundary of the known world. Whatever the origins, certain basic tenets underpin the cult and myth of St James, and the focus of its legend on Compostela. The most important of these was the belief that his body was

18

contained in the shrine there. St James the Greater, St Jacques, Santiago or St Yakob was the first of Christ's Apostles to be martyred. The son of Zebedee and brother of John, St James is reputed to have preached the gospel in the Iberian Peninsula, but without much success. Returning to Jerusalem, he was put to death by Herod Agrippa in AD42; his body and head being thrown to the dogs. Rescued by some of his disciples, the holy remains were conveyed in a miraculous stone boat to the coast of Galicia and interred nearby. The legend resumes early in the ninth century when a hermit, Pelayo, had a vision of a field of stars which guided him to the burial place. Summoning the local Bishop, Theodemir of Iria Flavia, the remains were uncovered on 25 July, the feast of St James, at the spot where the Cathedral of Santiago de Compostela now stands. The site became known as the 'field of stars' or *Campus Stellae* which, according to the legend, gave Compostela its name. A more probable explanation for the name, one supported by postwar archaeological work in the cathedral's crypt and precincts, is the location at the site of an ancient burial ground, or *compostum*. St James's miraculous powers also extended to the protection of pilgrims who worshipped at his shrine and included a spectacular and timely personal appearance at the Battle of Cavijo in AD 859 when he helped an outnumbered Christian army to massacre some 40,000 infidels. This earned him the title of 'Matamoros' or Moorslayer, as well as field promotion to patron saint of Spain.

For 1,000 years, without any significant interruption, people have journeyed along the 'Way of St James'. As a result, the pilgrimage to Santiago is frequently cited as one of the earliest manifestations of mass tourism, and comparisons are made between the pilgrim and the modern tourist seeking out certain places and objects in the belief that physical proximity will make one a better person for having been there.

Further parallels between pilgrimage and modern tourism can be discerned in the growth of the pilgrimage to Santiago and the organizational detail of the journey. As a destination, Santiago was marketed with energy and imagination by entrepreneurs, politicians and the church. As a propaganda instrument, the pilgrimage and St James's role as the Moorslayer were effectively interwoven within the wider political and economic struggle of Christian 'Reconquest' in Spain. From the eleventh century, a succession of leading secular figures such as Sancho the Great of Navarre, Alfonso VI of Castille and Sancho Ramirez of Aragón played an important part in sponsoring the commercial growth of the route, encouraging French craftsmen and merchants to settle along its length. So much so, that the most popular route across Spain became known as *the Camino Francés* or French Road, with towns such as Estella and Villafranca del Bierzo still bearing evidence in their names to the French communities which flourished there. Alfonso VI was also responsible for commissioning a range of infrastructure projects such as bridges, causeways and other road improvements, mostly under the supervision of two holy engineers, St Dominic and St Juan de Ortega. Another significant proponent of the pilgrimage was Diego Gelmírez, the first Archbishop of Santiago, who could probably be regarded as the Richard Branson of his day. An accomplished self-publicist and spiritual entrepreneur, he consolidated the international reputation of the city as one of the three great shrines of Christendom, ensuring effective market penetration beyond France to northern Europe and Italy.

Along the *Camino Francés* there grew up a complex support system of refuges, hostels, hospitals and churches to provide both physical and spiritual sustenance for pilgrims travelling to Santiago. At the forefront of this hotel and catering operation was the monastic order of Cluny, a sort of Trust House Forte equivalent. It is an indication of the organization of the route that, at the height of the pilgrimage, a traveller on foot, could probably count on having a simple bed and food at the end of each day's journey. Security was provided by the Templars, Hospitallers and the Knights of Santiago, militant church orders charged with the defence of the roads and the pilgrims. The Knights of Santiago operated under a particularly inventive performance bonus scheme. The Order's vast wealth was derived from royal donations, and here is the catch, initially in the form of Muslim-occupied lands which, of course, were not theirs to give away. However, this did not deter the Knights who were positively encouraged to sally forth and seize the land thereby adding to their own wealth, at the same time as expanding the territorial extent of the Christian Kingdom.

Apart from becoming a human and commercial highway, the Santiago pilgrimage routes also became cultural arteries for the transmission of craft skills, and artistic and architectural ideas. The most obvious examples are the Moorish motifs and influences clearly visible in some Romanesque churches in southern France, such as the portal to the abbey church at Moissac. Going the other way, French influence during the Gothic period is evident in the Spanish cathedrals of Burgos and Leon. The hands of the same itinerant masons, sculptors and architects can also be identified in a number of churches along the route. The five main churches associated with the pilgrimage routes – the cathedral at Santiago, St Martin at Tours, St Martial at Limoges, Ste Foy at Conques and St Sernin at Toulouse – were not only built within the same, relatively short, time frame, but also conformed to similar ground-plans and elevations. Constructed to monumental proportions, their long naves, wide transepts, apses with radiating chapels and ambulatory were all designed to marshall, circulate and disgorge, by way of the offertory box, as many pilgrims as possible with minimum interference to the liturgical proceedings.

The source to which most scholars turn for information about the practical details of the pilgrimage is the *Liber Sancti Jacobi,* a Latin manuscript also known as the *Codex Calixtinus* because its authorship was falsely attributed to Pope Calixtus II (1119–24). It was probably written in about 1139 by a French cleric, Aimery Picaud of Parthenay le Vieux, and is regarded as one of the first-ever travel guides, a sort of medieval Michelin. Almost certainly a marketing document sponsored by the Cluniacs, it was designed specifically to promote the pilgrimage to Santiago. It presents a rumbustious concoction of advice on what to see, where to go and what to watch out for. Apart from details of where not to drink the water, and of ferrymen, toll-collectors and innkeepers out to rip off the unsuspecting pilgrim, Aimery exhibits a degree of prejudice towards foreigners which, sadly, would not seem out of place on some modern-day excursions. For example, of the people of Navarre he writes:

> ... a barbarous people ... malignant, dark in colour, ugly of face, debauched, perverse, faithless, dishonourable, corrupt, lustful, drunken, skilled in all forms of violence, fierce and savage, dishonest and false, impious and coarse, cruel and quarrelsome, incapable of any good impulses, past masters of all vices and iniquities ... The Navarrese fornicate shamelessly with their beasts, and it is said that a Navarrese will put a padlock on his she-mule and his mare lest another man should get at them.

Being a human activity, pilgrimage was not always entirely spiritually uplifting, and yob culture was not unknown. For instance, until the sixteenth century, Santiago cathedral remained open throughout the day and night. The massive Romanesque Pórtico de la Gloria, like the portal to heaven of which it was a literal representation, was a doorless structure opening directly onto the plaza in front of the church. However, scandalous behaviour resulting from pilgrims sleeping in the cathedral led to the portal being enclosed by outer doors, and thereby obscuring for ever a sculptural masterpiece.

So far, we have looked at the pilgrimage to Santiago simply from the aspect of the support systems which were put in place to cope with a seasonal but chronic mass migration of people to a particular place. Inevitably, comparisons can be made with the elaborate infrastructure of modern mass tourism, since the basic demands of travellers for food, lodging and a safe journey remain timeless. But what of the pilgrim and the modern tourist: can we discern any shared experience particularly with regard to the material culture of the pilgrimage to Santiago? Clearly, the medieval pilgrim had a passion for relics and special places. Equally, there is no doubt that today's tourist can achieve some level of intellectual self-improvement by visiting the relics of an historical past, be they temples, castles, stately homes or objects laid out in museums and art galleries. Certainly, the added frisson to be gained from closeness to the real object or from standing at the scene of some historical event can give these objects and places a numinous power not dissimilar from that attributed by the pilgrim to the relics of martyrs. However, the personal expectations of the pilgrim and the tourist whilst, on the face of it, seeming to share a similar experience were, in fact, very different. For the pilgrim it was about the next life, the remission of sin, time off from Purgatory and proximity to God; for today's tourist it is probably going to be more about this life, a rounded cultural experience, the acquisition of knowledge and informed dinner-table discussion.

I would argue that the Santiago pilgrimage is particularly interesting for the way in which it has been turned on its head. The revival, during this century, in the numbers of people travelling the ancient routes to Santiago has really been illustrative of how the many surviving remnants of the medieval pilgrimage – churches, fragments of chapels, ruins of hospitals, even the tracks and roads – have themselves become the focus and purpose of the journey, taking on the status of relics in their own right. These relics are mediated and cared for on our behalf by the new priesthood of historians, travel writers, curators and conservators. They are part of an international patrimony of souvenirs on a vast scale, memories of an historical past which now enjoy the same or even greater cultural status as the shrine of St James itself. This is a change which has to be placed within the western European context of 300 years of movement away from spirituality as defined by organized religion and towards a cultural intellectualism built upon principles of rationality, scepticism and materialism.

For the pilgrim, the pay-off came after death. Material culture was immaterial to what should essentially be a spiritual experience. In Book One of the *Liber Sancti Jacobi*, a sermon known as the *Veranda Dies* set out the expectations.

> The way of St James is fine but narrow, as narrow as the path of salvation. That path is the shunning of vice, the mortification of the flesh, and the increasing of virtue … The pilgrim may bring with him no money at all, except perhaps to distribute it to the poor on the road. Those who sell their property before leaving

must give every penny of it to the poor, for if they spend it on their own journey they are departing from the path of God ... Goods shared in common are worth much more than goods owned by individuals. Thus it is that the pilgrim who dies on the road with money in his pocket is permanently excluded from the kingdom of heaven.

Some commentators see pilgrimage as a rite of passage, moving through three distinct phases. Detachment from a group or social structure; then a betwixt and between state of ambiguity, dislocation and movement represented by the journey; and finally, consummation and return to society and the mundane world. (All three states are probably also recognizable to anyone who has been on a Club 18–30 holiday.)

In the first phase, the would-be pilgrim obtained permission of his feudal lord for the journey, set his personal affairs in order, made confession of his sins and obtained the blessing of his priest. He would also put on the simple but distinctive dress which would identify him as a pilgrim. This consisted of a staff, tunic, scrip or pouch and a large, broad-brimmed hat sometimes decorated with a scallop shell. The scallop shell is the enduring icon of the Santiago pilgrimage, yet the origins of its association are unclear. As a corporate identity, however, it was hugely successful and advertised the pilgrimage in sculpture, paint, architectural detail and stained glass across the breadth of Europe. Scallop shells, metal badges and jewellery in jet were sold in Santiago as personal mementos and have been found in medieval graves across Europe. The modern tourist, of course, still has the opportunity to purchase all of these items of pilgrim dress and regalia in a variety of outlets in Santiago. The journey of pilgrimage, itself a metaphor for life, was supposed to bring spiritual enlightenment and the counterbalancing of good over evil. Along the journey, the pilgrim was constantly confronted by the threshold that exists between heaven and hell, the inevitability of final judgment and the horrendous doom awaiting the damned. The abbey church of Ste Foy at Conques presented the pilgrim with one of the most graphic and powerful representations of the last judgment, a sermon in stone on the tympanum designed to galvanize the weak and strengthen resolve. Here, good and evil could be seen in battle for possession of the soul, the torments and chaos of Hell were illustrated in fine detail, and portrayed the vision of a world without God in which evil was equated with human insanity. Such messages were repeated over and over again, all along the route. Powerful stuff indeed; oh, and by the way pilgrim, don't forget to pop inside the church and make your offering at the shrine of Ste Foy where you will see her martyred remains contained in a fabulous golden casket. Of course, we won't mention that these were stolen by one of our own monks from the nearby abbey of Agen in order to attract passing pilgrim trade to Conques.

For the medieval pilgrim relics and shrines played an essential part as a go-between in the process of spiritual salvation. Physical proximity to these vestiges of saints and martyrs transcended history and the threshold between heaven and hell. They acted as divine funnels through which the supplicant could be put in touch with the saving power of the Almighty. In this respect, the shrine of St James was regarded as a particularly powerful medium. Having attained a degree of spiritual salvation, a material memento to take home would seem rather trite. However, with the practicality which marked much of the experience, the pilgrim could obtain a *Corn postellana* as rather more tangible evidence of his having achieved the goal of salvation. This document was a plenary indulgence confirming the sought after remission from purgatory. Rather more pragmatically, it also granted trading rights on the *Camino Francés* and was therefore highly prized on the black market; a useful little contingency for that long journey back home.

3 Tourism and Material Culture in Turkey

JENNIFER SCARCE

Tourism, as in many countries with a Mediterranean shoreline, has become a major foreign currency earner in Turkey, together with the textile, clothing and food industries. Tourism is broadly divided between major cities such as Istanbul capital of both Byzantine Greeks and Ottoman Turks, inland sites of archaeological and environmental interest such as the extraordinary early Christian churches and rock formations of Cappadocia and coastal resorts such as Kusadasi, Marmoris, Fethiye and Bodrum where modest fishing ports have been transformed out of all recognition. Traditional crafts, however, still survive but are often modified to suit both internal and external tourist markets. Turks themselves are increasingly exploring the attractions of their country; Bodrum, for example, is mainly a Turkish vacation resort.

Any survey of tourism in Turkey should involve an exploration of the relationship between modern and traditional customs as seen, for example, in the reactions of tourists to local rituals of hospitality. Responses here to invitations which are conducted within a social framework natural to their Turkish hosts vary from confusion at the unfamiliar to acceptance and genuine appreciation. Other faces of the tourist relationship concern the survival and transformation of material culture in the production and sale of souvenirs which can range from objects of considerable imaginative and craft skill to trinkets and mementoes. Although tourism is regarded as a relatively modern phenomenon it is an industry with a securely documented historical foundation. Visits to centres in both the ancient and medieval world such as the oracle of Apollo at Delphi, the Holy Sepulchre at Jerusalem and the Kaaba at Mecca, easily combined the spiritual needs of pilgrimage with the material rewards of tourism gained through the provision of services, supplies of relics and souvenirs, and the management of rituals and festivals. These criteria are equally applicable to secular pilgrimage which developed, particularly from the eighteenth century onwards, in visits to fashionable spas and health resorts.

In historical terms Turkey's credentials as a tourist centre may be traced back to the Graeco-Roman world as the location of two of the Seven Wonders of the Ancient World,[1] the Temple of Artemis/Diana at Ephesus and the Mausoleum at Halicarnassus. These two major attractions further enriched the flourishing cities of Asia Minor as centres of trade and leisure. The Temple of Artemis had all the ingredients for a successful tourist site – accessible location, infrastructure of a great city, a defined focus, magnificent architecture and plenty of diversions. Ephesus, a port founded by Greek colonists c. 1000 BC on one of the trade routes supplying the western Graeco-Roman world with the products of the east, had developed as a prosperous city with well-planned commercial and residential quarters and a flourishing social and cultural life. While these alone would have ensured a steady flow of visitors Ephesus could boast of a unique attraction, the shrine of the goddess Artemis, who had been honoured there since the sixth century BC for her intercession in all matters of political and religious life. Her shrine, the Artemesium, was a magnificent structure whose architecture was famous throughout the Graeco-Roman world. Situated on a high terrace in a great courtyard which could accommodate crowds of pilgrims her temple constructed according to the best classical principles was a vast gleaming marble building enfolded on all sides by slender fluted columns with graceful curved Ionian capitals. After this temple was destroyed by fire in the fourth century BC it was rebuilt anew on a colossal scale.

Within the temple stood the cult statues of Artemis portrayed as a rigid figure wearing a tall headdress, stiff Oriental robes decorated with lions, sphinxes and griffins and a heavy neck garland of clusters of eggs symbolizing fertility. All Ephesus took part in her festivals with processions of officials, priests and priestesses, musicians and dancers, and sacrificial animals accompanying her statue around the city providing colourful entertainment for both locals and visitors. As the fame of Artemis and her temple spread a vigorous subculture developed to service the needs of the pilgrim tourists. By Roman times there was a brisk trade in small silver copies of both the temple and cult image which provided steady employment for the silversmiths of Ephesus. This souvenir industry did not meet with universal approval. St Paul visited Ephesus in the first century AD and preached against the silver images in the theatre of Ephesus (Acts 19, v. 23–34) where he was challenged by the silversmith Demetrius desperate at the threat to his livelihood. Cries of 'Great is Diana of the Ephesians' indicate the strength of his support. Others who profited from religious tourism were fortune-tellers, forecasters of oracles, and priests and priestesses who sold less durable souvenirs – leftovers of sacrificial meat. All these activities took place against the constantly noisy background of the city's traders, artisans, theatre and street performers. Ephesus stayed loyal to Artemis until the fourth century AD, when the Christian emperor Theodosius I closed her temple along with all pagan shrines.

Turkey's second ancient wonder, the Mausoleum at Halicarnassus (modern Bodrum) was more easily defined and managed than the somewhat unruly sanctuary of Artemis as it was visited for its architecture. Pliny the Elder, writing in c. 75 AD, lists the main facts rather like an entry in a modern guide book. Halicarnassus, originally a Greek colony founded c. 1000 BC, became prosperous as the capital of Mausolus (377–353 BC), ruler of the ancient provinces of Caria, Lydia, and Lycia and the islands of Chios, Rhodes and Cos. He was a great patron of town planning and architecture whose most impressive monument was the tomb-shrine, the Mausoleum which he began for his wife Artemesia and himself between 370 and 365 BC; it was only completed in 350 BC. Its size and lavish sculptured decoration made it famous throughout the classical world and from Roman times mausoleum became a general term for any large tomb. The Mausoleum was an enormous fusion of classical Greek, Lycian and Egyptian architectural influences. A colonnade of slender Ionian columns arose from a massive base and supported a pyramidal roof which rose in steps to a marble sculpture of a chariot with four horses. Sculptured friezes of battles between Greeks and Amazons, horses and charioteers all attributed to the most famous Greek sculptors adorned the sides. The Mausoleum survived the arrival of Christianity and Islam until it was damaged by earthquake during the 13th century. It survives as an intriguing ruin and as part of Bodrum Castle since the Knights of St John began in 1494 to remove blocks of green volcanic stone for repairs.

Turkey continued to attract pilgrims and admiring visitors. Constantinople, after the conquest by the Ottoman Sultan Mehmet II (1451–83) in 1453, flourished again as Istanbul a great imperial capital. It also functioned as a holy city through the custodianship of unique relics of the Prophet Muhammad, which enhanced the moral authority and prestige of the Ottoman sultans throughout the Islamic world that Istanbul was the most sacred place of pilgrimage after Mecca and Jerusalem.

The tomb of Eyup Ensari, companion and standard bearer of the Prophet is picturesquely situated at the top of the Golden Horn within an imposing architectural complex of mosque, theological college and almshouse, built by Mehmet II in 1458 and restored by Selim III (1789–1807) between 1798 and 1800. Eyup was killed during the first Arab siege of Constantinople of 674–78 and reputedly buried outside the city walls. His grave evolved into a venerated shrine after its miraculous and convenient discovery by Mehmet

II's spiritual adviser Askemsettin Sheyh ul-Islam during the siege of Constantinople. Religion and Ottoman legitimacy were further linked as the accession of a new sultan required him to visit the shrine where he was invested with the sword of Osman Gazi, the founder of the dynasty. Politics apart, Eyup was and continues to be visited by pious Muslims who process around his tomb now only visible through a silver grating in a chamber lavishly decorated with brilliantly coloured tiles and gilded candlesticks.

If Eyup provided an accessible focus of Muslim pilgrimage, even more prestigious relics were housed in the Topkapi Palace, residence of the sultans and centre of Ottoman administration from the late fiteenth to mid-nineteenth century. These relics were brought back by Sultan Selim I (1512–20) in 1517 as precious booty from his conquest of Egypt. They include hairs from the beard and a tooth of the Prophet Muhammad (d. 632), his cloak and standard, and the swords of his successors – the first four Caliphs of Islam – Abu Bakr, Umar, Uthman and Ali. Recognition of their immense religious and political importance – possession of them conferred the office of Caliph of the Islamic community on the Sultan – was shown by housing them in a suite of richly decorated rooms, the Pavilion of the Holy Mantle of the Topkapi Palace where access was originally limited to the Sultan, his family and senior officials.

Istanbul also had other attractions. The city was an essential destination for professionals doing business with the Ottoman civil and military establishment, diplomats, merchants and a host of pleasure seekers and tourists ready to admire its superb architecture, shop in its bazaars, sample its excellent cuisine and enjoy picnics and excursions along the shores of the Golden Horn and the Bosphorus. Such visitors included the traveller and antiquarian Thomas Hope in 1799 and a French naval officer Julian Viaud, who made the first of his many visits in 1876. Both took away tangible souvenirs of their voyages. Hope's Turkish waistcoat has survived, while in addition to his collection of clothes and *objets d'art*, Viaud, under his *nom de plume* Pierre Loti, recorded his experiences in a series of best-selling novels and memoirs (1877, 1906, 1921).

These highlights of some of the many wonders of Turkey's extraordinarily varied past may justifiably be regarded as tourist attractions. It is clear that one of the priorities of tourism in modern Turkey is heritage management which can provide local employment opportunities, encourage the survival and development of customs and crafts, and entice the visitor. It is a complex task requiring the expertise of archaeologists and historians, craftsmen and conservators, matched by managerial and financial resources. It is therefore revealing to examine how Turkey has recognized that tourism is best served by capitalizing on attractions which as in the past have generated their own material culture.

The presentation of classical sites is comparatively recent and owes much to survey and archaeological fieldwork. Apart from the two Wonders of the Ancient World Turkey has sites which demonstrate the sophistication and amenities of Graeco-Roman town planning such as the cities of Perge, Priene and Side, and a superb Roman theatre at Aspendos. Wealthy travellers of the eighteenth century visited these sites as 'romantic ruins' during the Grand Tours which were an essential part of their classical education, but it was the systematic excavations from the nineteenth century onwards which enabled these sites to be understood and made accessible to tourists. Management of the two Wonders demonstrates this process.

Ephesus, which declined after the closure of the temple of Artemis in the fourth century AD into a deserted, poverty-stricken village, has revived through tourism into a thriving, crowded attraction comparable with the city's status in classical times. Tourists arrive in buses on day excursions from the coastal resorts of Kusadasi and Bodrum or from the small local town of Seljuk which provides hotels and restaurants. The temple is now a waterlogged area with only a solitary column standing, but the city's amenities are more than adequate compensation. The site has been cleared so that visitors walk through the ancient streets admiring the substantial remains of houses and monuments, and the great library of Celsus reconstructed by international teams of archaeologists and conservators. They can enjoy seasonal performances in the great theatre where St Paul preached. Directional signs and labels, a wealth of illustrated guidebooks and the attentions of guides licensed by the Ministry of Tourism ensure that they do not lose their way. Ongoing excavations mean that the city is never static, as new attractions are revealed to tempt a return visit. On leaving Ephesus tourists encounter a situation comparable to that of their classical counterparts, stalls crammed with all kinds of souvenir – postcards, copies of Roman pottery lamps and figurines, leather, wool and cotton garments, textiles using the traditional technique of block-printing but in 'classical' designs, boxes of Turkish delight, and trinkets such as the ubiquitous blue glass eye beads bought in from wholesale outlets in Istanbul's Grand Bazaar. The excellent museum in Selcuk displays site finds, including two life-size opulent marble statues of the goddess Artemis, and offers small-scale reproductions for sale. Living religion has also contributed to the revival of Ephesus. According to Christian tradition the Virgin Mary lived there during her last years between 37 and 48 AD. While the site of her house had long been a place of pilgrimage for local Orthodox Christians, it only became a universal attraction after a German nun Catherine Emmerich (1775–1824) described what she had seen in a vision. In the late nineteenth century the Catholic Lazarist Fathers of Izmir investigated the site and found a building which they claimed matched this description. They now administer the shrine which is visited by many pilgrims of Roman Catholic, Orthodox and Muslim faiths especially on the annual Feast of the Assumption on 15 August. After their visit they can purchase a range of souvenirs – images of the Virgin Mary, rosaries, guidebooks, and prayer cards.

The revival of Ephesus contrasts with that of the second Wonder, the Mausoleum at Halicarnassus. The ancient monument is beyond reconstruction but it is presented as an archaeological site; an addition to the main tourist attractions of Bodrum. The site is now enclosed with a small museum displaying plans and photographs of recent archaeological work. Emphasis has now moved to the spectacular fifteenth century Castle of the Knights of St John which dominates the Bodrum shoreline, but the classical past continues to be exploited. Tourists can both explore the ramparts and towers of the castle and visit the reconstructions and cargoes of Bronze Age and Roman wrecked ships in a Museum of Underwater Archaeology and the sarcophagus and gold jewellery recovered from the tomb of Queen Ada, the sister of Mausolus. Souvenirs continue the classical theme with a pharmacy which stocks locally made blocks of soaps, shampoos, ointments and herbal remedies concocted from Greek and Latin recipes and sold to the tourists by sales assistants wearing tunics and sandals.

Management of Turkey's classical heritage is relatively contained as it concerns cultures which have long disappeared. The Ottoman heritage is still living. As the last Sultan only abdicated in 1924 many Turks have active personal memories of the period whose traditions of architecture, trade and crafts survive as striking visual evidence of a great imperial past. Unbroken continuity is seen, for example, in the practices of religious pilgrimage. Turks still venerate the shrine of Eyup Ensari. Muslim pilgrims of all nationalities visiting the Holy Relics of the Prophet Muhammad which are now freely accessible in the Topkapi Palace Museum mingle with the crowds of foreign tourists amazed at the treasures of this former imperial residence. Other Ottoman residences also contribute to Istanbul's status as Turkey's major tourism asset. The nineteenth century palaces of Dolmabahce, which dominate the waterfront of the Bosphorus and Yildiz, whose comparatively informal pavilions are discreetly hidden in a large park, now function as locations for official receptions, archival centres and museums. The charming summer palaces of Beylerbeyi and Kucuksu built in the late nineteenth century as holiday retreats for the sultans and their entourage continue this role in some way as they have been converted into museums with cafes so that both Turkish and foreign visitor can enjoy a leisurely afternoon's excursion before passing on to dinner in a fish restaurant. Conversion of palaces offers many opportunities for marketing Ottoman culture in the form of guidebooks explaining history, architecture and decoration, reprints of memoirs of the lives of their inhabitants, and in the case of the Topkapi Palace reproductions of some of the superb manuscript illustrations still housed in the library.

A more intimate involvement of the tourist in a version of Ottoman life is through hotel and restaurant culture which also perpetuates traditional crafts. The grandest hotel now in Istanbul is the Ciragan Hotel, a sumptuously restored and furnished late nineteenth century palace which had been destroyed by fire in 1910. Establishments, however, on a comfortable but more modest level give tourists an opportunity to enjoy themselves much in the manner of European visitors of the eighteenth and nineteenth centuries. Several of Istanbul's picturesque old wooden houses near the city's main tourist attractions of the Topkapi Palace, the cathedral of Ayia Sophia and the Blue Mosque, have been saved from demolition through conversion into small hotels under the guidance of The Turkish Touring and Automobile Club. They have been repaired and painted in pastel colours – green, yellow, blue. Inside the public areas and bedrooms have been furnished with sofas, divans, carpets, brass beds draped in lace-edged sheets and crochet covers, bureaus laden with candlesticks and flower vases, and window blinds of linen decorated with openwork embroidery framed by heavy swagged curtains to create a 'typical' late nineteenth century middle-class household. The equipping and furnishing of these hotels involves searching Istanbul's antique and second-hand markets and more significantly for craft survival and development the commissioning of furniture and fabrics in traditional designs from specialist workshops and items of crochet and embroidery from local women who welcome this opportunity to supplement their income. The concept of the Ottoman household hotel has spread to Ankara's old citadel quarter, to the small town of Safranbolu which consists entirely of traditional houses and has been declared a protected heritage site, and to coastal resorts such as Antalya where the harbour area has been completely restored. Visitor figures and comments indicate that tourists very much enjoy this type of accommodation. Once based in their hotel, they can sample Istanbul's many diversions – sightseeing, watching the colourful performances of the *mehter*, the Janissery military band, whose members are now recruited from the Turkish army, eating in the city's inexhaustible range of cafes and restaurants, and taking part in agreeable excursions such as boat trips up the Bosphorus. Excursions again prolong the Ottoman experience. Alongside the great religious shrine of Eyup at the tip of the Golden Horn is the Pierre Loti café, where the service of Turkish coffee and sweets is welcome after exploring the local sights. Guidebooks capitalize further on the French author's reputation by featuring Pierre Loti itineraries (see Everyman Guides, 1993). On the Asian side of the Bosphorus tourists visiting the wooded hills of Buyuk Camlica can take rides in an *araba* – a curtained ox-drawn carriage which once transported Ottoman ladies on excursions and visits, and nibble wafers of *gullac*, a local sweet.

All these diversions would be incomplete without the ultimate tourist experience of shopping and here Istanbul still fulfils its historical role as a great cosmopolitan trading centre in the choice of goods for sale. Its products also play an outreach role in the material culture of tourism as they are supplied to resorts throughout Turkey, where they supplement local specialities. There is, however, an area where the division between the Turkish and foreign market is eroded as they both contribute to the survival of craft and design traditions. This is seen especially in products inspired by the heritage of Ottoman design. Two major exhibitions of Turkish art held in Istanbul encouraged this development – *The Anatolian Civilisations* sponsored by the Council of Europe in 1983[2] which displayed objects in all media ranging from prehistory to the Ottoman period, and *Iznik, the pottery of Ottoman Turkey* sponsored by the Turk Ekonomik Bankasi in 1989,[3] which focused on the brilliant polychrome ceramics and tiles which furnished and decorated Ottoman buildings from the fifteenth to eighteenth centuries. Both exhibitions had excellent catalogues, were well-publicized and attracted deservedly good attendances.

Museum shops sold tasteful souvenirs, such as scarves, cushion covers, ceramic vases and tiles, silver jewellery and copperware, whose designs were inspired by those of the exhibits. The many designers and craftsmen who had been invited to contribute to this project continued to develop products long after both exhibitions had closed. The work of a large retail company and two designers in textiles are examples of this contemporary evolution of Ottoman art. It is also appropriate that these fabrics are still woven in Bursa the main textile production centre during the Ottoman period. Vakko is a long-established department store with headquarters in the fashionable Beyoglu district of Istanbul and branches in Ankara, Izmir and Antalya. It specializes in smart clothes and accessories for men and women and exclusive soft furnishing items, and also sponsors the work of Turkish artists through its galleries. Vakko chose to interpret Ottoman textile designs in ranges of scarves and cushion covers. Vakko scarves, coveted by Turks and foreign visitors alike, are luxury products woven in fine silk and screen printed in a range of jewel colours. In 1983 Vakko scarves featured boldly printed flower sprays on plain grounds inspired by the block-printed cotton head scarves traditionally worn by Turkish women. From 1989 onwards each year's designs have had an Ottoman court art theme. Silk squares, for example, were printed with the distinctive *cintamani* motif of triple spots and double ribbon-like bands in gold, black and blue on a choice of red, turquoise, green or brown grounds. Currently the motif has reappeared on cushion covers woven in gilt thread on a sombre maroon or dark green ground in the manner of velvets of the sixteenth century. The *cintamani* motif was taken up by other designers. Aykut Hamzagil commissioned lengths of fabric of width and weight suitable for curtains, cushion and loose covers, and also for women's jackets and waistcoats, printed again in a range of colour combinations such as brown and gold on black and blue and black on beige. Recent production by Sahin Paksoy, however, has concentrated on heavy furnishing velvets with designs closely resembling those of Ottoman textiles of the sixteenth and seventeenth centuries. Here oval foliate medallions, palmettes framed within pairs of serrated leaves, stylized pine cones and wavy bands of tulips are woven in silver and gilt threads on grounds of ivory, dark blue, olive green and crimson.[4]

A direct result of the Iznik exhibition was its influence on the techniques and designs of contemporary ceramics. Turkey's main centre here is Kutahya, where production has steadily continued since the late fifteenth century. Today its wares are divided between industrial ceramics, tablewares, and individual presentation pieces and gift items for both local and tourist markets. For many years Turkey's souvenir shops have been crammed with colourful plates, bowls, vases, cups etc. of varying quality decorated with designs inspired by those of Iznik ceramics. Both the exhibition of 1989 and the accompanying publication exposed superb pieces to the technicians and designers of Kutahya who realized that there was a market for products of comparable quality. Several of them have now refined their wares imitating the hard white ceramic fabric, the bright fresh colours and the clear unblemished glazes of the best Iznik wares. Their ranges include plates, dishes, vases, coffee and tea sets, tiles for kitchens and bathrooms all painted with Iznik designs including the ever versatile spots and ribbons of the *cintamani* motif.

All of these products reflect the top level of the heritage market. Turkey is, however, inundated with tourist souvenirs ranging from the gifts in smart hotel boutiques such as silk evening bags and spectacle cases embroidered with delicate flower motifs derived from the borders of traditional domestic textiles to the crowded displays of shops and stalls located near the main sights of Istanbul and in the coastal resorts selling postcards, jewellery, leather clothing, shell and ceramic knick-knacks, etc.

A discriminating search among this stock often reveals well-made local crafts such as socks and gloves knitted in traditional patterns, pieces of crochet and knotted needleworked lace worked in designs of extraordinary intricacy, scarves of handspun and woven silk. The tourist market here for the present guarantees the continuity of this aspect of material culture. One special Ottoman performing art, the Karagoz shadow puppet theatre, which bridges the gap between court and popular culture, has survived as a souvenir. This theatre, featuring the adventures of two contrasting characters, the noisy Karagoz and his ascetic companion Hacivat, was performed at weddings and other celebrations throughout the provinces of the Ottoman empire. Jointed painted leather puppets manipulated behind a lighted white cloth screen created a world of mobile, coloured mosaic. Performances have steadily dwindled in Turkey in the face of competition from cinema and television and were recently seen in the state-sponsored children's puppet theatre in Ankara and in the increasingly rare appearances of a few independent puppeteers. The images, however, of the two main characters are flourishing both as small leather puppets, figures painted on tiles, modelled in plaster and brass, embroidered on towels, printed on silk scarves and fashioned into dangling mobiles, all to tempt the tourist.

Notes

1   The Seven Wonders of the Ancient World are: the Hanging Gardens of Babylon; the Pyramids of Egypt; the Temple of Artemis at Ephesus; the Mausoleum of Halicarnassus; the Statue of Zeus at Olympia; the Colossus of Rhodes; and the Lighthouse at Alexandria.

2   Istanbul, 22 May–30 October 1983, held at the church of St Irene, and the Topkapi Palace Museum. Catalogue in three volumes sponsored by the Turkish Ministry of Culture and Tourism.

3   Istanbul, September–November 1989, held at the Museum of Turkish and Islamic Art. Accompanying publication, *Iznik, the pottery of Ottoman Turkey* by Nurhan Atasoy and Julian Raby, London 1989.

4   The collections of the National Museums of Scotland have a piece of a child's garment of early seventeenth century date (A.1884.65.17) and a length of fabric by Sahin Paksoy (K.1998.119) with the same design of tulip scroll.

References

Everyman Guides (1993), 'Pierre Loti Itinerary', *Istanbul*, London, pp. 354–5.
Loti, P. (Julian Viaud) (1877), *Aziyade*, Paris.
Loti, P. (Julian Viaud) (1906), *Les Desenchantees*, Paris.
Loti, P. (Julian Viaud) (1921), *Supreme Visions d'Orient*, Paris.
Pliny the Elder (1989), *Natural History*, XXXVI, IV, Loeb Classical Library edition, Vol. 10, pp. 30–1.

4 Reproducing India: International Exhibitions and Victorian Tourism

NICKY LEVELL

In an article that poetically explores the complex politics of identity, as articulated by late twentieth-century travellers' tales, Trinh Minh-ha (1994, pp.10–11) outlines the way in which:

> Journeying across generations and cultures, tale-telling excels in its powers of adaption and germination; while with exile and migration, travelling expanded in time and space becomes dizzyingly complex in its repercussive effects. Both are subject to the hazards of displacement, interaction and translation. Both, however have the potential to widen the horizon's of one's imagination and to shift the frontiers of reality and fantasy, or of Here and There.

Such narratives, that engender journeying through the memory, traversing time and space, and displacing the boundaries of the actual and the imaginary, are representative of those that generate and are themselves activated by souvenirs. Hence, the actuality of a souvenir is not necessarily contingent upon the spatio-temporal context of the cultural encounter between the subject and the object, as is often assumed in a reductive, literal interpretation, but rather its being is predicated upon the tale that can be told. From a Bakhtinian perspective, every narrative form is created by and reproduces its own particular 'chronotope'. That is to say, a specific field of interconnected temporal and spatial relations, that constitutes a 'whole complex of concepts, an integral way of understanding experience, and a ground for visualizing and representing human life' (Todorov, 1984, p.14). With these concepts in mind, this paper will critically explore the way in which, during the Victorian period, the 'Oriental chronotope', which engendered Orientalism, the nineteenth century master narrative, served to construct, visualize and represent the subcontinent of India, its peoples and their cultures as an exotic, distant other, frozen in time. By focusing on the development of the touristic gaze in relation to the production, display, and consumption of Indian material culture or what could be termed displaced souvenirs, at selected international exhibitions, this paper will scrutinize the representational strategies, along with the complex network of political, commercial and cultural relations, that served to exoticize, commoditize and objectify Indian cultures. Furthermore, it will reveal the way in which the reification and reproduction of this imaginary, which denied the social, political and economic conditions of the actual, entered the 'real' world and shifted the boundaries between reality and fantasy.

The Exhibitionary Spectacle

On 3 May 1851 Queen Victoria wrote a letter to her uncle, the King of Belgium:

> I wish you could have witnessed the 1st May 1851, the greatest day of our history, the most beautiful and imposing and touching spectacle ever seen … It was truly astonishing, a fairy scene. Many cried and all felt touched and impressed with devotional feelings (quoted in Greenhalgh, 1993, p. 29).

The event that evoked such reverential sentiments was the official opening ceremony of the Great Exhibition of Works of All Nations. The scene was composed of a crowd of over 500,000 spectators assembled at the Hyde Park Exhibition site and a further 30,000 (Beaver, 1970, p. 37) people gathered in the modern purpose-built exhibition building designed by Joseph Paxton. The immense scale of Paxton's innovative glass and iron construction and its glittering, 'fairy-like appearance' in the sunlight resulted in it being christened the 'Crystal Palace' by Douglas Jerrold, the former editor of *Punch*. It is, however, reductive to regard the Crystal Palace as merely a nineteenth century building designed to house exhibits: it was a monumental symbol of Britain's progress, on show to both the national and the international audience. The fact that it embodied state-of-the-art construction technology on an unprecedented scale – the structure covered nineteen acres of parkland and was composed of 293,655 panes of glass supported by 330 iron columns – rendered it 'the biggest and most extravagant of all the things on display' (Briggs, 1988, p. 54). Indeed the scale, scope, opulence and public success of the Crystal Palace, which was the first exhibition to be really 'international' in its remit,[1] set the precedent for the subsequent large-scale international exhibitions[2] that were held throughout Europe and the colonies in the nineteenth and twentieth centuries.

The Great Exhibition not only marked the dawn of the exhibitionary age, it also initiated a new mode of mass consumption: excursion tourism. From the outset, the British populace was actively encouraged to visit these vast, urban temporary exhibition sites and consume their modernistic commodity spectacles.[3] Travelling to these new leisure destinations was made possible by recent improvement in communication technologies, especially the railway networks. In addition, mid-nineteenth century legislation ensured that members of the working classes had recreational time to visit such events. For the remainder of the nineteenth century, international exhibitions, which were held in major cities across the globe,[4] were popular resorts where ephemeral Victorian tourists were able to visit other places, peoples and their cultures through the medium of display.

If the Crystal Palace's exterior spoke to the tourists of the nation's progressive architectural design, technological prowess and organizational abilities; its interior served to visually complement, reinforce, and legitimate the nation's dominant position in international affairs. Internally, it was spatially divided into western and eastern sides: the former was given over to Britain and her empire and the latter to the other participating countries and their empires. In total there were 13,937 exhibitors, over half of whom (7,381) were from the British Isles and Empire (Gibbs-Smith, 1950, p. 23). Throughout the nineteenth century and up until the first decades of the twentieth century, all exhibitions, whatever their scale or rationale, always managed to integrate colonized races into their displays. Their inclusion provided 'the points of differentiation around which to reinforce, whether consciously or through more subtle means, the certainty of European imperial superiority' (Coombes, 1994, p. 64). In 1851, as at all subsequent exhibitions, the Indian section was the centrepiece of Britain's display of empire.

Prior to 1851, the British public had not been systematically exposed to Indian products and manufactures. Although the India Museum, a cultural adjunct of the East India Company based at its headquarters in Leadenhall Street, had been in existence for half a century, its rather eclectic collection, coupled with its insufficient and unsuitable accommodation, plus its location in the City, did not render it a popular leisure destination. However, the general public's introduction to the Indian products on display in the Crystal Palace – exhibits that had been collected and arranged by the East India Company – seems to have stimulated their interest in this field. In 1851, the number of visitors to the India Museum sharply rose from 18,623 in 1850 to 37,490 (Desmond, 1982, pp. 39–41). Admittedly visitor numbers to the India Museum must be contextualized and positioned within the wider picture of tourism. The popularity of visiting the Exhibition and other tourist attractions was aided by the provision of cheap excursion traffic. From 1 May to 14 October 1851, for the duration of the Crystal Palace's five-and-a-half -month life span in Hyde Park, over six million visitors descended upon the metropolis and paid to enter the exhibition.

Constructing the Orient

Queen Victoria made a point of visiting the Crystal Palace's Indian Court on a number of occasions and confided in her journal that she was 'quite dazzled by the most splendid shawls and tissues' (ibid., p. 73). Even *The Times,* which had initially been apprehensive and scathing about the form and content of the 1851 Exhibition, singled out the Indian section for exalted praise, saying that it constituted 'one of the most complete, splendid, and interesting collections in Hyde Park' (quoted ibid.).

Eleven days before the official closing ceremony, the *Illustrated Exhibitor,* a weekly periodical that printed short articles on the exhibits, devoted over 60 per cent of its copy to the India Court display. In the leading article, the south Asian subcontinent was fantasized as:

> The glowing land, the gorgeous and the beautiful; India, the golden prize contended for by Alexander of old, and acknowledged in our day as the brightest jewel in Victoria's crown; India the romantic, the fervid, the dreamy country of the rising sun; India the far-off, the strange, the wonderful, the original, the true, the brave, the conquered; India, how nobly does she show in the Palace devoted to the industrial products of the world! We gaze upon the myriad objects, rare and beautiful ...; we examine the rich stuffs which cover her walls – velvet and silk, and muslin, and cloth of gold – and gazing upon the simple instruments and the still simpler people by whom they were produced – ... we are transported to a strange country, and carried back to the infancy of time (1851, pp. 317–18).

This evocative, albeit melodramatic, description of a display, which was capable of conjuring up images of 'Arabian Nights', 'Oriental potentates', 'Peri Banou', the 'fabled genii', 'Caliph Haroun Alraschid', and 'Noureddin and the fair Persian' (ibid., pp. 318–19), reaffirms Edward Said's contention that the Orient was 'almost a European invention, and had been since antiquity a place of romance, exotic beings, haunting memories and landscapes, remarkable appearances' (Said, 1978, p. 1). This romantic trope was certainly visually embellished by the exotic exhibits, such as the flamboyant state umbrellas, the silk palanquins, the highly decorative elephant howdah displayed on a stuffed elephant, and the antiquated weaponry and chain-mail arranged in trophy-like displays. Trophy-like displays of weaponry were a stock-feature of imperial displays (see Coombes, 1994, pp. 70–3). Ornate, old-fashioned Indian arms, such as shields, matchlocks, daggers and swords, were displayed as representative of recent manufactures and indicative of the state of firearm technology in India. However, as Mukharji noted in the catalogue, *Art Manufactures of India*, which was produced to accompany the artware at the Glasgow International Exhibition (1888), in the late nineteenth century India was manufacturing antiquated arms solely to sell to the Western market, to European tourists or collectors, for display in their domestic spaces (Mukharji, 1888, pp. 112–21). As his contemporary Major Thomas Holbein Hendley, District Surgeon and Principal of the 'Jeypore School of Art', explained, because tourists were creating a 'great demand' for old weapons, the Indian artisans, in reaction to market forces, were manufacturing and supplying 'a modern production ... made to look ancient' (quoted ibid., p. 117). Ironically, while the European consumer was devouring, both visually and materially, a romanticized Orient, divorced from the modern world and rooted in the 'infancy of time'; the Orient was at work reproducing this imaginary for the Western market. The double irony of this commercial venture is that it was ultimately controlled by the West.

The Indian government had established a number of art schools in the mid-nineteenth century.[5] The ideological rationale behind these institutions was the amelioration and preservation of 'traditional' Indian crafts' (Burns, 1901, p. 629). However, these schools were not located in the great centres of Indian art and industry, but rather 'at the principal seats of government, which were also the centres of Anglo-Indian university life and of European commerce' (Havell, 1910, p. 274). Although seemingly eager to stem the 'degradation' of Indian crafts, the government's promotion of the craft sector was, to a large degree, economically motivated. Participation in international exhibitions was, according to the Revenue Department, a sure-fire way 'of increasing the demand for such art-wares, widening the overseas markets and facilitating their supply through the agency of traders in Oriental works' (Swallow, 1998, p. 157). Because the art schools were supposed to function on a semi-commercial basis, they were encouraged to play a leading role in orchestrating the production and display of the commodity spectacle, the imaginary India, which was being 'sold' to the nascent tourist at international exhibitions.

In the late nineteenth century, there was, however, a marked deterioration in the quality and design of the 'traditional' Indian crafts being produced for the overseas market. The fate of Indian handicrafts entered into the debate that was taking place in the British art establishment regarding the deleterious effects of industrialization on taste, standards and creativity. Although the polemic was primarily centred on the deterioration of British design and craftsmanship, there was a growing concern that Indian manufactures – which had previously been promoted as exemplars of the harmony of design produced by pre-industrial societies – were rapidly degenerating due to western influences. The poor quality of the Indian craft products on display at the 1878 *Exposition Universelle* in Paris, the majority of which had been supplied by the three older art schools in Madras, Bombay and Calcutta prompted a massive petition. The petition, which was underscored by leading arts and crafts practitioners, such as William Morris, Edward Burne-Jones, and Philip Webb, centred on 'the rapid deterioration of the great historical arts of India'. The undersigned not only blamed western industrialization for the demise of handicrafts but also the way such crafts were being manipulated by the Europeans in charge of the Indian art schools. While William Morris was publicly proclaiming that Indian 'art is dead and the commerce of modern civilisation has slain it' (quoted in Archer, 1986, p. 265) the British public was consuming a 'romantic primitivist' image of the Orient in the form of, what Sir George Birdwood, organizer of the 1878 exhibition, derogatorily termed, 'mongrel articles'.

Reproducing the Oriental Chronotope

The notion that the visuality of exhibits could stimulate the spectators' imaginations and transport them, albeit temporarily, into a chimerical India was a recurrent topos promulgated by the nineteenth century media. Yet, the spectator's ability to penetrate the Oriental chronotope was, for the most part, contingent upon the creativity of the individuals responsible for producing the exhibition. As Greenhalgh (1993, p. 29) argues:

> all expositions had to do with fantasy. Their raison d'être was unreality ... regardless of their socio-political intentions, they always attempted ... to represent a world which does not actually exist, but one which the organisers would like to see exist.

Throughout the 1850s, John Forbes Royale, an East India Company employee and a leading proponent of economic botany, was responsible for coordinating the Indian section at the various international exhibitions. Because of the Company's commercial interests, India's raw materials – coal, oil, precious stones, saltpetre and spices- were made prominently visible. In fact, they dominated, both in quantity and importance, the manufactured goods in the imperial displays (Barringer, 1998, p. 12). In 1858, however, following the events of the Indian Mutiny, the East India Company was dissolved; this factor coupled with the death of Royale had a marked effect on the form, content and organization of India's contribution to subsequent international exhibitions. For the last four decades of the nineteenth century, the creative responsibility for the overall representation of India resided with a close-knit group of Indophiles. The key members of this home-based delegate were: Caspar Purdon Clarke, Sir George Birdwood, Sir Henry Cole, Owen Jones, Matthew Digby Wyatt, Henry Dyce and Richard Redgrave (MacKenzie, 1995, p. 119).

At a number of exhibitions, Caspar Purdon Clarke, who was later Keeper at the South Kensington Museum (renamed the Victoria and Albert Museum in 1899), was given the responsibility for the architectural design of the India display area. For the 1878 *Exposition Universelle* in Paris, which attracted 16 million visitors, he designed an 'Indian Pavilion' to house the exhibits. This Oriental edifice, which occupied 'the place of honour' in the exhibition hall, was the archetypal construction for all subsequent representations of India (*Journal of Indian Art*, 1884–6, p. 21). An article appearing in the 1878 *Art Journal*, described the pavilion as a 'compound structure two hundred feet long, coloured a deep red approaching chocolate, with its dusky gold domes and brilliant spires' (quoted in Metcalf, 1989, p. 147). A construction which would conjure up the image of an exotic East. Notwithstanding the poor quality of the art school exhibits, the pavilion housed an impressive selection of 'traditional' Indian pottery, glass, metalwork, textiles and embroideries, which were gifts that the Prince of Wales had received on his 1875–6 tour of India (Birdwood, 1878). At the centre of the display was the prize piece, a 300 year old carpet; *ensemble* the exhibits were said to reveal the diversity and 'ancient beauty' of India's traditional crafts. There was, however, another message being conveyed. Dominating the entrance to the pavilion was an equestrian statue of the Prince of Wales. The positioning, scale, and form of the sculpture functioned as a visual metonym for cultural imperialism (Metcalf, 1989, p. 147). Furthermore, the difference and distance between Britain and India and the legitimation of Empire were also visually reinforced at a macro-level, in terms of the whole exhibition hall. The British section consisted of a series of house facades charting the evolution of decorative art. There was: the Queen Ann style; the Elizabethan, fifteenth-century half-timbered; the William and Mary era country house, and the recently invented semi-Gothic, terracotta frontage (ibid.). The social evolutionary narrative that informed the British presentation of itself as a progressive, evolving race, also underscored the representation of India as a 'timeless', primitive other, and served to further endorse the tutelary relations between the colonial power and the possessed.

Purdon Clarke's most memorable oriental construction appeared at the 1886 Colonial and Indian Exhibition. This was the most popular in a series of major exhibitions that were held between 1883 and 1886, at the Royal Albert Hall site, west of Exhibition Road.[6] Technically speaking it did not constitute an international exhibition because the exhibitors were drawn exclusively from the British Isles and the British Colonies. However, the sheer scale of the event – it attracted over 5.5 million visitors – and the fact that the Indian section played such a dominant role, warrant its inclusion in this chapter. Moreover, it serves a valuable case study in the light of the contention that from the 1880s, the message conveyed through the representation of Empire at international exhibitions shifted from being one of 'complacent pride' to one of 'propagandistic defence' (Greenhalgh, 1988, p. 58). One of the justifications for this shift is that the scramble for Africa had left the British apprehensive of their European rivals' imperial ambitions and concerned about the safety of British colonial possessions.

The Colonial and Indian Exhibition was an expensive exercise in imperial propaganda and, as usual, centre-stage went to India. The Indian exhibits alone covered 103,000 square feet and cost £22,000. Usually the structural and architectural facets of the Indian displays were funded by the Indian government, the British government and private enterprise, such as wealthy tea syndicates; however, for the Colonial and Indian, all the monies came from governmental sources.[7] The Exhibition was organized by Sir Philip Cunliffe-Owen, Director of the South Kensington Museum and Secretary to the Royal Commission, a body headed by the Prince of Wales (see Cundall, 1886, p. 3), and, from the outset, the propagandistic motivation behind the event was made explicit. Its publicized aim was to strengthen the 'bond of union between her Majesty's subjects in all parts of the Empire' (quoted in Metcalf, 1989, p. 147). In order to achieve this objective, towards the end of 1885, the Prince of Wales appointed the firm Thomas Cook and Son to act as the General Passenger Agents, to help ensure that everyone, from Maharajas to British workers, would be afforded the opportunity to visit the event.

Thomas Cook and Son had already proven their organizational abilities at the 1851 Exhibition. Having been persuaded by Joseph Paxton, the architect of the Crystal Palace, and John Ellis of the Midland Railway Company (the latter had invested a substantial amount of money in new rolling stock in anticipation of the increase in trade) Thomas Cook, a Leicestershire printer, organized regular excursion trips to the Great Exhibition. As well as negotiating contracts with railway companies, Thomas Cook and his son John, distributed printed fliers, held meetings, encouraged the formation of savings clubs, and ultimately escorted 165,000 members of the British public to and from the Exhibition site. By the time of the second *Exposition Universelle* in Paris, in 1867, with the support of Raymond Le Play, the director-general, the firm 'Thomas Cook and Son' was able to offer a complete package deal, including accommodation at 'Cook's Anglo-American Exhibition Hotel' (Brendon, 1991, p. 110). In the 1850s, 'Cook's Tours' had been synonymous with working and lower middle class travel and, as such, they were often summarily dismissed by members of the middle and upper classes. However, as Cook and Son's enterprises extended to the continent, the firm started to attract members of the bourgeoisie, and consequently, it was able to enlarge its programme of continental and world tours.

The royal endorsement of Cook and Son's services for the Colonial and Indian Exhibition not only had a marked impact on the company's public image, it also stimulated its commercial interests in the Indian subcontinent. In the early 1880s, India was not one of the popular, exotic tourist destinations; in fact it had received negative reviews in *Murray's Handbooks*. However, Thomas Cook was aware of the public's growing interest in, and the commercial potential for, travel in India, so he established an office, a reading room and a meeting point at the 1886 Exhibition site (ibid., p. 205). The firm benefited from its presence at the Exhibition: it not only started acting as the travel agency for many of the rulers of India's 600 semi-independent states, it also embarked upon a new series of package tours to India.[8]

The Indian component of the 1886 exhibition was designed and constructed to give the impression of 'stepping into the "exotic" world of the Orient' (Metcalf, 1989, p. 147). From the entrance on Exhibition Road, the visitor passed through the vestibule into the Indian Section and was confronted by the ornately carved Jaipur Gateway, which had been contributed by the Maharaja of Jaipur and formed the entrance into the 'Rajputana Court', the first of the regional 'Art Ware Courts'. Each court was enclosed by carved wooden screens, the production of which had been funded by a grant established by the Royal Commissioners. Although the screens were supposed to be representative of the 'living form of decorative art' found in the specific province (*Colonial and Indian Exhibition, 1886. Special Catalogue of Exhibits by the Government of India and Private Exhibitors*, p. 2), it is insightful that Major Hendley of the 'Jeypore School of Art', had issued the following directive to his screen-carvers: 'as great a variety of pattern should be employed as possible, the ornament to be purely Indian and no attempt be made to work other than traditional lines' (ibid., p. 191). The patterns on the Indian carpets were also being dictated by the colonial authority, as a journalist from *The Illustrated London News* (17 July 1886, p. 82) reported: 'with respect to the alluring carpets ... the influence of the Government Schools of Art at Bombay, Lahore and Madras is being steadily exercised to restore and uphold the standard of pure colours and true Oriental designs'.

The Indian artisans' creativity was suppressed in order to satiate the imperial demand for exotic wares; commodities that would appeal to the western perceptions of the Orient.

At the heart of the Colonial and Indian Exhibition were Purdon Clarke's Indian Palace and Durbar Hall. The overt hybridity of their architectural styles was described by *The Graphic*:

> A Hindu structure is made the entrance to a Mahomedan *serai* and Sikh modern carved woodwork has been adapted in the interior fittings of an ancient Mahomedan palace, and, still more incongruous, old English stained windows have been added to this aggregation of ideas (quoted in Barringer, 1998, p. 24).

The form and function of the highly ornate Durbar Hall, carved by Punjabi artisans for the Prince of Wales' official receptions or 'durbars', visibly signified both the richness of India's past and Britain's present role in preserving it. Formerly, *durbars* were organized formal events, which involved lengthy rituals of gift-giving in honour of Mughal emperors.[9] The Victorians had consciously striven to regenerate *durbars*, in India, as a means of officially and ritually consolidating their imperial position.

In accordance with a 'typical Oriental Palace', there was the *karkhaneh*, workshops for the palace artists. For the 1886 Exhibition, live exhibits – carpet-weavers, potters, woodcarvers, printers, dyers, metalworkers, etc. – brought to Britain by Dr J. Tyler, Superintendent of the Agra Jail, could be seen at work in the *karkhaneh*. Not only were tourists expected to 'gaze' at this tableau-vivant, they were also encouraged to interact with the exhibits by purchasing their wares. In addition to this living diorama, there was a 'model of a native village', consisting of a row of shops and life-size figures of traders, which had been exhibited three years earlier at the Amsterdam International

Exhibition. These reconstructions enabled the visitor to physically enter the oriental chronotope, as *The Times* explained:

> at a single step, the visitor is carried from the wild, mad whirl of the individual competitive struggle for existence to which civilisation has been reduced in the ever changing West, into the stately splendour of that unchanging antique land of the East, the tradition of which has been preserved in pristine purity only in India (quoted in Metcalf, 1989, p.146).

Prior to the incorporation of live exhibits, peoples from the Indian subcontinent were objectified, commoditized, and displayed at the majority of the international exhibitions in the forms of models.

In 1851, an extensive series of life-size models, representing Indian artisans, was displayed on the ledge surrounding the India court. Reports of the day described them as thin, scantily-clad, 'barbarians' working with the 'rudest, roughest implements'. For example, the weaver was depicted 'sitting in holes in the earth before the handful of rickety sticks which constitute the loom' (*The Illustrated Exhibitor*, 1851, p. 319). The spatial layout of the Exhibition, ensured that this 'primitive' technology was spatially juxtaposed with Britain's contribution to the machinery section: 'within a few feet of each other were displayed the exotic offerings of the East and the mechanical and scientific triumphs of the West' (Beaver, 1970, p. 47). This was social evolutionary theory translated into a visual format and writ large. As well as the life-size models, a regular feature at international exhibitions was the large numbers of realistic miniature clay figures representing different castes and occupations.[10] These small portable figures, based on visible traits and idealized types, were predominantly made for the Western tourist market. Miniaturization provided an ideal means of appropriating, scrutinizing while simultaneously maintaining a comfortable distance from the objectivized. Furthermore, because miniature souvenirs refer not to the time of production but to the time of consumption,[11] they constituted what Marx termed 'fetishes', completely dissociated from the human relations that operated to produce them.

The earliest display of 'live exhibits' appeared at the 1867 *Exposition Universelle* in Paris (see Greenhalgh, 1988, p. 85), thereafter colonial peoples became a stock component of the displays of empire. By the early 1880s, the British were regularly incorporating Indian peoples in their oriental pavilions. At the first Glasgow International Exhibition in 1888, one of the main tourist attractions was the 'Indian Street', where Indian artisans plied their trades and supplied souvenirs of jewellery, pottery, carved work and sweetmeats. Another popular entertainment was to be served by an Indian waiter on the veranda of the Royal Bungalow or in the Indian and Ceylon Tea Rooms (see Kinchin and Kinchin, p. 35; MacKenzie, 1995, p. 86). The Indian component, for the first Glasgow exhibition, was coordinated by three steering committees. These had been established in Calcutta, Bombay and Madras, the homes of the main, government-funded, art schools, to manage the selection, collection, shipping and display of the exhibits. The resultant display was a 'rich bazaar of art wares, fabrics, carpeting, carved furniture, and curiosities catering to the European consumer's conception of India' (MacKenzie, 1995, p. 35). One of the main aims of the Glasgow Exhibition had been to encourage tourism in west Scotland and with 5.75 million visitors, this objective was met.

From the 1880s, the British regularly set-up Ceylonese and Indian tea rooms with exotically attired waiters. The centrality and grand-scale of the tea rooms was achieved because the Indian Tea Syndicate regularly sponsored the Indian displays. At the 1889 *Exposition Universelle* in Paris, the central hall for the sale of tea and light refreshments and the long veranda, replete with 'traditionally' dressed, turbaned waiters, were the most dominant features of the Indian pavilion. The socioeconomic reality of life in parts of India was completely effaced from this idealized representation of the peoples of the Empire. This fact did not evade the French critic Maurice Talmeyr, who wrote:

> why is starving India incarnated in well-coiffed, well-nourished, well-clothed Indians? Because famine is not and never can be an Exposition attraction … For this land of enormous and sumptuous trade is equally that of frightening local degeneracy, of horrifying indigenous misery (quoted in Greenhalgh, 1988, p. 60).

The 1889 *Exposition Universelle* was the first occasion on which India was exhibited, for the tourist market, on a purely commercial basis. The British monarch, like virtually every other European monarch, had declined to attend the event because it was being held to commemorate the centenary of the Revolution. Although the monarchy refused to participate, as a token of goodwill towards the French government and, above all, in the 'interests of commerce', the British government agreed to assist any exhibitors in anyway they could. A select committee of gentlemen with Indo-centric and/or commercial interests, including Sir George Birdwood, and Lord Brassey, was established to oversee the proceedings and Purdon Clarke was commissioned to design a pavilion of 'sufficiently ornamental character'. The pavilion was constructed with bays, which housed the 20 retail outlets, all of which were staffed by colonial subjects in traditional costumes. Framgee Pestonjee Bhumgara, a Bombay merchant, who had been awarded 18 medals from various European exhibitions, had two shops in the pavilion selling pottery, metalwork and embroideries. Liberty and Co. also had a large display area where they exhibited a selection of Indian wares, including carved and inlaid sandalwood boxes from Bombay, which were 'suitable for small gifts and souvenirs' (*Journal of Indian Art,* 1889–90, p. 21). Arthur Liberty, the founder of the company, had entered the 'oriental' retail trade, after seeing the Eastern wares on display at the 1862 International Exhibition in South Kensington. Having successfully exhibited at previous exhibitions, he opened a shop – a satellite of his 'East India House' store on Regent Street (established in 1875) – in Paris, on the Avenue de l'Opéra, in order to capitalize on the number of tourists visiting the *Exposition Universelle* (Duncan, 1992, p. 16).

The fact that the European monarchy had boycotted the 1889 event does not appear to have diminished its popularity. A record-breaking 32.4 million visitors flocked to the French capital. Thomas Cook and Son escorted over 200,000 British tourists to Paris to see this ephemeral new town of palaces, pavilions, temples and pagodas, and the infamous Eiffel Tower. As well as dealing with all the travel arrangements, the firm offered a complete package deal, including accommodation and daily sightseeing excursions around the 100-acre site, that stretched from the Champs de Mars to the Trocadéro (Briggs, 1988, p. 90). The touristic act of travelling across time and space, consuming other places, peoples and their cultures through exhibitionary spectacles, served to widen the horizon's of the Victorian's imagination and simultaneously shifted the boundaries of the actual and the imaginary.

The 'traditional' India, which was represented by hybrid oriental architectural styles and exotic exhibits, at the large-scale national and international exhibitions throughout the nineteenth century, was, in part, a product of the European imagination. This product – a land, its peoples and cultures – was constructed within the Oriental chronotope, by the West for the West. By consuming this imaginary, European tourists were not incorporating it into their reality; they were also ensuring the reproduction of this fictional Orient in cultural institutions at home and abroad. As Bakhtin explained, inside the chronotope:

> The work and the world represented in it enter the real world and enrich it, and the real world enters the work and its world as part of the process of its creation, as well as part of the subsequent life, in a continual renewing of the work through

the creative perception of listeners and readers (quoted in Morson and Emerson, 1990, p. 429).

Notes

1   Prince Albert, the President of the Royal Society of Arts, and Henry Cole, an active Society member, initially had the idea for the 1851 Exhibition. Since 1847, they had been staging exhibitions on 'Art Manufacture' in London. These had been inspired by the Parisian model. In Paris, large-scale, national exhibitions had been regularly organized since 1798. See Reeves, 1986, p. 2.

2   The terminology for large-scale 'international exhibitions' varies depending on the country where they were hosted. In Britain they were generally referred to as 'international' or 'universal' exhibitions; in Paris as *'Expositions Universelle'*, and in America as 'World Fairs'.

3   For a discussion of international exhibitions as mass-produced consumer spectacles. See McClintock, 1995, p. 56.

4   After the inaugural international exhibition of 1851 in London, 26 others took place in the second half of the nineteenth century, namely: 1853 – Dublin, 1853/4 – New York, 1854 – London, 1855 – Paris, 1862 – London, 1865 – Dublin, 1867 – Paris, 1871, 1873, 1874 – London, 1872 – Moscow, 1873 – Vienna, 1876 – Philadelphia, 1878 – Paris, 1880 – Melbourne, 1883 – Amsterdam, 1883 – Calcutta, 1885 – Antwerp, 1888 – Barcelona, 1888 – Glasgow, 1888 – Brussels, 1889 – Paris, 1893 – Chicago, 1894 – Antwerp, 1897 – Brussels. For a comprehensive list covering twentieth century exhibitions see Greenhalgh, 1993, p. 32.

5   For a detailed historiography of schools of art in India see Mitter, 1994, pp. 27–61.

6   The themes of the other exhibitions were: 1883, fisheries; 1884, health; and 1885, invention. For visitor numbers see *The Times*, 11 November 1886.

7   The Indian government contributed £10,000; the Royal Commission (effectively the British government) £3,000; the Bombay Exhibition Grant £6,850 and the Commission Screen Grant £2,500. See Greenhalgh, 1988, p. 60.

8   Three years later, the success of the package tours prompted an article in *Cook's Excursionist* stating that 'the whole of India has been opened out to tourists' as a result of the firm's innovative coupon system. Quoted in Brendon, 1991, p. 20.

9   For a detailed explication of the reinvention of the Durbar tradition see Cohn, 1983.

10 In 1851, 150 small 'caste' and 'occupation' figures from the Bengal district were displayed. Similar figures, made specifically for the Western market, appeared at the Colonial and Indian Exhibition (1886) and at the Glasgow International Exhibition (1888). In addition, at the latter exhibition, the Jeypore School of Art displayed 144 'caste' heads, modelled in papier-mâché, depicting the different Hindu caste groups found in Rajastan.

11 For a detailed discussion of the construction of miniature souvenirs see Stewart, 1993.

References

Archer, M. (1986), 'Lockwood Kipling and Indian Decorative Arts', *Apollo*, April, Vol. CXXIII.

Ata-Ullah, N. (1998), 'Stylistic Hybridity and Colonial Art and Design Education: A Wooden Carved Screen by Ram Singh', in T. Barringer and T. Flynn (eds), *Colonialism and the Object. Empire, Material Culture and the Museum*, London and New York: Routledge.

Barringer, T. (1998), 'The South Kensington Museum and the Colonial Project', in T. Barringer and T. Flynn (eds), *Colonialism and the Object. Empire, Material Culture and the Museum*, London and New York: Routledge.

Beaver, P. (1970), *The Crystal Palace. A Portrait of Victorian Enterprise*, Chichester: Phillimore.

Birdwood, G. (1878), *Paris Universal Exhibition of 1878. Handbook to the British Indian Section*, London.

Brendon, P. (1991), *Thomas Cook. 150 Years of Popular Tourism*, London: Secker and Warburg Ltd.

Briggs, A. (1988), *Victorian Things*, London: B.T. Batsford Ltd.

Burns, C. (1901), 'The Function of Schools of Art in India', *Journal of the Royal Society of Arts*, 2985, 57.

Cohn, B. (1983), 'Representing Authority in Victorian India', in E. Hobsbawm and T. Ranger (eds), *The Invention of Tradition*, Cambridge: Cambridge University Press.

Colonial and Indian Exhibition (1886), *Special Catalogue of Exhibits by the Government of India and Private Exhibitors*, London: The Royal Commission.

Coombes, A. (1994), *Reinventing Africa. Museums, Material Culture and Popular Imagination*, London and New Haven: Yale University Press.

Cundall, F. (1886), *Reminiscences of the Colonial and Indian Exhibition*, London: The Royal Commission.

Desmond, R. (1982), *The India Museum, 1801-1879*, London: HMSO.

Duncan, A. (1992), 'Art Nouveau', in S. Calloway (ed.), *The House of Liberty: Masters of Style and Decoration*, London: Thames and Hudson.

Gibbs-Smith, C.H. (1950), *The Great Exhibition of 1851*, London: HMSO.

Greenhalgh, P. (1988), *Ephemeral Vistas. The Expositions Universelles, Great Exhibitions and World's Fairs, 1851-1939*, Manchester: Manchester University Press.

Greenhalgh, P. (1993), 'The Tradition of Expositions Universelles', *The Panoramic Dream: Antwerp and the World Exhibitions, 1885. 1894. 1930*, Antwerp: Frank Vanhaecke.

Havell, E. (1910), 'Arts Administration in India', *Journal of the Royal Society of Arts*, 2985, 58.

The Illustrated Exhibitor (1851), 'India and Indian Contributions to the Industrial Bazaar', No. 18, 4 October.

The Illustrated London News (1886), 17 July.

Journal of Indian Art (1884–86), Vol. 1.

Kinchin, P. and Kinchin, J., *Glasgow Exhibitions*, Oxon: White Cockade Publishing.

MacKenzie, J. (1995), *Orientalism: History, Theory and the Arts*, Manchester: Manchester University Press.

McClintock, A. (1995), *Imperial Leather. Race Gender and Sexuality in the Colonial Conquest*, London and New York: Routledge.

Metcalf, T. (1989), *An Imperial Vision. Indian Architecture and Britain's Raj*, London: Faber and Faber Ltd.

Minh-ha, T. (1994), 'Other than myself/my other self', in G. Robertson, M. Mash, L. Tickner, J. Birk, B. Curtis and T. Putnam (eds), *Travellers' Tales. Narratives of Home and Displacement*, London and New York: Routledge.

Mitter, P. (1994), *Art and Nationalism in Colonial India, 1850–1922*, Cambridge: Cambridge University Press.

Morson, G.S. and Emerson, C. (1990), *Mikhail Bakhtin. Creation of a Prosaics*, Stanford, California: Stanford University Press.

Mukharji, T. (1888), *Art-Manufactures of India*, Calcutta: Government Printing.

Reeves, G. (1986), *The Palace of the People*, London: Bromley Library Service.

Said, E. (1978), *Orientalism. Western Conceptions of the Orient*, London, New York, Ontario and Auckland: Penguin Books Ltd.

Stewart, S. (1993), *On Longing. Narratives of the Miniature, the Gigantic, the Souvenir, the Collection*, Durham and London: Duke University Press.

Swallow, D. (1998), 'Colonial Architecture, International Exhibitions and Official Patronage of the Indian Artisan: The Case of a Gateway from Gwalior in the Victoria and Albert Museum', in T. Barringer and T. Flynn (eds), *Colonialism and the Object. Empire, Material Culture and the Museum*, London and New York: Routledge.

The Times (1886), 11 November.

Todorov, T. (1984), *Mikhail Bakhtin: The Dialogical Principle*, trans. W. Godzich, Manchester: Manchester University Press.

5   From Earliest Contacts: An Examination of Inuit and Aleut[1] Art[2] in Scottish Collections

BRIONY CROZIER

This chapter examines collections of Inuit and Aleut art in Scotland over 170 years. They include items gathered on explorative journeys by Sir William Parry during the 1820s; collected by Scots during the nineteenth century, and produced for the late twentieth century art market.

The author finds it useful to envisage Inuit and Aleut objects brought to Scotland for almost two centuries as 'souvenirs' to those who collected them. The product of imported ideas and materials, the souvenir is a reliable gauge of the degree of contact between cultures. Though not immediately recognized as souvenirs upon first appraisal, objects of Arctic artwork in Scotland in fact illustrate poignantly the history of contact between Scots and their associates of the far north.

On examining the products of Inuit and Aleut (or Eskimoaleut) art in museums in Edinburgh, Orkney, Aberdeen, Peterhead, Dundee and Glasgow, I have set out to explore the degree to which they can be thought of as representing souvenirs to their European collectors. Relying on the ever faithful *Oxford English Dictionary*, I have found that, as a noun, the word refers to a 'memory' or 'keepsake'. In the museum context, which I inhabit, these definitions are pertinent: what museums do, after all, is collect and display objects, or keepsakes, for the purposes of stimulating memory.

The *OED Supplement* gives 'souvenir' a verb form, 'to appropriate, to pilfer, steal'. This definition, too, is relevant for those concerned with museums, and has of course been applied to a variety of ethnographic material in European collections.

For Arctic collections in Scotland, however, all the indications are that we might sleep easy in our beds. Due to the harsh climate and the difficult terrain, European visitors have tended to rely upon the goodwill of its inhabitants. What they have brought home with them has predominantly been fairly traded. In fact, some observers have complained about pilfering in the opposite direction. Kane, for example, wrote that during his search for Franklin an axe, a saw, knives, and wood from his India-rubber boat, went missing, but due to the urgent need of his party for meat, 'I could not afford to break with the rogues' (Kane, 1861, p. 124).

While Eskimoaleut art objects can now be bought quite easily on the European and American market if one knows where to look, numbers of tourists, in the modern sense of the word, to the north polar region itself are still small. To go there, you have to be very single-minded, and wealthy to boot (see Pelly, 1998, p. 3), and consequently, Scottish collections have benefited little in recent years.

However, from the eighteenth century to the present, explorers, whalers, ships' captains, traders, scientists, and a small number of late twentieth century museum curators have all brought items of such artwork to Scotland. Whether collected under specific instruction for museum purposes, gathered to aid survival, kept for sentimental value or brought here as didactic aids, they all serve to imbue, and provoke, memory. As such, they might all be described as souvenirs.

Art produced for, or influenced by, the 'market' can always be measured in two ways. Firstly, it incorporates materials not locally available. In the Arctic these, until the last few decades, have been metals of various kinds, glass beads, woven cloth, dyes and paints. In many cases they have led to the production of objects of local form using foreign materials.

Metals used in tools suggest that trade between peoples in Alaska and those in Siberia was probably established early in the Christian era; and that, by around 1200 AD, Norse iron was used in Greenland and eastern Canada (Oswalt, 1979, pp. 279–80). The products of Asia and Europe, then, have affected work of the far north for far longer than is historically documented. It is quite possible that, through trade, Eskimoaleut products have reached European shores for an equal period of time.

The second force of change is that corpus of influence which can broadly be termed 'ideas', and have resulted in altered, or totally imported, forms. Among the Inuit, traceable changes in this category are more recent and include forms such as the nineteenth and twentieth century cribbage boards, baleen baskets and 'modern' sculptures pictured in almost any book on Arctic art one cares to lift. It is partly with such objects, but also with earlier souvenirs that this chapter deals.

Since the eighteenth century, hundreds of Scots have been recruited to man ships travelling to polar regions. Particularly during the nineteenth century, many more joined the Hudson's Bay Company. As a result, Scottish collections encompass objects from northern Canada, Greenland and Alaska.

In this article I shall introduce some of those 'souvenirs' to which collectors' names are attached. Some are linked with specific geographical areas. For others I have relied on paper archives and previous research, and have attributed to them rough locales on stylistic grounds. As is so often the case, only a tiny minority is identified with particular artists. Their names are included in this article where possible.

The earliest identified group of Eskimoaleut 'souvenirs' in Scotland is at the National Museums of Scotland in Edinburgh, and relates to the explorative excursions of William Edward Parry around Melville Peninsula while attempting to discover the northern sea route to the Far East, the Northwest Passage, in 1821–23.

During this voyage, Parry observed the presence among the people now known as the Iglulingmiut of glass beads, brass, knives of European form, and copper kettles, and the ability to make 'clumsy' model umiaks, a sort of boat they did not use (Parry, 1824, pp. 503, 507). If these people had not had contact with Europeans prior to this, they were certainly involved in indirect trade to acquire European goods, probably emanating from trading sloops which began regular operations in the Churchill area of Hudson's Bay between 1750 and 1790 (see Oswalt, 1979, p. 283). Since Parry's first voyage, to Greenland, in 1818, he had been accustomed to carry items such as '... shirts, umbrellas, needles, looking-glasses, cowrie-shells, glass beads ... to attract the attention of people in an uncivilized state' (Fisher, 1819, p. v); and such items were no doubt also eagerly acquired by the Iglulingmiut on their contact with his ships.

Paradoxically, though, of the items in Scotland relating to Parry, very few contain non-native materials. Among them are a man's and a woman's knife (Figure 5.1), with iron and copper blades, and a salmon hook, fishing rod and arrow containing iron components. In the polar region, meteoric iron had been available even before the arrival of imports (see Oswalt, 1979, p. 120), and copper was mined at a number of sites (Issenman, 1997, p. 60). Detailed materials testing could identify the origins of the metals in the tools concerned, but at present there is no evidence to ascertain whether or not they were derived from local sources.

In the Arbuthnot Museum in Peterhead, there is a model kayak, given in 1893, which is documented as having been 'made by one of Captain Crozier's

Figure 5.1   A woman's knife

officers'. Crozier accompanied Parry in his three arctic voyages between 1821 and 1827, and in 1836 co-captained a voyage with Captain James Clark Ross to Davis Strait and Baffin Bay. On which of these four journeys the kayak was collected is not recorded. However, there is scant record of non-Inuit making such models and it may therefore be one piece of evidence in a Scottish collection to the early provision of diminutive Inuit products to British voyagers.

The collections in Edinburgh have benefited from other early travels, most notably Frederick Beechey's, in 1826–27 aboard the *Blossom*, to attempt the Northwest Passage. Within this group, there is little more in the way of imported materials than in Parry's, revolving instead around items made of wood (see Figure 5.2), leather and ivory.

However, it must be remembered that, in contrast with the present discussion, these explorers were not interested in the incorporation of European materials within native artwork. Instead, as regards ethnographic objects their remit, guided by the Lords of the Admiralty, was to collect 'rare and curious specimens in the several departments of science ...' (Beechey in Bockstoce, 1977, p. 10). Nevertheless, the results of their efforts are fascinating records of an artistic stage prior to regular contact between Eskimoaleut and Beechey, Parry, and their kind.

Of objects collected during explorative voyages, the next important group in Scotland was gathered by the Orcadian, Dr John Rae, during his surveys of the polar area between 1846 and 1860 and his searches for the fate of Franklin in 1847 and 1850.

Rae's collection was made a little later than those of Parry and Beechey but still contains sparse reference to the importation of European products. Like his predecessors, Rae was aware of the value of carrying such items as 'a small box of beads and cutlery of various kinds for the natives' (Rae, 1854, p. 370), for which he could trade non-edible native items, which, unlike most of them, he used for his own survival (Idiens in Bunyan, Calder, Idiens and Wilson, 1993, pp. 78–85). These included such articles as 'pieces of moose skin for repairs of moccasins, thongs of deer skin for mending sledges, Eskimos' spectacles etc.' (see Rae, op. cit.).

'Collecting' in the course of private use, the objects Rae later donated to Scottish collections are chiefly functional, and include knives, harpoons and arrowheads from the Mackenzie and Coppermine Rivers, a salmon spear from Repulse Bay, and his own moccasins. Again, the copper and iron could have come from one of the many previous visiting ships to the area, or extracted locally: neither can be definitively ascribed to a European source.

Figure 5.2   Wooden figure from the collections in Edinburgh

Among the non-utilitarian items Rae gathered are a pair of labrets (Figure 5.3) of white limestone and blue glass, from the Mackenzie River. Beechey noted in Western Alaska in 1831 that men and boys readily removed their labrets to trade them (see Bockstoce, 1977, p. 88), and several writers have remarked upon the early preference for the colour blue in the area (see Ray, 1977, p. 17). The glass itself may have come from the west: Siberian trade was probably expanding within North America by the time of the first European contact (see Bockstoce, 1977, p. 71), and 'Russian' blue glass beads were widely used on both functional and decorative items in the Mackenzie River area and Alaska at the time.[3]

The most substantial early involvement of Scots in the Arctic was as whalers. Dundee and Peterhead, both important whaling ports, hold some of the most interesting objects derived from the Arctic during their heyday. At the Arbuthnot Museum, Peterhead, for example, there is a pair of suspenders collected in Greenland between 1849 and 1891 (Figure 5.4)[4] by a Captain David Gray. Made of soft, white leather to hold up inner boots or socks, they are backed with white European linen and were indubitably made for Gray's own use or for one of his men.

The McManus Galleries, Dundee holds a number of interesting items associated with the whaling trade. Among the most tantalizing are an ivory rosary (Figure 5.5), crochet hook and paper knife brought back by Brymer, a crewman on the *Active*, which operated in the Davis Straits in the 1890s. Poignant examples of the early impact of European form on local style, they almost certainly come from Greenland, where missionary presence had been felt since 1721 (see Rink, 1877, p. 34). Material associated with missionary influence is also to be found in Stromness Museum, Orkney, which holds photographs and records of Henry and Joseph Linklater, both captains of Moravian mission ships to Labrador.

I have mentioned cribbage boards as a clear reminder of the presence of Europeans in Eskimoaleut territory. Cribbage became popular during the gold rush in Nome, Alaska during the 1890s, and I have found three boards in Scottish collections. At the Marischal Museum, Aberdeen, there is a board collected by John Livingstone, a Hudson's Bay Company employee between 1913 and 1941. It is at present documented to be from Cape Dorset, but Livingstone could also have acquired it during his brief farming period in western Canada in 1924. In Orkney, there are two further boards from James ('Jimmy') Sinclair (Figure 5.6), who served on Baffin Island in the east and as post manager at Herschel Island and Letty Harbour, both in the Western

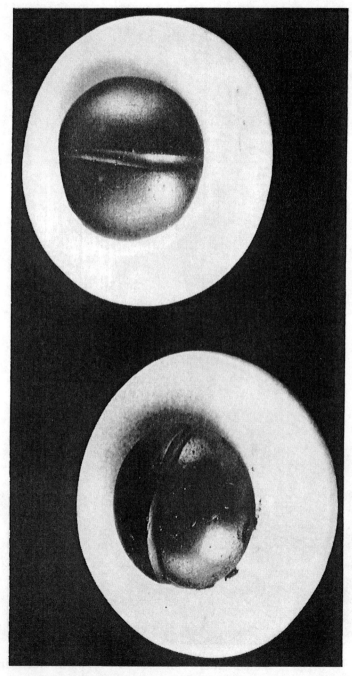

Figure 5.3   A pair of labrets from the Mackenzie River

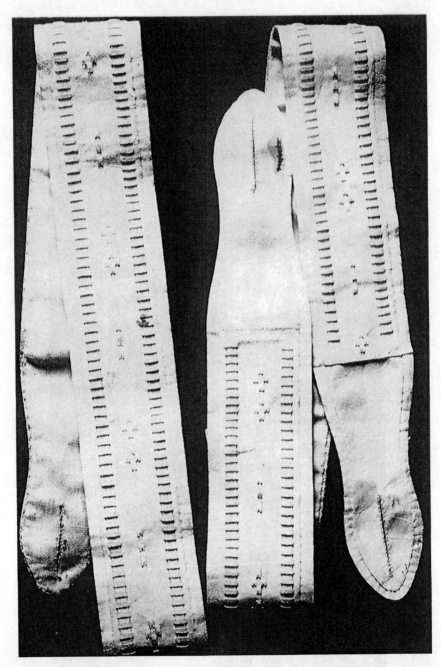

**Figure 5.4   A pair of suspenders collected in Greenland between 1849
and 1891**

Figure 5.5   An ivory rosary brought back by Brymer

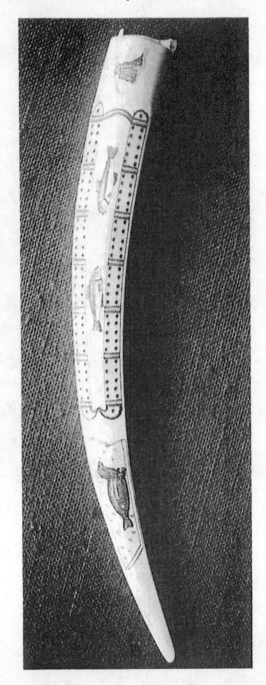

Figure 5.6   A cribbage board fom James ('Jimmy') Sinclair

Arctic, between 1931 and 1935.[5] He is thought to have collected the boards while revisiting old haunts in the 1960s.[6]

The people of the Western Arctic during the late nineteenth and early twentieth centuries were quick to incorporate ideas drawn from magazine illustrations and whalers' scrimshaw art into their own (see Ray, 1977, pp. 43–4). The Western style of pictorial art is present on each of the boards listed above. Art made for sale in the Alaskan region slumped following the influenza epidemic in 1918, when many artists died (ibid.), but cribbage boards were still being made for sale in the latter part of this century.

Non-indigenous script was another new feature applied to objects by Alaskan Inuit during the early twentieth century. At the Kelvingrove Museum, Glasgow, there are two bags, one made from a seal-flapper, inscribed in glass seed-beads with 'Sitka' (a city in Alaska) and 'Sitka 1900'. These were collected by Mrs Wilkie, while visiting her brother-in-law, Bishop Peter Trimble Rowe, of the American Episcopal Church (Lovelace, 1990). By 1900, Sitka had been subject to over 100 years of extensive white contact (ibid.), and its native inhabitants would have been well aware of the sort of souvenirs a visitor like Mrs Wilkie might wish to take home.

Late nineteenth and twentieth century Arctic collections of course contain more reference to the influence of European materials and forms than those made earlier. Several useful examples are within the collection of Roderick Ross MacFarlane, a Hudson's Bay Company clerk and chief trader between 1852 and 1920. MacFarlane explored the Anderson River in 1861 and collected prolifically, from which the Smithsonian Institution, in particular, has made gains (Vanstone in Sturtevant and Damas, 1984, p. 352). Perhaps because his home ground was the Isle of Lewis, however, some of MacFarlane's collection is also at Edinburgh and represents some of the best 'contact' art of this period in Scottish collections. All the objects were collected from the Mackenzie River area and include firebags, a bunch of dress charms (Figure 5.7),[7] and ivory needle cases all decorated with European seed-beads or 'Russian' beads. The presence of glass beads, in many parts of the world, is a well-known early material indicator of the presence of outsiders. However, all of these objects take previously existing forms.

It has already been seen that souvenirs gathered by employees of the Hudson's Bay Company are substantially represented within Scottish collections. Because of his lasting effect on Inuit art in the eastern Arctic, one who is due special mention is Lord Tweedsmuir.

Tweedsmuir, son of the author John Buchan, was taken on by the HBC in 1938 and was stationed at Cape Dorset, Baffin Island. During his two-year

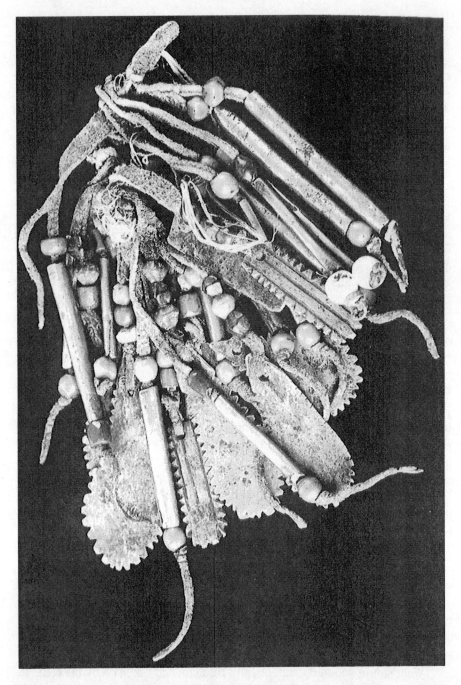

Figure 5.7   A bunch of dress charms from the Mackenzie River area

stay there he became friends with Peter Pitseolak, the 'paladin of his race' (Tweedsmuir, 1951, p. 15), who was later to become one of the finest Inuit artists of his day. Particularly famous for his paintings, Pitseolak first encountered the art-form when watching Tweedsmuir use a sketchbook and box of paints. Encouraged by his interest, Tweedsmuir sent to his mother for a block of paper and 'the largest paint box that money could buy'[8] for Pitseolak: 'Two years later, I received Pitseolak's paintings. These were the first paintings that he had ever attempted' (see Lord Tweedsmuir in Eber, 1980, p. 54), and are now in Montreal. Pitseolak was probably the first on Baffin Island to represent his life in the European, two-dimensional tradition.

Pitseolak was famous also for his carvings, widely illustrated in catalogues of Arctic art (see, e.g. Swinton, 1972, pp. 454, 459). In 1997, the National Museums of Scotland acquired one such carving, one of 37 Inuit items from Tweedsmuir's collection,[9] made by him. It depicts a woman standing on the back of a walrus holding a mug and pail (Figure 5.8); the details are executed using (imported) red and blue paint. The carving is thought to be that described by Tweedsmuir as 'a companion to the carving that he did of myself ... I look puny and ineffective clutching a snow-knife, while my large strapping wife ... towers over me' (see Tweedsmuir, 1951, p. 166). This, surely, is a souvenir as personal as one might collect!

Arctic peoples of today are internationally renowned for multiple art forms, including stone sculpture, printmaking, basketry, painting and textile arts. Many, though not all, of these are the result of special projects, generated by outsiders. One such project was that started by Brower, a trader at Point Barrow, Alaska, who in around 1905 suggested the creation of baskets made of baleen, the hornlike substance growing from the palates of some species of whale. Made by a small number of men, these baskets were probably copied from willow baskets traded into Alaska from Athapaskan Indians (see Ray, 1977, p. 49).

A recent example, made by the artist John Hanks of Point Barrow, was collected by Jonathan King, a curator at the British Museum, on behalf of the National Museums of Scotland in 1994. More rounded in shape, it is however not very different to those collected in the 1930s by the intrepid botanist Miss Isobel Hutchison.[10] Over a period of 60 years, the form has changed little.

Hutchison collected nearly 300 Inuit items from Alaska and Greenland in the 1920s and 1930s, which are now in the National Museums of Scotland.[11] Among the most interesting in Edinburgh, in 'souvenir' terms, is a Greenlandic doll, dressed in a red wool shirt, with an elaborate collar of glass beads, complete with bloomers (of which only one leg remains) and a pair of miniature

Figure 5.8   A woman standing on the back of a walrus holding a mug and pail from Tweedsmuir's collection of Inuit items

leather knee-boots (Figure 5.9). She was made by Otto Rosing, a Danish missionary at Umanagg. His wife, a Kalallit, was responsible for dressing the doll and provided her own hair.

James Houston has written widely on his encouragement, starting in 1948, of sculptors and graphic artists who could produce work for the first time for the outside market, which could help them survive within an increasingly monetized economy (see, e.g. Houston, 1995). In Scotland there are a small number of sculptures made in the eastern Arctic for sale. The largest is a 1960s soapstone carving in the National Museums of Scotland of an Inuit boy with a seal, carved by a younger relative of Pitseolak (Figure 5.10).[12] Its size is representative of Baffin Island art made for the market during the mid-late twentieth century, when, because larger works commanded higher prices, scale rose from the diminutive to the very large (see Swinton, 1972, p. 141).

Of contemporary Eskimoaleut art, Scottish museums hold very little. Although since Houston's time the art market has developed rapidly, due to a drastic reduction of Scottish presence in the Arctic during the same period, very little produced over the last 50 years has reached our shores. My own visits to private homes have shown that much more in Scotland lies in the hands of collectors who have lived in Canada further south, and returned to Scotland on retirement.

In 1997, Frances Pelly, a Scottish artist based in Orkney, visited Cape Dorset to gain experience and inspiration from the artistic community there. She was disappointed to find that many carvers now 'seem only to produce carvings when necessary – a fuel or grocery bill to pay' (see Pelly, 1998, p. 3).

Throughout the Arctic, in an environment where artistic production is now, for some, a specialized activity, and where industry to generate alternative sources of income is unevenly distributed, art for sale will continue to be made. In Scotland, the future of Inuit art seems bright. Frances Pelly hopes soon to set up a return visit by a Cape Dorset artist, Arnaunau Ashevak, to Orkney. If her plan comes off, what he will produce will be a 'souvenir' of his Scottish experience.

Souvenirs from the Arctic are recognized in Scottish museums to be of great relevance as material reminders of our cultural exchange. They still offer new opportunities to invigorate existing artistic practice. For this reason, it is hoped that museums in Scotland will have sufficient resources to continue to collect them.[13]

Figure 5.9   A Greenlandic doll collected by Isobel Hutchison

**Figure 5.10 Soapstone carving of an Inuit boy with a seal, carved by a
younger relative of Pitseolak**

Notes

1   The Inuit and Aleut, known collectively as the Eskimoaleut, constitute a linguistic family of the Arctic, extending from Greenland in the East, along the north and northeastern Canadian coastline and into Siberia. Forming two physically and culturally distinguishable groups, the Aleut inhabit the Aleutian Island chain and the Alaskan Peninsula; and the Inuit are traditionally placed on the northern coasts of Canada and Alaska, and in some parts of Greenland. Activities taking Scots to Arctic regions have brought them into contact with both groups; and both Aleut and Inuit objects are included in this article. I recognize however that groups within these territories is some cases distinguish themselves from one another, using other group names. While the use of the terms 'Inuit', 'Aleut' and 'Eskimoaleut' here is employed as a tool to discuss their art, where it is comparable, the author does not overlook these distinctions.

2   I use 'art' as a term referring to all items of artistic production, not exclusively to those which may be judged as 'art' for purely aesthetic reasons. It is beyond the scope of this chapter to enter into the distinction between art and artifact.

3   These beads may not have been made in Russia, but traded from Asia. See Dubin, 1987, pp. 274–5.

4   There is a question as to whether these suspenders were collected by Captain David Gray senior, or his grandson of the same name, both of whom were whalers. At present they can therefore be dated only approximately. The Grays were an important whaling family, who were involved in the Arctic for longer than any other in the British Isles. For more information, see Smith, 1993, pp. 27–35.

5   I am indebted to Judith Hudson Beattie of the Hudson's Bay Company archives for information about the careers of John Livingstone and James Sinclair.

6   Information from Bryce Wilson, Stromness Museum, Orkney.

7   In the opinion of James Houston, the well-known Canadian artist and author who has worked extensively with the Inuit, this bunch of dress charms was possibly imported from Siberia (verbal report, 11 March 1998).

8   For this inclusion I am indebted to Lord James Douglas-Hamilton, son-in-law of Lord Tweedsmuir, who passed on a copy of a personal record written by Lord Tweedsmuir of Pitseolak's first encounter with painting. Date unknown.

9   His collection had been on loan, for a number of years, at the Scott Polar Research Institute, Cambridge, who passed the collection to the National Museums of Scotland upon their purchase of it in 1997.

10   Isobel Hutchison was born at Kirkliston, Scotland in 1889, and died in 1982. 'In 1928–9 she spent a year in North Greenland, [and] went around the coast of Alaska in 1933, reaching Aklavik on the Mackenzie River in Canada in the winter by dog-team'. All information contained in this paper on Isobel Hutchison comes from Gwyneth Hoyle, a research associate at Trent University, Ontario, who is writing her biography.

11   In 1933, Isobel Hutchison also collected on the Alaskan coast for the Museum of Anthropology and Archaeology in Cambridge.

12   The documentation for this piece implies, but does not state, that it was made by Pitseolak Ashoona, famous for her prints and drawings (see, for example, Eber, 1971). Recent surveys of the piece by Terry Ryan of the West Baffin Eskimo Co-op Limited, and James Houston, suggest that it was in fact by a younger, male relative of Peter Pitseolak, of the same name.

13   I wish to acknowledge David Bertie at the Arbuthnot Museum, Peterhead; Mark Hall at the

Perth Museum and Art Gallery; Charles Hunt at the Marischal Museum, Aberdeen; Maire Noonan at the Kelvingrove Museum, Glasgow; Bryce Wilson at Stromness Museum, Orkney; and Adrian Zealand at the McManus Gallery, Dundee, for their help in preparing this article.

References

Bockstoce, J.R. (1977), *Eskimos of Northwest Alaska in the Early Nineteenth Century*, Oxford: Pitts Rivers Museum.

Bunyan, I., Calder, J., Idiens, D. and Wilson, B. (1993), *No Ordinary Journey*, Edinburgh: National Museums of Scotland.

Dubin, L.S. (1987), *The History of Beads*, London: Thames and Hudson.

Eber, D. (1971), *Pictures out of My Life*, Montreal and Oxford: Design Collaborative Books and Oxford University Press.

Eber, D. (1980), *Peter Pitseolak (1902–1973): Eskimo Historian of Seekooseelak*, Montreal: McCord Museum.

Fisher, A. (1819), 'Journal of a voyage of discovery to the Arctic regions performed between the 4th of April and the 19th of November, 1818, in His Majesty's ship Alexander, Wm. Edw. Parry Esq. Lieut. and Commander', in *New Voyages and Travels: Consisting of Originals, Translations and Abridgements*, London, Vol. 1, Richard Phillips.

Houston, J. (1995), *Confessions of an Igloo Dweller*, Toronto: McLelland and Stewart Inc.

Issenman, B.K. (1997), *Sinews of Survival: the Living Legacy of Inuit Clothing*, Vancouver: UBC Press.

Kane, E.K. (1861), *Arctic explorations: The Second Grinnell Expedition in search of Sir John Franklin 1853, '54, '55*, London: T. Nelson.

Lovelace, A. (1990), 'Two Alaskan masks in the reserve collections at Glasgow Galleries and Museums', unpublished.

Oswalt, W.H. (1979), *Eskimos and Explorers*, Novato, California: Chandler and Sharp Inc.

Parry, W.E. (1824), *Journal of a Second Voyage for the Discovery of a North-West Passage from the Atlantic to the Pacific, performed in the years 1821–3, in H.M. Fury and Hecla*, London.

Pelly, F. (1998), 'Report from Frances Pelly on a Study Visit to Cape Dorset', unpublished.

Rae, J. (1854), *Autobiography relating to the dates 1813 to April 1854*, unpublished, Scott Polar Research Institute Cambridge MS 787 1–2, Vol. 3.

Ray, D.J. (1977), *Eskimo Art: Tradition and Innovation in North Alaska*, Seattle and London: University of Washington Press.

Rink, H. (1877), *Danish Greenland: The People and Its Products*, London: Henry S. King and Co.

Smith, R. (1993), *The Whale Hunter*, Edinburgh: John Donald Publishers Ltd.

Sturtevant, W.C. and Damas, D. (eds), *Handbook of the North American Indians*, Vol. 5, Washington: Smithsonian Institute.

Swinton, G. (1972), *Sculpture of the Eskimo*, London: C. Hurst.

Tweedsmuir, Lord (1951), *Hudson's Bay Trader*, London: Spottiswoode Ballantyne and Co.

6 Exotic Souvenirs of the Travelling Surrealists

LOUISE TYTHACOTT

Almost all members of the Surrealist movement were concerned with identifying, collecting, displaying and revering certain types of 'things'. Most became avid collectors; some amassed large and significant collections of so-called primitive art. In the 1920s and 1930s, André Breton, the leader of the Surrealist movement, frequented the *marché aux puces* on the outskirts of Paris, wandering, searching for and often finding in the labyrinth of stalls objects – or souvenirs – he could identify as 'Surreal'. Breton recognized at these flea markets the fullest possibility for 'chance encounters', for unexpected, novel associations, for the discovery of objects torn from one set of circumstances and thrown into another.

The non-Western artefacts discovered in these markets were used as a means of subverting European aesthetics. In their provocative art exhibitions in the 1920s and 1930s, for example, a Duchamp 'ready-made' might be juxtaposed with a New Ireland *malagan* carving in an attempt to question the notion of 'art' traditionally used in the West. Surrealists used objects from other cultures as a means of transgressing or reshuffling the orders of Western classificatory systems. By deliberately juxtaposing different cultural realities, they believed they could bring into question the very nature of our own reality (Clifford, 1988).

Many Surrealist works are concerned with a collage-like fragmentation and realignment of cultural norms. Their domestic displays in particular exemplify this strategy of juxtaposing artefacts from different realities. Breton's apartment, as photographed in the late 1950s and 1960s, is a good example. On display were stuffed birds, cases of tropical butterflies, decorative boxes filled with marvellous objects, coins, minerals, crystals, glass bottles, objects made by psychiatric patients, books, photographs, paintings by Henri Rousseau, prints by Edward Munch, drawings by Seurat and Adolf Wölfi, sculptures by Giacometti, *objets trouvées* discovered in the Parisian flea markets and a rich variety of masks and sculptures from Africa, Asia, Oceania

72

and the Americas. Photographs of the apartment depict an intensely crowded domain with something of the air of a Cabinet of Curiosities. Objects adorn the walls and the shelves, inhabit boxes, glass cases and belljars – even overflow onto Breton's desk. So dense and crowded was the apartment with these rare and strange objects that George Melly likened the atmosphere to that of a museum. Some of the spaces were designed in museum-like classifications: there were over 30 *kachinas* from the American South West laid out in several in rows, surrounded by paintings. Across another wall Breton's collection of Inuit masks was hung. He mounted his Easter Island carvings on perspex and interspersed pre-Columbian heads with Northwest Coast masks. Breton once said of these objects:

> For my part, I often feel the need to return to them, to awaken looking at them, to take them in my hands, to accompany them back to the places from which they came in order to be reconciled with the places where I am (Cowling, 1992, p. 180).

Breton had his favourite *malagan* sculpture prominently placed, reverential and almost totem-like on his desk, and he apparently used to touch and stroke some of his favourite ethnographic pieces. He is often depicted in these strange, atmospheric images, seated at his desk, or smoking a pipe – a dominating presence, the only human amongst a plethora of exotica, as if presiding over a strange world of objects from far away places, or as Dawn Ades (1995) once suggested, he is like a 'fetishist' amongst his 'fetishes'.

Both Breton and his close friend and Surrealist associate, Paul Eluard, amassed large collections of ethnographic objects in the 1920s and 1930s which were put together from wandering around these flea markets, from dealers' shops, auctioneers or through contact with travellers arriving back from abroad. Surrealists seemed to be in constant search of Oceanic pieces at this time, which they considered to be strangely beautiful:

> There was a time wrote Breton, when every trip abroad that I and my friends made, was motivated by the hope that we would discover after incessant day-long searching, some rare Oceanic object (Cowling, op. cit.).

Elisabeth Cowling argues:

> it became Breton's mission to reinvest Oceanic objects with the 'surreal' power once native to them but since lost through mis-appropriation by the colonialists, missionaries and ethnographers who had brought them to Europe as so many 'curious' trophies of peoples in a state of still-unnregenerate savagery. In buying

up Oceanic art in the curio shops, flea markets and auction houses of Europe the Surrealists believed they were saving it from defiling hands (ibid., p. 181).

Many of the activities of the Surrealists were concerned with seeking out and attributing sacredness to banal, forgotten, devalued things in a deliberate attempt to defy Western systems of value. Surrealists were concerned to reinstate materials or revalue objects that had been excluded, degraded or debased by the West. Hence Duchamp's bottle rack or urinal, or those waste materials – newspapers, bus tickets, magazines, debris, found and chosen objects – that Kurt Schwitters so tenderly enmeshed into collages. Other Surrealist creations reveal a respectful, reverential, even obsessive relationship to otherwise unconsidered material. The collection and display of non-Western masks and sculptures found a place within these Surrealist acts of cultural usurpation and redefinition.

The range of ethnographic objects collected by Breton and Eluard is witnessed in 1931 when in response to financial difficulties they auctioned their collections at the Hôtel Drouot in Paris. The sale, which consisted of around 310 non-European objects, is considered to be one of the most important 'Primitive art' auctions held in Paris between the wars (Maurer, 1984, p. 546). The catalogue reveals the variety and size of their combined collection, with masks from Africa, the Pacific and the Americas. Almost half (149) were from Oceania, 125 were from North or South America, and only 30 from Africa.

Breton's main ethnographic love had always been Oceania. The very first 'primitive' object he bought as a child was a figure from Easter Island. In his novel *Nadja* (1926) he writes of a conical mask from New Britain made of reeds and red elder fibre; an Easter Island figure is also illustrated. So moved was Breton by the art of the Pacific art that he declares that 'he development of surrealism' was 'inseparable from the power to seduce and fascinate that Oceanic art possessed in our eyes' (Ades, 1978, pp. 463–4).

Breton collected *kapkaps* from the Solomon Islands, jade *tikis* from New Zealand (see Figure 6.1). It is easy to imagine how these small objects could be transported across oceans to Europe, emerging as if by chance in a Parisian flea market, attracting the eye of a wandering Surrealist searching for *objets trouvé* and integrated into an eclectic domestic display. Breton sustained a passionate obsession with Pacific artefacts throughout his entire life and was even buried with his favourite oceanic piece (Cowling, 1991, p. 180).

There were many other Surrealists who collected Oceanian objects, some of whom even travelled to the Pacific archipelago. Paul Eluard, Max Ernst,

Figure 6.1 *Hei-tiki* (personal ornaments: pendant), nephrite, nineteenth century. Maori, New Zealand. Copyright: Board of Trustees of the National Museums and Galleries on Merseyside (Liverpool Museum)

Roberta Matta, Tristan Tzara, and Wilfredo Lam – to name but a few – amassed collections from New Guinea, New Ireland and New Caledonia. Surrealists also included Pacific objects in their journals, art magazines and exhibitions. The catalogue cover to a display of paintings by Man Ray in March 1926, for example, illustrated a photograph entitled *The Moon shines above the Island of Nias* in which a Pacific sculpture from Breton's collection takes central place in a dreamy lunar landscape, with a large round moon in the left-hand side.[1] The exhibition included over 60 sculptures from Indonesia and the Pacific Islands from the collections of Breton, Eluard, Aragon and others, placed alongside recent photographs and paintings by Man Ray.

If the focus of Surrealist exotic souvenir collecting in the 1920s and 1930s was Oceania, by the 1940s their gaze had shifted to the Americas, largely as a result of the physical relocation of the Surrealist movement to the USA after the German invasion of France. Here, in an entirely new continent, Surrealists were able to nurture their obsessions and desires for ethnographic art. Breton and Max Ernst forged a close alliance with the French anthropologist, Claude Lévi-Strauss and together the three wandered around flea markets, bric-à-brac shops and the ethnographic museums of New York. They discovered and collected pre-Columbian ceramics, Hopi *kachinas* and Northwest Coast and Inuit masks – objects that were then relatively hard to find in quantity in Europe.

Hopi culture in particular began to fascinate many of these Surrealists in exile. The small wooden *kachinas* increasingly appear in Surrealist collections from the 1930s on: Breton, Ernst, Marcel Duchamp and Roland Penrose all acquired these figures. During a trip across the USA in 1945 Breton even visited Hopi villages, reputedly taking notes on certain rituals and way of life. But it was Ernst more than any other who came to know the Hopi culture. In the spring of 1946 he bought a plot of land in Sedona, Arizona, where he lived in relative isolation for the next seven years. The Indians were one of the things that most attracted him to this landscape. He made friends with Hopi people and continued to collect *kachinas*.

The vibrant, multicoloured and often hybrid masks of British Colombia also attracted the Surrealist gaze. Ernst, Breton, Aragon and Eluard acquired Northwest Coast masks. Kurt Seligman and Wolfgang Paalen amassed the finest collections; the latter travelled widely in British Colombia and Alaska during the 1930s and was commissioned to collect for both the National Museum of Anthropology in Mexico City and the Musée de l'Homme.

Inuit, or what were then termed Eskimo, artefacts were also greatly admired by wandering Surrealist collectors. The Breton-Eluard sale in 1931 consisted of items such as carved ivory tusks from Alaska, ivory toggles, decorated tusks, small model sleighs and masks. In the 1940s and 1950s Breton had amassed a superb collection of Inuit shamanic masks, many of which he displayed prominently along his apartment walls.

Finally, Surrealists collected a range of souvenirs from travels around Latin America. Antonin Artaud was the first to visit Mexico in 1936, remarking that the few weeks spent among the Tarahumara in the remote northern Sierra region were the happiest times of his life. Benjamin Péret, the Surrealist poet, spent much time amongst the Indians in Mexico and also lived in Brazil, later on publishing a collection of indigenous myths (1960). Paalen settled in Mexico in 1939 and collected pre-Columbian art, owning a Mayan relief from Campeche depicting Chac, the god of rain. Breton, who visited Mexico in 1938, was also haunted by Mesoamerican art and writes of the aura surrounding these ancient ceramic pieces.

Conclusion

Collecting exotic souvenirs became a crucial activity for members of the Surrealist movement, and perhaps for Breton, a complete obsession. Many Surrealists constructed small domestic museums populated with strange, wonderful, curious souvenirs gathered from bric-à-brac shops, auctions or on their travels around the world. And the resulting displays, with their syncretic groupings, gave the impression more of Cabinets of Curiosity than nineteenth or twentieth century museums organized along scientific or typological classifications.

While Surrealist collections and displays may on first sight appear eclectic, crowded or chaotic, they are, as Cowling suggests '... always guided by a consistent aesthetic' (Cowling, 1978, p. 458) – by the desire to transgress bounded notions of art, aesthetics and beauty and to redefine and reclassify the orders and categories of the twentieth century European world. Surrealist souvenir collections deliberately juxtapose objects which are mutually alien, strange and foreign – according to European classificatory systems – but which are united by a perceived notion of marvellousness and aura to the initiated Surrealist collector.[2]

Notes

1   The island of Nias is located to the west of Sumatra in the Indian Ocean.
2   This chapter is taken from the author's monograph on *Surrealism and the Exotic*, 1999, Harwood Academic Publishers.

References

Ades, D. (1995), lecture on *Fetishism and Surrealism*, University of Brighton.

Clifford, J. (1988), 'On Ethnographic Surrealism', in J. Clifford, *The Predicament of Culture: Twentieth Century Ethnography, Literature and Art*, Massachusetts and London: Harvard University Press.

Cowling, E. (1978), 'Another Culture', in D. Ades, *Dada and Surrealism Revealed*, catalogue, Hayward Gallery Exhibition, published by the Arts Council of Great Britain, London.

Cowling, E. (1992), '*L'oeil Sauvage*: Oceanic Art and the Surrealists', in S. Greub (ed.), *The Art of the Northwest New Guinea*, New York: Rizzoli International Publications.

Maurer, E. (1984), 'Dada and Surrealism', in W. Rubin (ed.), *Primitivism in 20th century art: Affinity of the Tribal and the Modern*, New York: Museum of Modern Art.

7   Women's Suffrage Souvenirs

KATHERINE BRADLEY

Before I begin to examine suffrage souvenirs, I will give a brief history of the suffrage movement.[1] The debate on women's suffrage began in earnest with the publication of *The English Woman's Journal* (1858) and John Stuart Mill's book *The Subjection of Women* (1869). By the early 1870s organized groups of suffrage supporters existed in London and all the major provincial cities. Petitions were organized and presented to parliament annually and public meetings were regularly held all over Britain. In 1897 the various groups formed an umbrella organization, the National Union of Women's Suffrage Societies (NUWSS), under the leadership of Millicent Fawcett. The NUWSS was a large non-militant organization which campaigned peacefully, holding public meetings and demonstrations, as well as collecting signatures for petitions to parliament and lobbying MPs. In 1903 Emmeline Pankhurst and her daughter Christabel, formed the Women's Social and Political Union (WSPU), a breakaway group. In 1905 they began their more militant activities and eventually became known as the suffragettes.[2] This militancy was a result of their frustration with the lack of progress in granting women the vote. They quickly attracted a large membership, some of whom were arrested and imprisoned on charges arising from militant demonstrations. When these women went on hunger strike, as a demonstration against their treatment as Second Division (criminal) prisoners, rather than First Division political ones, they were often brutally force fed. Their treatment aroused much public sympathy for the suffrage cause. However, by 1914 public support for women's suffrage had been undermined by their increasing militancy. From 1897 the suffrage groups' object was for women to be given the vote on the same terms as men, that is, dependent on existing property qualifications. Eventually in 1918 under the Representation of the People Act, women householders and wives of householders over the age of 30 were granted the vote. Finally in 1928 all women over 21 were enfranchised, giving women equal suffrage rights to men.

In this chapter I will concentrate on the WSPU, since they were the first female political group to market their goods and were first class entrepreneurs

(Atkinson, 1992, p. 18). They have long fascinated historians by the way in which they broke the boundaries of Edwardian conventional behaviour. The WSPU managed to capture the public imagination, then and now, partly as a result of their behaviour and actions, and partly as a result of their conscious portrayal as a feminine and feminist group of women, who paid close attention to the way in which they presented themselves to the public, both in their dress and their propaganda. Closely connected to this was the way in which they marketed their goods and how these goods have then been used by historians, feminists and modern collectors to help piece together their history.

Three leading suffragettes were mainly responsible for marketing the WSPU. They were Sylvia Pankhurst, who designed the WSPU logos and most of their goods; and Emmeline and Frederick Pethick Lawrence who were responsible for promoting the WSPU's image and ideas as well as their marketing and fundraising strategies. Unlike the NUWSS and the smaller militant group the Women's Freedom League (WFL), the WSPU did not have a specific group of artists to create their imagery.[3] Instead they relied on Sylvia Pankhurst for their main designs. Other artists contributed drawings and cartoons, but these were mainly confined to the suffragette journals, *Votes for Women* and later *The Suffragette*.

Sylvia Pankhurst (1886–1960), the second daughter of Emmeline and Richard Pankhurst, was a trained artist who had studied at Manchester Art School in 1901 and then won a scholarship in 1904 to the Royal College of Art. In 1906 she left the Royal College and devoted her time to the WSPU, as an artist and writer. She first designed the WSPU membership card and then nearly all their visual material, until at least 1910. Eventually in 1914, after a disagreement with her mother and sister, she formed the East London Federation of Suffragettes, later the Workers' Suffrage Federation.

The Pethick Lawrences were a wealthy couple who joined the WSPU in 1906. Emmeline Pethick (1867–1954) and Frederick Lawrence (1871–1961) were married in 1901. That year Frederick, a wealthy Cambridge graduate, took on the responsibility for the finances of the London evening newspaper, *The Echo* and in 1903 became its editor. He then edited various other publications. Emmeline Pethick had been a settlement worker. In 1906 she was appointed the WSPU Treasurer and quickly reorganized its chaotic finances. In 1907 Frederick began to publish *Votes for Women* which soon became the official WSPU weekly newspaper. Although Frederick did not have an official position within the WSPU he helped his wife edit and write for *Votes for Women*. Together with Christabel Pankhurst they controlled WSPU appointments, finances and publications. In 1912 they broke away from the WSPU, due to disagreements with the Pankhursts over the more extreme use of militancy and the following year formed the Votes for Women Fellowship, later the United Suffragists. *Votes for Women* remained in their hands, whilst Christabel Pankhurst edited a new journal, *The Suffragette*.[4]

Because of its range of activities and propaganda, the WSPU had a vast expenditure, larger than any other suffrage organization. This increased rapidly from £2,705 (income £2,959) in 1906–07 to approximately £36,896 (income £46,876) in the financial year, 1913 to 1914 (*Women's Social and Political Union, Annual Reports*, 1907–14). At first the money came from subscribers and members as well as collections at public meetings. But as the WSPU expanded it found that it was not raising enough money to pay for its activities. By 1909 the WSPU employed 45 office staff and 30 organizers (Rosen, 1974, pp. 63, 69 and 130). Activities also increased which needed more funds and this resulted in additional fundraising activities such as tea parties, concerts and self-denial weeks, together with the marketing of a variety of goods. Thus from 1908 more funds were needed to pay for the court fines of suffragettes who were arrested, charged and then fined, as well as for advertising the increasing number of public events, hiring halls for public meetings and the expanding administrative staff.

In 1906 the Pethick Lawrences reorganized the WSPU's accounting system and formed as eparate literature section, the Women's Press, and engaged a shopkeeper, Alice Knight, to manage it. At first the shop sold books, pamphlets, badges and postcards of photographs of WSPU leaders. The Women's Press itself began as a publishing imprint and distribution house, based in the WSPU headquarters, 4 St Clements Inn. To begin with its profits in 1906 were £60. Gradually it expanded and produced a variety of goods, so that by 1910 its profits increased to £12,000 (*Women's Social and Political Union, Annual Reports*, 1906–07 and 1912–13). That year it moved to larger premises at 186 Charing Cross. Two years later it moved again to the new and larger WSPU headquarters at Lincoln's Inn House in Kingsway. From this time until 1914, however, the WSPU reduced its activities and made its priority the production of literature and propaganda. It discontinued the production and sale of its other goods. This was due to the increased use of militancy which took the form of a window smashing campaign (government offices and West End department stores), and resulted in the split between the Pethick Lawrences and the Pankhursts; followed in 1913 until the beginning of the First World War by an arson and letter box campaign.[5] Added to this between 1913 and 1914 the headquarters were periodically raided by the police.

To raise more funds, the WSPU, with the help of the Pethick Lawrences and Sylvia Pankhurst, designed new methods of marketing their ideas. This was done by widening the remit of the Women's Press and adopting colours which would identify their goods and activities. Stocks from the Women's Press were sold at public meetings, demonstrations and in shops in London and the provinces. Goods were produced specifically for the WSPU, packaged and embellished with their colours, purple, green and white; their slogan, 'Votes for Women' and the various logos.[6]

Between 1908 and 1912 an enormous variety of goods and literature were sold. These can be divided into four groups: paper goods, clothing, foodstuffs and miscellaneous goods. The first group included boxes of stationery, blotters, songsheets, greeting cards including Christmas cards, albums, signed photographs of leading suffragettes, such as Annie Kenney,[7] souvenir programmes of demonstrations, posters and calendars. Clothing articles were mainly decorative, such as hat trimmings, buttons, buckles, broaches, necklaces, pins, rosette ribbons, ties, shantung motor scarves (one of the most successful items as it could be adapted as a stole, a motorveil or as trimming for a straw boater), silk scarves, shoulder sashes, ribbons, belt ribbons, linen, cotton and paper handkerchiefs and bags including 'the Emmeline' and 'the Christabel bag'. White muslin blouses (white was the colour which women were encouraged to wear at demonstrations) were also sold. Foodstuffs included marmalade, chocolates and tea. Miscellaneous items ranged from board games such as Pank-a-squith, 'the highly artistic Table Game that helps to Spread the movement ... PUZZLES, AMUSES, TEASES, EXCITES, SETS EVERYBODY LAUGHING',[8] puzzles, card games, such as 'The Game of Suffragettes', all devised by the WSPU and other manufacturers; to packets of sweet pea seeds, boxes of buttermilk soap, suffragette dolls, cigarettes, the 'Pethick' tobacco pouch, and 24-piece tea sets, designed with embellishments by Sylvia Pankhurst and manufactured by Williamson of Longton, Staffordshire in 1909. All were advertised by the Women's Press and *Votes for Women*.

Some of the larger groups in London and the provinces had their own shops. By 1911 there were 17 shops in London covering the area between Bow and Wimbledon and there were 15 outside London, for example in Manchester, Liverpool, Oldham, Reading and Bath. In Bath the shop, in rented premises in the town centre, survived from September 1910 until at least 1913. Here members sold WSPU goods as well as home-produced goods such as lavender bags, sweets, cakes and needlework. Bath WSPU members also sold goods at public meetings and at the local market. The money raised contributed to their local funds and the WSPU nationally (*Votes for Women*,

10 September 1909).[9] Other groups such as Oxford had a temporary shop
which was set up in November 1910 for a month, possibly to take advantage
of the Christmas demand (ibid., 11 November and 23 December 1910).[10]

One of the more spectacular ways in which the WSPU promoted its ideas
and simultaneously raised funds was the 'Women's Exhibition' held at the
Prince's Skating Rink, Knightsbridge, between 18 and 26 May 1909.[11] Here
it marketed not only the goods produced by the Women's Press, but local
groups contributed stalls; refreshments were provided; a photographic history
of feminism was displayed; the Actresses' Suffrage League performed suffrage
plays and some members taught ju-jitsu. There were also contributions by the
major London department stores, Liberty, Derry and Toms and Peter Jones,
and from the South Moulton Street and Bond Street milliners. A polling booth
was set up where the public could vote on a different issue each day. WSPU
members from all over the country flocked to this exhibition. In fact special
excursions were arranged for members to visit it. It was a great success,
enrolling more than 250 members and raising £5,664. At the exhibition a
presentation of a car upholstered in the WSPU colours was made to Emmeline
Pethick Lawrence, to help her with her propaganda and fundraising work.

As a result of the Exhibition's success, similar events were put on
elsewhere, such as the Grand Bazaar at St Andrew's Hall, Glasgow in April
1910 (King, 1993, p. 140). Here the Scottish WSPU sold similar wares but
added to the goods the decoration of the Scottish thistle which conveniently
matched WSPU colours. Christmas and Flower Fairs were also held
intermittently in London on a similar basis to the Exhibition.

All suffrage groups had their own colours. These were first introduced by
the NUWSS in 1907 and were red and white. Green was later added in
November 1909. However, the first group to consciously choose its colours
was the WSPU in May 1908. These were chosen by Emmeline Pethick
Lawrence. She explained the symbolism behind them in *Votes for Women*.[12]

> Purple as everyone knows is the royal colour. It stands for the royal blood that
> flows in the veins of every suffragette, the instinct of freedom and dignity ...
> White stands for purity in private and public life ... Green is the colour of hope
> and the emblem of spring.

These colours were worn at demonstrations and were first used at the Women's
Sunday on 21 June 1908 in London (*Votes for Women*, 2 July 1908). Here,
under the direction of Mrs Pethick Lawrence, 700 banners were decorated,
thousands of flags carried and sashes were worn over white dresses. During

this demonstration like all the others, WSPU goods were sold. Street vendors also capitalized on the large numbers of participants and carried suffragette rubber dolls on their trays and offered 'heverlasting soiveneers of the grite de-mon-steration' (ibid.).

Soon other suffrage groups adopted their own colours, as did the anti-suffragists, and it became easy to identify both literature and groups and individuals at suffrage and anti-suffrage meetings and demonstrations. For example, the WFL held a referendum in 1908 and their members chose green, white and gold. In 1910 the NUWSS in their journal *Common Cause* announced that their colours were also symbolic. White portrayed 'serene faith in ideas which makes the soul divine'; green 'the perpetual reflorescence of hope and youth into the fruit of well-doing'; and red 'the passion and blood of martyrs and of heroes' (*Common Cause*, 26 May 1910).[13]

In terms of marketing, other suffrage organizations stuck to producing literature, posters, postcards and banners. This was not because they were not in need of funds, although none had the heavy expenditure incurred by WSPU militant actions. Indeed they were all less affluent, and all held fundraising events and made frequent appeals, but they relied on more traditional methods. Possibly they did not approve of WSPU fundraising methods in the same way as they disapproved of their militancy.

The opposition to women's suffrage, which by 1908 had formed the Women's Anti-Suffrage League, later the National League Opposing Women's Suffrage, also adopted their own colours, white, pink and black. Like the suffragettes they used them to decorate meetings, literature and badges. They also attempted to market goods, such as badges, posters, cartoon postcards and pottery, which often caricatured the suffragettes, for example, a Royal Doulton virago inkwell.[14] On the whole they had no problem in attracting funds since much of their membership was wealthy, paid large subscriptions and organized fundraising social events. These items have not been collected in the way suffragette artefacts have, possibly because they were the losers and represented ideas which have become unpopular.

As the suffragettes became better known some of the main London department stores cashed in on the possibility of gaining new customers. As Atkinson (1992, p. 21) comments:

> Evidence suggests that takings rose in the weeks before a major rally or procession in London, but that leading stores and smaller shops all over the capital kept a regular stock of purple, white and green items.

They advertised in all the main suffrage journals as well as in *The Anti-Suffrage Review*. In *Votes for Women* there were also regular articles on fashion from 1909, headed 'Concerning Dress'. In 1909 the first West End department stores to take advantage of this new market were Peter Robinson and Liberty, followed by Derry and Toms. They stocked fashion accessories in WSPU colours including shoes. They were soon followed by many Bond Street shops and the jewellers, Mappin and Webb, who advertised and sold by catalogue jewellery in the WSPU colours, for example a gold brooch with an emerald, pearls and amethyst, priced £8 10s. 6d. (*Votes for Women*, 17 December 1909). Many other companies cashed in on this new market such as the bicycle company, Elswick, which sold painted bikes in WSPU colours, price 10 guineas (ibid., 25 June 1909). All these goods could be ordered through the WSPU, who made a profit from their sales.

Between 1910 and 1914 the WSPU ran two other schemes to promote its ideas and increase its membership. The first of these was to encourage members to organize a holiday campaign whilst on their summer holidays, as a means of 'political tourism'. Many suffragettes spent their holidays in different towns at 'suffragette' bed and breakfast accommodation in coastal resorts such as Brighton, (advertised in *Votes for Women*), or visiting their friends in other areas. These campaigns were undertaken either in conjunction with an existing branch or where no branch existed and were then a means of recruiting members to form a branch, for example, Oxford and St Ives (ibid., 23 July, 13, 20 and 27 August 1909).[15] Here they sold WSPU literature and badges and even goods and addressed open air meetings. Judging from the reports in *Votes for Women* they were successful. Indeed, by 1913 the holiday campaigns had become more sophisticated and were given individual titles, for example 'By the Silver Sea' (Kent), 'Shakespeare's Country', 'the English Riviera' (Devon and Cornwall) and 'the Island Campaign' (the Isle of Man) (*The Suffragette*, 1 and 8 August 1913).

The second scheme was the 1910 'Circulation Scheme' (*Votes for Women*, 1 July and 23 October 1910). This was a complicated competition for increasing the circulation of *Votes for Women* during the summer months. Prizes were awarded to members and local groups who sold the largest number of copies of the journal to newsagents and at meetings, as well as to groups who persuaded newsagents to exhibit suffragette posters. There were first, second and third prizes and these included a bicycle inscribed with 'Votes for Women' and the name of the winner, books, a green metal watch, bound volumes of *Votes for Women* and unspecified mementos. Although not strictly speaking souvenirs, I have included this scheme because it helped to establish a pattern of rewards and a recognition of exceptional devotion to the cause, which was given to suffragette prisoners.

One of the WSPU mottos, 'Deeds not Words', succinctly describes the WSPU expectations of their members, that is, that they were required when possible to participate in non-violent demonstrations which could lead to a prison sentence. In prison many went on hunger strike. The form of reward for this was particularly treasured by the recipients. They have also become collectors' items, perhaps the most valued since they are both rarer and help to identify individuals who actively participated in the WSPU. Interestingly the WFL, which also required its members to perform deeds of self-sacrifice such as refusal to pay taxes, did not reward their members for these services. Instead they followed a philosophy of altruistic self-sacrifice.

There were two types of reward for these WSPU members. The first was for those suffragettes who were imprisoned for their actions at demonstrations and later for participating in the window smashing and arson campaigns. The second was for those who went on hunger strike. For imprisonment, suffragettes received a badge decorated with WSPU ribbons. Hunger strikers were awarded medals which represented a prison's portcullis and chains in silver, pierced by a convict's enamel arrow in WSPU colours and were engraved with dates of the suffragette's hunger strike. They also received illustrated scrolls and their names inscribed on a list of honour. All were designed by Sylvia Pankhurst. To further commemorate these individuals and to raise additional funds, photographs of suffragette prisoners and bags decorated with the convict's arrow, were also sold.

In some ways the historian is not only a tourist of the past, but a collector of the remains or souvenirs of the past. In a similar way to the tourist, the historian makes a journey, not to a particular resort, but to a specific period and subject, and like the tourist relies on memories and more concrete reminders, such as documents and objects. The picture of past holidays are never complete, just fragmented memories of places and events. The more concrete reminders are the souvenirs. The historian, like the tourist, gives these fragments a new identity as well as preserving them for posterity. Thus the visible remains of the suffragette movement are in effect rather similar to the souvenirs which tourists take home.

Some historians of the early twentieth century and of women's history have focused on women's suffrage, its feminist ideas and contribution to extending liberal democracy and women's public role, in particular the suffragettes. Much of the evidence comes from the legacy of material described earlier. Some of these objects have survived in museums and are displayed as suffragette collections. One of the earliest is in the People's Palace Museum, Glasgow (King, 1993, pp. 123 and 138), acquired in the early 1950s, when surviving Scottish suffragettes decided to donate their memorabilia. The largest collection is probably in the Museum of London. The main collections of documents are scattered in libraries, mainly the Fawcett, Bodleian and Manchester City Libraries. Yet more documents and artifacts are in the hands of private collectors, for example, the film director, Jill Craigie. From the 1960s onwards, coinciding with the advent of second wave feminism, much of this material has been reproduced as postcards, posters, as well as on goods, such as mugs and badges for the modern consumers of their history. The marketing of these replicas is integrated into museums and libraries as part of their wider facilities. The WSPU colours have also been used by groups of feminists such as the women camping at Greenham Common in the 1980s and more recently the Women's Peace Alliance in Northern Ireland, as well as covers of women's history books, such as *Women's History: Britain, 1850–1945* (Purvis, 1995)[16] and to advertise feminist conferences. Thus, like tourists, historians and museums have given these artefacts a new identity and have helped in their preservation. However, in the last few years collections of suffragette goods have also been collected by an increasing number of individuals, either out of interest, or to make money. As a result the prices of these souvenirs have risen, so that it is difficult for historians and museums to compete.

Thus in effect the surviving visible suffragette remains have become souvenirs, both at the time when they were produced, when they were bought and often kept as a reminder to their owners of past events and places and more recently when they have been used by historians and museums to remind us of the suffragettes' contribution to political and cultural life. This is not surprising since historians need past documents and artefacts to help them reconstruct the past. It could also be argued that because the suffragettes left such a rich heritage of their history and ideas in the form of mementos or souvenirs, that this has contributed to many historians concentrating on this particular group of campaigners for women's suffrage, rather than the non-militant suffragists or other women's groups. Hence the suffragettes have unwittingly provided historians and collectors with a great deal of colourful material which has enabled them to reconstruct their past. This is, I would argue, because they were successful both as entrepreneurs and propagandists. Thus the suffragettes have contributed to their own survival.

Notes

1   There is a great deal of literature on women's suffrage (see References). For an excellent overview of suffrage history and the way in which propaganda was produced and disseminated, see Tickner, 1989.

2   Until 1906 supporters of women's suffrage were known as suffragists. As militancy increased the media and the different groups felt there was a need to distinguish between the different supporters. Members of the WSPU and the WFL were known as suffragettes. The word was first used by *The Daily Mail*.

3   The two main groups of artists to support women's suffrage were the Artists' Suffrage League (1907) and the Suffrage Atelier (1909). They produced much of the suffrage propaganda material between 1907–14. See Tickner, 1989, pp. 15–26.

4   *The Suffragette* continued until the outbreak of the First World War, when Emmeline and Christabel Pankhurst changed its name to *Britannia*. It survived until 1918.

5   The WSPU's arson campaign commenced officially in November 1912 and continued until the outbreak of the First World War. WSPU members burnt down empty private and public buildings and set pillar boxes alight. The campaign gradually extended to cutting telephone lines, slashing paintings in art galleries and finally attacking churches. It illustrated the growing frustration of the WSPU with the government's broken promises and the lack of legislation.

6   Between 1907 and 1911 Sylvia Pankhurst designed four different logos. This did not seem to have an adverse effect on sales.

7   Annie Kenney (1879–1953) was a former cotton mill worker. She campaigned with Christabel Pankhurst in Manchester and later became one of the leading WSPU organizers. Like most other organizers she was arrested and imprisoned several times.

8   For an illustration of this and some of the other items marketed by the WSPU see Atkinson, 1992.

9   The Bath shop was officially opened on 14 September 1909 and remained open until mid-1913. At times it was closed due to a lack of volunteers.

10 The shop was in Oxford High Street.

11 Between 14 January and 4 June 1909, *Votes for Women* reported the arrangements, the Exhibition itself and the financial outcome in detail.

12 Editorials in 1908 frequently stressed the importance of the colours and their role in providing the WSPU with a separate identity, particularly at large demonstrations in London.

13 Other suffrage groups which adopted colours were:

Artists' Suffrage League – blue and silver;
Suffrage Atelier – blue, orange and black;
Women's Conservative and Unionist Franchise Association – blue, white and gold;
Writers' Suffrage League – black, white and gold;
Votes for Women Fellowship – purple, white and red;
Church League for Women's Suffrage – white and gold;
East London Federation of the Suffragettes – purple, white, green and red;
Jewish League for Women's Suffrage – royal purple and celestial blue;
Actresses' Franchise League – pink and green;
Free Church League – buff, blue and green.

14 The Royal Doulton Inkwell can be found at the Sir Henry Doulton Gallery, Stoke-on-Trent.
15 Three members of the WSPU on holiday in Oxford, held open air meetings and sold literature in the summer of 1909. As a result of their work an Oxford branch was eventually established. From 1909 until the summer of 1914 WSPU members on holiday held open air meetings and sold literature in St Ives, Cornwall. They never managed to establish a branch there.
16 The cover is an illustration reproduced from *The Suffragette*, 11 July 1913. It is a photograph of two suffragettes selling *The Suffragette* at the Henley Regatta.

References

Primary Sources

The Anti-Suffrage Review.
Common Cause.
The Suffragette.
The Vote.
Votes for Women.
Women's Social and Political Union, Annual Reports 1907–14.

Secondary Sources

(The literature about the women's suffrage movement is vast. The titles given here are a small selection of books which have been used for this chapter.)

Atkinson, D. (1990), *Votes for Women*, Cambridge: Cambridge University Press.
Atkinson, D. (1992), *Suffragettes in the Purple, White and Green*, London: Museum of London.
Atkinson, D. (1996), *The Suffragettes in Pictures*, Stroud: Sutton Publishing.
Balshaw, J. (1997), 'Sharing the Burden: The Pethick Lawrences and women's suffrage', in A.V. John and C. Eustance (eds), *The Men's Share? Masculinities, Male Support and Women's Suffrage in Britain, 1890–1920*, London and New York: Routledge.
Brittain, V. (1963), *Pethwick-Lawrence: a Portrait*, London: George Allen & Unwin.
Kenney, A. (1924), *Memories of a Militant*, London: E. Arnold.
King, E. (1993), 'The Scottish Women's Suffrage Movement', in E. Breitenbach and E. Gordon (eds), *Women in Scottish Society*, Edinburgh: Edinburgh University Press.
McDonald, I. (1989), *Vindication! A Postcard History of the Women's Movement*, London: Deirdre McDonald Books.
Pankhurst, C. (1987), *Unshackled: the Story of How We Won the Vote*, London: Cresset Women's Voices.
Pankhurst, E. (1914), *My Own Story* (ghosted by R.C. Dorr), London: Eveleigh Nash.
Pankhurst, R. (1979), *Sylvia Pankhurst: Artist and Crusader*, London: Paddington Press.
Pankhurst, S. (1978), *The Suffragette Movement*, London: Virago.
Pethick Lawrence, F. (1943), *Fate Has Been Kind*, London: Hutchinson.
Pugh, M. (1995), *Votes for Women in England, 1865–1928*, London: Historical Association.

Purvis, J. (ed.), *Women's History: Britain, 1850–1945*, London: University College Press.

Raeburn, A. (1973), *Militant Suffragettes*, London: Michael Joseph.

Raeburn, A. (1976), *The Suffragette View*, Newton Abbott: David & Charles.

Romero, P.W. (1987), *E. Sylvia Pankhurst: Portrait of a Radical*, New Haven and London: Yale University Press.

Rosen, A. (1974), *Rise up Women! The Militant Campaign of the Women's Social and Political Union, 1903–1914*, London: Routledge & Kegan Paul.

Strachey, R. (1978), *The Cause: a Short History of the Women's Movement in Great Britain*, London: Virago.

Tickner, L. (1989), *The Spectacle of Women: Imagery of the Suffrage Campaign*, London: Chatto & Windus.

8 'Souvenir-gifts' as Tokens of Filial Esteem: The Meanings of Blackpool Souvenirs

GERALD MARS AND VALERIE MARS

Introduction and Argument

This paper discusses mementos bought at the seaside, particularly at Blackpool, and brought home as gifts, mainly to the industrial north of England, roughly between the 1880s and the 1950s. Our major concern is with small white ceramic ornaments (hereafter called 'ceramic ornaments'). They were industrially produced for the working class, and comprised either printed views of town landmarks such as the Tower, the Giant Ferris Wheel, the Piers and the Promenade or 'crested china', that is, bearing prints of the Blackpool town crest with its motto *Progress*.[1] These were inspired by the higher quality china products of the Goss factory[2] and for the most part, being cruder, cheaper and made of pottery, can be regarded as 'sub-Goss' (Figure 8.1).

The bringing home of souvenirs by travellers has a long history ranging from lowly valued pilgrims' badges and fairings to paintings and antiquities brought back from the Grand Tour (Wilton and Bignami, 1997). Though some were expensive artefacts at the time of purchase, others acquired value only later. Some appear unlikely ever to increase in value. It seems almost universal, however, for travellers to have returned with souvenirs of their journeys, though the role of souvenirs as gifts has, as we shall see, more complex implications.

We concentrate on Blackpool's ceramic ornaments partly because they have proved more durable than most Blackpool souvenirs, partly because we have a collection of them but mainly because they tell a significant tale. It is a tale with two aspects. First it considers collecting outside its normal treatment as 'the accumulation of prestige artefacts that reflect the wealth and discrimination of the owner' (a practice shown by Johnson, 1986 to be near universal). Our items, of course, are not inherently prestigious and are generally considered kitsch. Furthermore, they offer a kind of prestige that is specific

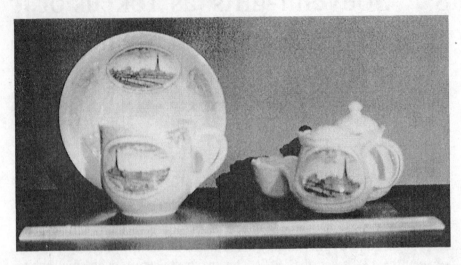

Figure 8.1   **A mixed selection of typical ornaments with crests and views. These are anonymous with the exception of the cruet and the jug and basin by SHO Bavaria, a tea-pot stand by Shelly and an ashtray by Mount Pleasant. The mermaid is simply marked 'Germany'**

Figure 8.1 cont'd

only to their recipients; when a recipient dies this is lost and the objects are typically dispersed. Second, when such artefacts are not just souvenirs but also gifts, and when giving and receiving them is expected and regularized, in a word, is institutionalized, then, as here, it can offer meanings that transcend more usual academic concerns. Thus, linking a souvenir's exotic source to its everyday destination (Cohen, 1990) and relating its power as a gift that embodies a bond between donor and recipient (Mauss, 1954) creates a new category of artefact. 'Souvenir-gifts', it will be argued, being more than just souvenirs and more than just gifts contain elements of each and offer understandings that transcend both.

To deconstruct the social role of souvenir-gifts, it is first necessary to understand the time and place from which they have come as well as that to which they are taken. We shall then see how in this example, ceramic ornaments reflected the relatively exotic 'other' that Blackpool represented to its holidaymakers and how they contributed to the gender based conflict that was built into the north of England's working-class households. We aim to answer six questions:

1   what were bought as souvenir-gifts;

2   who bought them;

3   who were they bought for;

4   what happened to them when they were taken home;

5   what meanings did they have for donors and recipients;

6   what meanings do they have for contemporary collectors – such as the authors?

The Historical Context of Gift-giving by Blackpool Holidaymakers

Buying ceramic ornaments at Blackpool was a feature of 'Wakes Week' holidays. 'The Wakes' involved the closure, in rotation, of whole towns so that workers could enjoy an annual holiday at the seaside (Walton, p. 35). This yearly exodus owed its impetus partly to the industrial solidarity of industrial workers and to the construction of the railway in 1848 which linked what had been a small watering place to its rapidly expanding industrial hinterland.[3]

Thereafter, the town's emergence as the UK's premier proletarian holiday resort was rapid. By 1857 *Porter's Guide to Blackpool* was able to list one column of 'Hotels and Inns' as against 10 of 'Lodging Houses'. The same issue also lists four dealers in souvenirs, some with more than one outlet. By the turn of the century the town had three piers (as against Brighton's two), most of its seven mile promenade, lavish 'Palaces of Varieties' and, dominating the skyline, a giant Ferris wheel and the 515 foot tower. By 1889 the town's official 'Popular Guide' boasted: 'Blackpool's markets are numerous and will be replete with everything to suit the taste of souvenir-seekers.' In a frank aside, it added: 'it will be remarkable if by chance a curious customer escapes their [the stallholder's] toils without making some purchase "for the good folks at home".'

Bringing back 'presents' 'for the good folks at home' was institutionalized as an important, even binding, obligation on holidaymakers. One aspect of present-giving, the main focus of this paper, involved ceramic ornaments that were largely bought by daughters for their mothers. They were, however, only one of several types of gift. Two others were postcards and seaside rock. It might be useful to briefly discuss these, since they too illustrate aspects of the social context of our ceramica and its domestic role in the period.

Whilst it is still usual for holidaymakers to send postcards home, those of this period, appear more strongly to have reflected aspects of their buyer's everyday lives than is currently the case. Postcards, for instance, showing cartoons that emphasized the difference between time-constrained work back home and free leisure at the seaside, were sent to workmates. with captions such as: 'I'm as free as air at Blackpool' and 'I've forgotten work at Blackpool.' In addition, a raft of postcards emphasized various aspects of the battle between the sexes that often featured small, cowed men dominated by enormous, harridan wives. There were also saucy taboo-breaking postcards in the Donald McGill and Arnold Taylor tradition, which were sent to peer equals. These ranged from the saucy (e.g. the depiction of a young woman in tears at a railway station, being seen off by five equally sorrowful young men (Howell, last unnumbered page)), to the blatantly obscene (e.g. a grotesquely fat man looking down at a small boy: 'Oh, yes, I had a little Willy once but I haven't seen him for a long time' (Calder-Marshall, 1966, front cover, no notation). Finally, innocuous postcards of photographed and printed views were sent to relatives and members of the older generation.

The second major item brought from the seaside was, and still is, Blackpool rock – baton-shaped novelty candy with the name of the town embedded throughout, and usually bought for children. Almost as ephemeral was a whole range of cheap presents including shell and chalk ornaments. Our informants tell us that shell ornaments were notoriously prone to break, whilst the chalk ones usually ended up with children as markers for hopscotch games played on pavements.

Though postcards and rock are still bought and given as gifts, ceramic ornaments, particularly those embellished with the town's crest and motto, are now part of a quickly receding past. They are today mostly found for £2 or £3 in shops selling junk or curios. Their role, and the intriguing place they once played in working class family organization, no longer applies, since the economic base and the symbiotic social order upon which it depended are no more.

Though we here focus on the more familiar and smaller ceramic ornaments, our collection also includes items large enough for use, such as mugs, spill vases ribbon plates, cups and saucers. These are printed with black and white or coloured views. Locating their purchasers and/or recipients has been more difficult. Ribbon plates were traditionally collected by canal narrow boat bargees. They were tokens of domestic pride, displayed in vertical lines for all to see near traditionally decorated cabin doors (Figure 8.2).

Other scenically decorated items reflect the wider economic range of tourists who holidayed at Blackpool before World War II. A selection of Blackpool views were pictured on English and foreign china. These may have acted as topics for polite comment, in the same manner as Soyer suggests in *The Modern Housewife* (1856). Ceramic wares decorated with views offered during the nineteenth century ranged from palatial urns to small souvenir vases while pictorial subjects were featured on elite dessert services throughout the century. Soyer suggested there should be a pause of 10 or 20 minutes before the dessert is put out after dinner: 'This gives an opportunity for my guests to admire the beautiful Sevres dessert plates, containing views of different French chateaux; this of course gives a subject for conversation to those who have visited them.' Although we have not found any dessert services featuring Blackpool views, views on ceramics might well have similarly acted as conversation pieces or, as in Soyer's example, as fuel for discussion.

The piers, the Giant Ferris Wheel, the Tower, a rough sea and a glowing sunset were some of the views of the distinctly 'other' world that Blackpool offered and that were illustrated on these more modest tablewares, and that made them too, suitable as conversation pieces. Holidaymakers, for instance, were persuaded they could get 'two sunsets in one evening', one at ground

**Figure 8.2   Ceramic ornaments of possible domestic use. Ribbon
plates (left to right) marked 'Schuman Bavaria',
'Germany' and 'Foreign'. The coffee cups and saucer and
mug are anonymous. The spill vases are marked 'Foreign'**

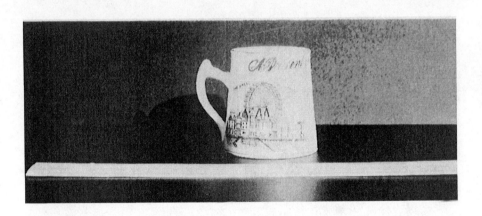

Figure 8.2 cont'd

level and the second by speedily taking a lift to the top of the tower for a second view (Ward Lock Cos, 1902). A plate with a blazing sunset was a true souvenir of this exotic other – even if it was only 50 miles from Manchester.

Gender, Poverty, Erratic Incomes and Inbuilt Conflict: The Filial Gift-giving of Ceramic Ornaments

For the working classes of Victorian England, incomes were not only low but essentially erratic, a situation that lasted until World War II. Endemic illness, payment by the piece, the operation of trade cycles and a minimum level of social security, all contributed to the insecurity and erraticism of domestic incomes. The only economic security available to men, as primary wage-earners, lay in their ability to demonstrate collective solidarity against their employers. In dealing with employers, therefore, working men could not afford the luxury of division, Their need for solidarity, forged in the workplace and the trade union, was bonded and reinforced in the pub by social drinking and gambling.

Drinking and gambling are effective ways to dissipate capital and certainly precluded its accumulation. Drinking was, in a very real sense, a case of 'pissing it up against the wall' (Mars, 1985).[4] In doing so, it insured against the possibility of emergent and potentially disastrous social divisions in the male workforce. Douglas and Isherwood (1980, pp. 166–9) discuss this form of egalitarian drinking in the context of Dennis' et al. (1956) study of 'Ashton', a coal-mining village in Yorkshire. In our experience, however, capital dissipation had much wider provenance throughout the industrial north of England.

Dennis et al. (p. 146) showed that the drive to male egalitarianism extended even to the consumption of tobacco. Only limited ranges of price and brand were considered appropriate. A mounting scale of sanctions, but most commonly ridicule, was applied to 'deviants' whose consumption or other behaviour was seen to threaten the male model of conformity.[5] In the early 1950s GM was once followed through the streets of Leigh, Lancashire (a homogeneously working class mining town) by a jeering crowd of youngsters. He was carrying an umbrella – seen then as unequivocally ostentatious.

Married women operated in a different social and economic milieu from men. The consistent demands by married women on erratic incomes for food, rent, clothes and fuel made for chronic dissonance between most of the consumption needs of husbands and wives. This was frequently exacerbated for wives because it was common for husbands to assert control over domestic spending (ibid., p. 201) (this generally applied even when women earned). Despite various self-help, cooperative and credit schemes that attempted to even out the supply of and demand for ready money, day to day responsibility for attempting to square this circle devolved upon the women. It is not surprising then, that the roles of husbands and wives should have conflicted, with both competing for the same limited resources. Nor, as a result, that mothers were often revered by their children for their heroic domestic capability and personal sacrifices.

Unlike their men, whose social lives were collective, married women's social lives were based upon mutually dependent but looser-knit support networks of female kin and neighbours. The home was to women what the pub and the workplace were to men – a centre for social interaction and source of identity and support. Here kin and neighbours would gather for cups of tea and gossip (ibid., pp. 203–5). But neither the work of women nor their social interactions were as constrained by egalitarian pressures. as they were for men. Women were freer to compete but did so by being 'houseproud'. They did not do so by demonstrating display items such as carpets, curtains, furniture or ornaments – the purchase of which was controlled and limited by husbands. One exception, possibly the only one, to this narrowing of competition from displaying goods to displaying performance, lay in the collections of ceramic ornaments given them by daughters.

Several informants confirmed that ceramic ornaments were bought by daughters for their mothers, rarely for fathers and that they were put on display to be viewed by other women as demonstrations of filial regard. Daughter to mother gift-giving, therefore, short-circuited husbands' control over the spending of household resources and the consistent husband-wife conflict it involved. In doing so it also affirmed and consolidated female gender links between the generations. The domestic and gender location of ceramic ornaments is evident from the form of many of them: egg-cups, miniature cheese covers, flat-irons, cruets, and spill vases, – not sports regalia, pint pots or shaving mugs (Figure 8.3). The male gender link was also confirmed across the generations but achieved outside the home – through work, the union, drinking and the support of football teams. Fathers we were told, typically did not receive souvenir gifts.

One informant from Wigan, a lady of about 60, told us that her mother, as was usual, displayed her collection on the mantelpiece and the sideboard. Display cabinets were not common. That ceramic ornaments essentially comprised display items is evident, not only from their miniature size, which

**Figure 8.3   Crested miniatures and sub-Goss novelty shapes. All are
anonymous except for the seat marked 'Foreign' and the
coal scuttle marked 'Gemma'**

made most of them useless for utilitarian purposes, but also because many had elaborate gold trims. Such ornamentation which is expensive to put on china and porcelain, is only found on the outer face of these ornaments (Figure 8.4).

Collections were essentially cumulative; the 'pool' of demonstrated filial affection grew as the collection grew, with its total social value being greater than the sum of its parts: the more extensive the collection the more esteem accrued to the mother.

We have not been able to determine the cost of ceramic ornaments. But relative to earnings at the time, their price was considered not insignificant and the obligation to buy them was strong. Our Wigan informant, whose own experience was of Blackpool in the period immediately following World War II, asserted that holidaymakers always bought their presents early in their holidays, 'before they'd spent up'. GM's experience, as the son of a Blackpool landlady in the 1940s, confirms this tradition; it was common for visitors (the native term for holidaymakers) to insist on paying their (boarding house) bill at the beginning of the holiday. Then they would go out and buy their presents.

Miller (1998) notes that objects, as essentially social things, have to be assimilated into the everyday accepted life of any new context to which they are moved. One of our informants showed this was done by recounting how these items were incorporated into routinized domestic cleaning schedules: 'They were dusted once a week and washed once a fortnight.'[6] Another informant recalled that her mother had used a hollowed crested swan that came down to her from her mother and in which she placed her husband's bus fares every evening, ready for him to take to work the following morning. It is in these routine (and routinizing) ways then, that ceramic objects, derived from 'the other' and which represented the holiday as 'time out of time' (Turner, 1969)[7] became part of the familiar and mundane domestic world of the industrial, time-constrained, north of England.

Civic Consciousness and Town Crests: The Rise of the Goss Factory and Its Imitators

China ornaments sold as souvenirs had first been produced on a small scale by the Goss factory in the 1870s. Goss's factory had been founded by William Henry Goss in 1858. Trained at the Government School of Design at Somerset House, he subsequently worked for the Copeland Spode Pottery. Designers at both were innovators, earnestly aiming not only to promulgate the new

Figure 8.4   False utility: frontal gilding on various anonymous pieces and an impractical cruet marked 'Foreign'

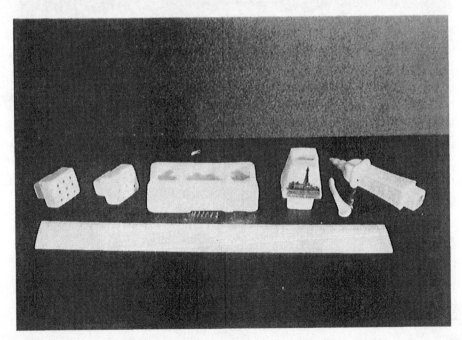

Figure 8.4 cont'd

technical advances of the time but to combine them with educational and aesthetic improvement. Goss's work encompassed skills both as chemist and designer. It was his more entrepreneurial son, Adolphus, however, who, joining the firm in 1881, first introduced town crests on the firm's exclusive ivory ware (Pine, 1994).

This was a shrewd marketing ploy. Municipal consciousness was becoming marked in the late Victorian era and town crests were beginning to be widely displayed on municipal buildings, uniforms, vehicles and even on school notebooks. To a town's residents their own town's crest was extremely familiar, even mundane. In contrast the crests of other towns such as Blackpool's, were seen, if not as exotic, then certainly as 'other'.

Goss's crested porcelain was consciously vested with elements of symbolic capital (Bourdieu, 1979). Crests were transferred on to miniatures of archaeological finds and historic monuments emphasizing contemporary heraldry and antiquarian interest. But the quality of the pieces also reinforced their status (Mars, 1997, pp. 271–5). The vast majority of crested china sold in Blackpool, however, was far removed from the high minded ideals of Goss, and for the most part, was made of lower quality pottery (Figure 8.5).

Goss's marketing of symbolic capital, so shrewdly targeted at the socially aspirant did not appeal to Blackpool's consumers. Yet more Goss souvenirs were produced for Blackpool than for any other resort.[8] This was achieved with an entrepreneurial flair typical of the resort's traders (Mars, 1958). A Mr Naylor, Blackpool's Goss agent after 1913, was the firm's best salesman. He increased his profits by an agreement to purchase all the factory's 'seconds' though they still retained the Goss factory mark. Their original descriptions, usually printed on the base, were often removed for Naylor (Pine, 1999) who then had them printed with Blackpool's coat of arms. Alien 'bodies' such as Lincoln Imps, Harvard University and Manx Cottages were among over 50 examples which were thus stripped of their previous symbolic capital. Naylor, with a shrewd understanding of his customers' taste, also requested the factory to add gilt embellishments to these pieces which were usually only decorated with coloured arms.[9]

In 1904, Goss racked up the level of symbolic capital even further. A National League of Goss Collectors was established, with a 2s. 6d. membership fee and the lure of a free collector's vase. Collectors gained further trophies after two, four and six years membership. Later a didactic journal was introduced and display cabinets advertised so that the divergence from Blackpool's products became even more marked. Goss's superior ivory china was imitated by makers of Blackpool's ornaments such as Willow and Shelly,

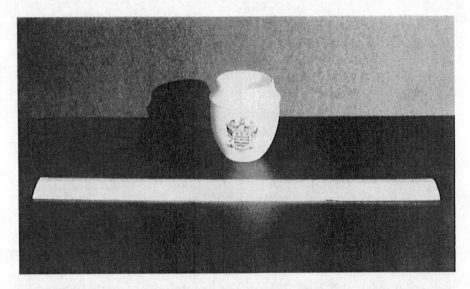

Figure 8.5   **A Goss urn (above) and (below) sub-Goss ornaments by named English makers. From left: suitcase, Florentine China; fishing basket, Swan China; Ferris Wheel, Willow Art China, Longton; Cottage, Carlton China, W&R, Stoke-on-Trent; Elephant, Willow Art China, Longton; Vase, 'The Duchess' China, H & Co., Longton (338449); Tulip Vase, Florentine China**

which in its turn, was imitated by anonymous cheaper crested ware made both in England and the continent. It is these which comprise most of our collection . By this time, however, civic identity was being merged into wider local and geographic identities and the prevalence of town crests declined. A new emphasis on 'the other' emerged in a growing preference for printed landscapes, major landmarks and buildings.

Dispersal or Retention?: Factors Determining the Value of Souvenir-gifts in General and Ceramic Ornaments in Particular

The significance of these collections lay not in their market exchange value but in a value more akin to that placed on heirlooms: they had a meaning and value only within a specific sphere of exchange (Bohannan, 1963).[10] Unlike heirlooms, however, and though cherished, displayed and regularly cleaned, their value was specific only to the individual mother to whom they had been given. When she died, her key role ceased, and the collection, regarded now as having no personal and little intrinsic value, was typically not retained as an entity. Some pieces were likely to be distributed among family members; others, treated as rubbish, were thrown away or otherwise disposed of to curio and junk shops. Such dispersal, of course, negates the idea of a collection as being greater than the sum of its parts.

This pattern of dispersal is typical of households of this type which have a relatively shallow time-depth. An aristocratic family with its identity sustained over time, and buttressed by ownership of land and property, tends, on the other hand, to ensure that its goods are not dissipated, particularly by restricting inheritance through the principle of primogeniture and through universalist knowledge inherent to the keeping of inventories. Chinese ornaments brought back to Burghley House by several generations of aristocrats have, for instance, stayed on the same shelf for decades. Even if not considered valuable at the time of purchase they seem destined to appreciate.

Thompson (1979) suggests that the transfer of goods classed as rubbish, to appreciation as collectables, owes much to their being so defined by the elite groups who own them. They have both a vested interest in asserting their value and the knowledge necessary to validate them. Such elites, of course, also confer value by provenance. None of these features presently apply to Blackpool's ceramic objects.

Present Day Collectors of Crested China

Crested china is not presently manufactured. Many old pieces now seem to be collected by people who have moved from their home town and wish to demonstrate a link to their past. In making collections, new gift networks are forged and affirmed as friends and relatives find more pieces for their collectors. Currently but in a very different social context, personal identities are again confirmed through prestation and cumulative display. These new collections, however, now serve not to confirm and consolidate collectors and donors as family members, firmly enmeshed in a *gemeinschaft* community: instead, they now affirm a more anomic, less group and more network based individualism. It must be admitted too that they often seem to offer their collectors the kind of inverted superiority that comes with self-conscious displays of kitsch. Whether today's Blackpool kitsch will turn into valuable antiques remains to be seen.

Conclusion

The ceramic ornaments that have been discussed are more than just a repository of memory; the reminder of a time and a place apart. This is the function of the souvenir. But when souvenirs also have an institutionalized role as gifts, when they are 'souvenir-gifts', they have had to go through additional and specific social processes appropriate to, and only understandable, by reference to their contexts of origin and destination. In this case ceramic ornaments as 'souvenir-gifts' can be said to have travelled:

1   as souvenirs from 'the other', representing the strange and the relatively exotic, to the familiar and the mundane;

2   from representing holidays as unscheduled, 'free', 'time out of time', to being incorporated, as gifts, via routinized domestic cleaning schedules, into the 'industrialized' time prevailing at home;

3   from being individual items with no social baggage to being part of a collection where their cumulatively increasing total offers greater prestige than the sum of its parts;

4   from being the prestation of one individual to another to representing and consolidating the generational transmission of the gender divided family;

5   finally, they are being recycled. After their dispersal and possessing little intrinsic or symbolic value they are being collected as self-conscious kitsch and sources of aspirant symbolic capital.[11]

Notes

1   Awarded 1876.
2   Black transfer printed crests, hand coloured on ivory bodies.
3   In 1848 nearly 14,000 people left Oldham over five days in special trains. In 1865 the figure had risen to 24,000 (Peter Fox, Oldham Museum, personal communication).
4   A very similar example is found among dockworkers in Newfoundland whose insecure economic work and domestic organization both parallel that here.
5   'This is seen in even the slightest things. Someone [in a pub] produced a rather expensive brand of tobacco. The cry immediately went up, "My, aren't we posh" and the middle aged collier concerned put the tin away in confusion. Again someone using a slightly unusual word such as "proximity" will find himself the butt of "good natured" banter' (Dennis et al., 1956, p. 146 n.; also quoted in Douglas and Isherwood, 1980).
6   We have observed similar processes of incorporation in contemporary London suburbs (Mars and Mars, 1993).
7   'Time out of time' as used here, is a concept of Turner's 1969, by which he defines time that has been abstracted and 'removed' from the routine and the 'normal'.
8   Nicholas Pine, personal communication.
9   Pat Welbourne, personal communication.
10   'Spheres of exchange' define aspects of the economy that do not normally merge. Heirlooms for example, though they may well possess an exchange value, do not normally enter the money economy.
11   Further details of ceramic marks and manufacturers of ceramic ornaments discussed here are to be found in Henderson, 1974. We would like to thank members of Reminiscence Groups and all the individuals who have discussed Blackpool souvenirs with us including: Lyn Fade at the Grundy Art Gallery and Mrs P. Hansell at the Central Library, Blackpool; Dr Leonard Mars, University of Wales at Swansea, Nicholas Pine of The Goss Museum, Waterlooville, Portsmouth; Peter Fox at the North West Sound Archive, and Staff and Volunteers at the Wigan Pier Museum. We would also like to thank those generous friends and relations who have given us so many of our ceramic souvenirs.
     Dr Gerald Mars is an anthropologist; Dr Valerie Mars is a social historian.

References

Blackpool (1889), *The Popular Guide to The Official Publication by The Mayor and Corporation.*

Bohannan, P. (1963), *Social Anthropology*, New York: Holt, Rinehart and Winston, Inc.

Bourdieu, P. (1986), *Distinction. A Social Critique of the Judgement of Taste*, tr. R. Nice, London: Routledge & Kegan Paul.

Calder-Marshall, A. (1966), *Wish You Were Here: The Art of Donald McGill*, London: Hutchinson & Co.

Cohen, E. (1990), 'Tourist Arts', in C . Cooper and A. Lockwood (eds), *Progress In Tourism; Recreation and Hospitality Management*, Vol. 4.

Dennis, Henriques and Slaughter (1956), *Coal is Our Life: An analysis of a Yorkshire mining community*, London: Eyre and Spottiswood.

Douglas M. (1978), 'Cultural Bias', *Occasional Paper No. 35*, London, Royal Anthropological Institute, reprinted in (1982) *In The Active Voice*, London: Routledge and Kegan Paul.

Douglas, M. and Isherwood, B. (1980), *The World of Goods: Towards an Anthropology of Consumption*, Harmondsworth: Penguin Books.

Emery, N. (1969), 'William Henry Goss and Goss Heraldic China', *Occasional Paper 1*, Berkshire Reference Library and Information Service.

Henderson, I.T. (1974), *Pictorial Souvenirs of Britain*, London: David & Charles.

Howell, G. (1977), *The Penguin Book of Naughty Postcards*, Harmondsworth: Penguin Books.

Johnson, R. (1986), 'Accumulation and Collecting: An anthropological perspective', *Art History*, Vol. 9, No. 1, March.

Mars, G. (1958), *Blackpool's Golden Mile*, mimeo, Blackpool Central Reference Library.

Mars, G. (1985), 'Drinking Among Canadian Dockworkers', in M. Douglas (ed.), *Constructive Drinking*, Cambridge: Cambridge University Press.

Mars, G. and Mars, V. (1993), 'Two Contrasting Dining Styles, Suburban Conformity and Urban Individualism', in G. Mars and V. Mars (eds), *Food, Culture and History*, Vol. I, London: The London Food Seminar.

Mars, V. (1997), *Ordering Dinner: Victorian Celebratory Domestic Dining in London*, PhD thesis, University of Leicester.

Mauss, M. (1954), 'Essai sur le don', *L'Anneee Sociologique*, NS 1, Paris (1923–4), tr. as *The Gift*, London: Cohen and West.

Miller, D. (1994), 'Artefacts and the Meaning of Things', in T. Ingold (ed.), *Companion Encyclopedia of Anthropology*, London, Routledge (1969), *Occasional Paper No. 1*.

Pine, N.J. (1994), *Goss and other Crested China*, Shire Album 120, Princes Risborough, Aylesbury, Bucks: Shire Publications Ltd.

Porter, W. (1857), *Porter's Guide To Blackpool; Directory of Blackpool*, Blackpool: Blackpool and Fleetwood Chronicle.

Soyer, A. (1856), *The Modern Housewife or Menagere*, London: Simpkin, Marshall & Co., (first published 1848).

Thompson, M. (1979), *Rubbish Theory: The Creation and Destruction of Capital*, Oxford: Oxford University Press.

Thompson, M., Ellis, R. and Wildavsky, A. (1990), *Cultural Theory*, Boulder, Colorado: Westview Press.

Turner, V.W. (1969), *The Ritual Process, Structure and Anti-structure: a demonstration of the use of ritual and symbol as a key to understanding social structure and process*, London: Routledge & Kegan Paul Ltd.

Walton, J.K. (1978), *The Blackpool Landlady: A social history*, Manchester: Manchester University Press.

Ward Lock Cos (1902), *Illustrated Guide to Blackpool, Lytham and St Annes*.

Wilton, A.and Bignamini, I. (eds) (1996), *The Grand Tour, the Lure of Italy in the Eighteenth Century*, London: Tate Publishing.

9 Transformations of the Tourist and Souvenir: The Travels and Collections of Philla Davis

ANDREW WEST

Philla Davis was once summed up as a 'delightfully eccentric person' with a 'colossal personality' and a 'very charismatic character' – but 'probably not photogenic'. Her life and her extensive travels in the latter half of the twentieth century, pose a number of questions around tourism, material culture and collecting. As a tourist she endeavoured to travel as cheaply as possible; as a craftswoman she sought out places to visit that fulfilled her interest in basketry manufacture; as a collector she looked for samples of local craft methods and examples of textiles and basketry.

This chapter looks at a collection of baskets and textiles made by Philla Davis on her travels around the world. The process of 'identifying' material in the collection raised questions about the notion of 'authentic' artefacts, and demonstrated how objects become transformed in different contexts and associations. Similarly the exploration of Philla Davis's life realized the complexity of identity, and the changes that occur in time and place.

Introduction

Women travellers have been the focus of academic and popular attention in recent years (see, for example, Allcock and Young, 1991; Keay, 1994; Mills, 1991; Russell, 1986). Some of these women, such as Gertrude Bell, Mary Kingsley and Freya Stark, are generally well known. But there are many who are less famous, as indicated by Robinson's (1990) anthology of some 400 women travellers. What all of these women have in common is that they left behind some documentation, even if only letters, although most had published books about their journeys. There must be many others who left no writing and whose travels are not remembered.

There are no known surviving travel writings by Philla Davis, but she did leave behind a large collection of textiles and basketry when she died in 1988. After her death, part of the collection was almost certainly destroyed, but much ended up divided among four museums.[1] Most went to the Collection of Southeast Asian Art and Traditional Craftsmanship at the Centre for Southeast Asian Studies at the University of Hull.[2] However, no documentation for the collection has either survived or was passed on except a few boxes of slides and a very few photographs.

Essentially there arrived in Hull a miscellany of baskets, textiles and a few other items, and no information. The material from Philla's house was accepted by the museums concerned because it fitted in with existing collections[3] (three were museums with 'ethnographic', that is, foreign collections, and the fourth included local history and British ethnography). The criteria used in this process of acceptance ultimately depends upon a notion of authenticity: that an object is distinctively from and perhaps somehow representative of a particular area or time. Effectively the objects supposedly fall into what Graburn (1976, pp. 5–6) classifies as indigenous, traditional or pseudo-traditional arts.

In Hull, the initial association of the artefacts with a region such as Southeast Asia then begged for more precise identification: to ascribe use, date and place. This can only be done through evidence from comparison with other material, published illustrations, etc. In so doing, a new value necessarily accrues (in the sense of cultural capital), a social construction of the object. This construction is dependent on the significance of, for example, age, aesthetics, rarity, or even, in the case of baskets, a provenance of place because most undocumented basketry is notoriously difficult to identify. Through 'identification' the objects become transformed in individual value and what was a miscellany of artefacts is given new internal and external relationships and categories in terms of use, place or significance. To help identify the objects it was necessary to investigate the collector's life story, which provided additional assessments of many pieces and began to articulate the significance and meaning of the collection to Philla Davis herself.

The identification of artefacts in the Philla Davis collection raised questions about the various categories used to evaluate material culture collections, especially the notion of *authentic* artefacts contrasted with, for example, *tourist* objects. Artefacts are transformed over time as they pass through different contexts and associations, such as the purpose of their manufacture, acquisition by others, the use subsequently made of them, their association with a particular collector, and their age. Similar problems are evident in the allocation of identities to individuals. How should Philla Davis be described, categorized or identified? A range of possibilities include, for example, tourist or traveller or anthropologist or fieldworker; collector or hoarder or souvenir gatherer. These social categories are also each associated with different status, dependent on circumstances and who is making the attribution. There are parallels in the transformations of the ascribed identities of individuals, and the shifting values accorded to objects: also in the difficulties of placing an artefact in a single category.

In looking at some of these issues and transformations I shall follow the process as it unfolded in practice. Lewis Hill and I[4] began working on the collection itself, cataloguing the objects; I started gathering oral history and other material about the collector to create a biography. Below, a brief description of the collection is followed by some examples of textile transformations and the problem of authenticity, a short biographical sketch of Philla Davis, and then some consideration of her life as tourist and collector.

The Collection

The material now in Hull is only part of what was probably quite a large collection, principally of basketry, with a smaller group of textiles. The collection as a whole covers a wide geographical range, from Asia, Africa, Europe and America and is but an indication of what, it transpired, were her worldwide travels. Philla Davis is now known to have visited parts of Europe, North and West Africa, South and Southeast Asia, Australia, North America, and possibly also to East Asia and South America. But the extent of her travels was not known when the collection was first received. There were around 150 basketry-based pieces and 30 textiles in Hull.

Obviously, in the move of the collection from her house in Church Stretton to the University of Hull an initial transformation occurred. For Philla Davis the assembly of objects had a range of personal meanings, for example, being associated with when and where she acquired them, and what use she made of them. The transfer of a collection to an institution, and the process of listing and cataloguing, can freeze or fix artefacts in a new social construction. This process is based on judgments of what they are, their use, where they are from and when they were made. The new construction is built from the perspective of the institution: in Hull one focused, as its title suggests, on 'traditional art and craftsmanship' in Southeast Asia.

When the material arrived in Hull, the slides were tantalizing, indicating that Philla had been touring Southeast Asia. It is easy to begin with the assumption that Philla Davis collected them 'on the spot' or 'in the field', and in pristine condition, rather than second or third hand. But in ascribing the pieces to Southeast Asia and subsequently to particular locations and cultures, several issues emerge. For example, how do we know where these objects are from, and what criteria are acceptable to make an artefact a genuine or authentic Southeast Asia piece. Must it have been bought there? and if so, is there a difference between a shop purchase and an acquisition in the field? is there a difference between acquisition from the maker or from the user of the artefact, whether given or bought?

Authenticity

Even this potential range of criteria demonstrates some of the constructions of value that can be accrued by, or assigned to artefacts. The range indicates criteria used by museums to assess an object, but these criteria are not valueless. One major difference between a museum and an auction house is that the latter highlights the monetary worth of an object, which is partially dependent on the vagaries of fashion, whereas the former is able both to emphasize other categories and to prize a piece that is worth little financially. Both institutions share many criteria, for example, of age, rarity, documentation, known provenance.

The example of 'tourist' souvenirs is an example of a shifting category. Once both auction houses and ethnography museums may have shown little interest in the (often cheap) items produced in multiple for sale to tourists; for many museums this is now changing as such items are appreciated as a record of changes in society and economy. Yet these artefacts are usually without intrinsic worth – that is, they are not highly regarded as art, or made of precious materials. The importance of provenance, and especially documentation, becomes clear. It is the documentation that is the souvenir, or makes the object a souvenir, a record of being there, concerned with time, place, people and interaction, albeit in a shop, house, street, field, etc.

The question of 'authenticity' then means going beyond the current appearance and use of the object, in order to consider its transformations over time and physical location, etc.[5] Difficulties immediately arise with a large cloth that has been made into cushion covers, such as an ikat cloth possibly from Timor (Hull number 1990.14.8). This cut up cloth presents a horror to museum curators seeking indigenous representative pieces, but in the context of tourist souvenirs says something about the collector who acquired it to use, rather than store, a use probably very different from what its maker envisaged. Other textiles in the Philla Davis collection show signs of use, obviously having been displayed and nailed to the wall. Similarly, one of the baskets had clearly been used as a fruit bowl and become slightly distorted in shape.

In the museum such damage done through re-use, with nails, etc., might be decried, because in such institutions these objects tend to be valued for their presumed earlier association as cultural artefacts rather than the souvenir collection of a tourist. But as Graburn (1976) has shown, there is not a simple dichotomy of choice, for example between authentic and tourist, as his schema illustrates in focusing on the production of art. Some of the complexity of issues of authenticity and documentation of artefacts can be illustrated through examples of ikat textiles in the Philla Davis collection.

Textiles

There are several pieces of ikat cloth in the Philla Davis collection. Ikat is a process where the threads, usually only the warp threads, are dyed in patterns before weaving. Two cloths in the collection are double ikat, where both warp and weft threads are dyed before weaving, which requires skill and care in making them up in order to create the desired patterns. These two cloths have intricate representations of seated and kneeling human figures. They are fragile, and look older than other pieces in the collection. This type of cloth, called *geringsing*, is readily attributable to a particular village, Tenganen in Bali.

Another two warp ikat cloths fortuitously arrived in Hull with a label pinned on, and an accompanying leaflet. These are *t'nalak* cloths from Mindanao. The leaflet offered an explanation, indicating an origin from the T'Boli people of Lake Sebu in the Philippines. However, such T'Boli textiles and crafts from Lake Sebu have been advertised and sold through fair trade shops and catalogues, such as *Traidcraft* (see, for example, *Traidcraft*, 1991/2 and *Oxfam* 1990, 1991). Philla could have acquired them in England, and one informant notes that she bought textiles from Oxfam shops 'if she knew the fabric', suggesting that Philla had some concern for 'authenticity', that is an understanding of place or people of origin.

From the slides it was apparent that Philla had been to both Bali and the Philippines, and this was supported by some basketry pieces from those places. An inlaid picture including the lettering 'Philippines' was supplemented by one basket full of craft items and another bearing a customs stamp, since emptied, but with the remains of newspaper packing from the islands. From Bali the basketry collection included some distinctive ceremonial decorations associated with Balinese Hindu festivals.

It is possible that these ikat pieces might be juxtaposed, one bought locally when travelling in Southeast Asia and the other bought in a shop in Britain. In fact we discovered that they were both purchased from shops. The *geringsing* cloths were both bought by Philla from an antique shop in the Netherlands, and the *t'nalak* from the Santa Cruz Mission shop in the Philippines. Does the evaluation of these two cloths change when we discover that both were purchased in shops? Is there a difference between a tourist shop selling crafts, and an antique shop selling second hand artefacts, and a charity shop selling fair trade items? Does the age of the piece matter? They might be contrasted as old double ikat cloths from Bali, and recent ikat cloths from the Philippines, but each of the latter *t'nalak* is now at least 25 years old. The two *geringsing* were a souvenir of Philla's visits to the Netherlands in the early 1970s: the *t'nalak* bought around the same time in the Philippines.

One difference between the two types of cloth seems to depend upon the purpose for which they were made and correspond to notions of authenticity: the older piece classified as indigenous, the more recent as traditional but made for sale and so seen as a 'tourist' item. In writing of Nepal, Teague notes items that are 'classifiable as "tourist art", [but] nevertheless they are appropriate artefacts to represent the social and cultural changes occurring in Nepal in recent times. They thus have "authenticity" as ethnographic museum objects' (1995, p. 54). This corresponds to the *t'nalak*, produced for sale and demonstrating aspects of the current economy – or rather the economy in the 1970s. But the *geringsing* represents social and cultural changes of a different kind: of the transformation of this textile from production for ritual use in Bali, to potential consumption as an antique in the Netherlands, where it might be not only a souvenir of the past but of the colonial past. Yet it was probably once acquired in Bali as a souvenir of the present. How sustainable is the categorization of tourist art and artefact over time? Is it connected with the moment, place and mode of acquisition, or the purpose of production?

Layton (1992) draws on Graburn (1976) to contrast 'inward directed' arts and 'those made for outside sale [which] project an ethnic image determined to some degree by the alien purchasers' values' (Layton, 1992, p. 137). Such an 'ethnic image' would apply when buying an ikat cloth in the Philippines or in Britain: a major difference in the purchase would be the environment, but the construction of an image, albeit different, would exist in both places. The *geringsing* also was bought away from its original locality, and may perhaps be associated with a broader set of images dependent on the purchaser. All of these might be concerned with the appropriation of culture, through the acquisition of material culture.

Two other ikat cloths in the Philla Davis collection indicate further complexities. One is a Batak man's cloth from Sumatra, another of the few which arrived with a label pinned on. There is also an ikat man's cloth from East Sumba – this one identified as such by comparison with other cloths. This 'provenance' gives an idea of where these two cloths are from: but that may not mean much because, as indicated above, it is not necessarily the same as where it was purchased. The Batak cloth was probably collected in the field by Philla; perhaps a modern piece at the time but 25 years old on accession in Hull. The East Sumba piece has been suggested as probably made in the 1930s as a commercial item, made for export to shops such as Liberty's.[6] Perhaps this cloth was bought by Philla on her travels in Europe or on her travels in East Sumba – offering different representations and memories for her.

What connects these cloths from Bali, the Philippines, Sumatra and Sumba is the buyer, for whom they were souvenirs from her travels, and for whom they also filled unique places in her collection. This connection recalls another issue, raised earlier. How are we to consider Philla Davis? As a tourist gathering souvenirs, as a collector who travelled, appropriating or exchanging, etc.? There is one consistent characteristic of most of the pieces in her collection: they were acquired by Philla when she was on holiday.

Life and Travels[7]

Philla Davis was born in 1915. She lived for the early and later part of her life at the family home in Church Stretton in Shropshire. Philla went to Badminton School in Bristol where her contemporaries in the school included Indira Gandhi and Iris Murdoch. After school she studied for three years on a Diploma in Architecture at the University of Liverpool, but left before completing the course. This withdrawal may have been on the instigation of her father, who apparently was not keen on her studying, and/or been influenced by the outbreak of war (see West, 1996).

The 1939–45 war seems to have brought Philla a measure of independence. Throughout the war she was involved in work on food dyes and welfare work, and she took a Certificate in Social Work 1942–44. By 1945 she was warden of a YWCA hostel in Sheffield. After the war Philla travelled at least once to the Netherlands by motorbike. By the early 1950s Philla had a job as Rural Craft Organizer for Herefordshire. She continued working for the local authority as a craft worker/instructor until taking retirement in 1975 shortly after her sixtieth birthday.

Before the early 1950s some of the main themes of her life were established, and might be broadly defined in five groups (a sixth, of music, could be added) as: outdoor pursuits such as camping and walking; botany; craft making, particularly basketry and other handicraft work related to twisting and plaiting techniques; travelling and her motorbike. We might see these themes as linked, for example, travelling by motorbike to camp and take part in botanical fieldwork, the knowledge of which informed basketry. A further major interest, in the history and spread of techniques of basketry developed from the practical craftwork. These themes in Philla's life are briefly examined below.

In her outdoor activities Philla participated in the Girl Guide Association, as an adult, for 38 years, from 1942–80, and held positions such as District and Division Commissioner. She led camps, taught handicrafts, outdoor craft skills and probably introductory botany, beginning with the naming of plants and trees. Philla's friends at Liverpool in the 1930s remembered her keen interest in botany. In the late 1970s Philla was recorded as having a practical knowledge of the botany of West Africa and of Alaska. In 1982 she registered for a PhD studying the ecology and vegetation of the Long Mynd in Shropshire.

Basketry was a key feature of her jobs as a crafts organizer. She taught various craft skills in schools (and also to the Guides) and co-wrote two books on mainly British straw work (Sandford and Davis, 1958, 1964). Philla was an early member of the Society for Folk Life Studies (an association to promote the study of British and Irish ethnology), served on its committee and undertook some recording of craft techniques in Wales and Ireland.

A major part of Philla's life was her travels and the more we discover, the more important these are. From the early 1950s or before to the mid-1970s it is quite possible that she travelled abroad at least once every year, probably not usual for a council employee at that time. By the 1970s there may well have been two overseas trips annually. She often visited continental Europe, particularly the Netherlands, around the new year, and in summer made a longer tour of different regions of Southeast Asia. In addition, she frequently participated in the annual meetings of the Society for Folk Life Studies and attended guide camps. Her travelling periods were limited by her job to school holidays.

In Britain and on the continent Philla frequently travelled by motorbike. She apparently cut a fine figure, a large woman wearing home-made clothes often with a sewing machine strapped to the back of the bike. Jeremy Sandford (1991, p. 10) recalls Philla visiting his mother:

> She [Lettice Sandford] was introduced to corndollies by Miss Philla Davis, a council craftworker who travelled by motorcycle and passed a night at Eye once a week to give classes in the school or village hall. The motorcycle of this remarkable women was hung round with whatever was needed for that week of craft work; vital bits of hessian, old legs for restored stools, rope and straw, bolts of cloth, men's boots, goggles, rush for chair seats, dummy figures, half upholstered chairs.

The motorbike was remembered by one informant as 'huge and powerful'. It may have been her major extravagance. In her years working in Herefordshire Philla lived for at least part of the time in a caravan situated at the edge of a field.

Philla's early travels were by motorbike overland to the European continent and then in the 1950s on to North Africa including Algeria, Morocco and the Sahara. She must have subsequently visited West Africa and North America (including Alaska), certainly before the late 1960s. Her attention then switched to Southeast Asia, and in the 1960s she visited Vietnam and Burma (and possibly also Hong Kong and Japan). In the early 1970s Philla toured Indonesia and the Philippines over several summers, and visited Australia.

Philla's retirement in 1975 curtailed her travelling as she moved back to Church Stretton to look after her mother. Despite Philla's worsening arthritis, and her mother's increasing ill health and dependency, Philla completed an Open University degree between 1976 and 1981. In the early 1980s she began to travel again, up the west coast of North America and then, in 1986 to Morocco and in 1988 to India, Bangladesh and Nepal. She died shortly after her return from South Asia.

Her travelling was done as cheaply as possible. In Java she at first used public transport but then hired a bicycle. Philla had two sets of good contacts: first, from school, where many of her friends 'married into the diplomatic service', and second, through the Girl Guides. Most of her travels were undertaken alone, except in the late 1980s and on some of the North African journeys.

Tourist and Collector

Just as the objects in her collection defy easy categorization, and may cross over boundaries and become transformed, likewise the life and identity of Philla Davis rejects simplistic analysis. The consistent description of her by various correspondents as a 'remarkable woman' hints at the complexities of her character and life.

She was certainly a multifaceted traveller. Philla raised money for trips through a frugal lifestyle and, in the early 1960s by designing and selling 'tea towels with patterns of traditional straw knots' (various, personal communication). Travelling the world, Philla apparently made use of her school contacts and the networks generated through the international Girl Guide movement. She occasionally stayed in hotels, and she stayed in the homes of some museum curators in Europe. But she also frequently slept rough, as remembered by one Welsh informant: 'she usually came to Folk Life meetings after days of sleeping in the open air under a ground sheet – usually in a remote place such as the Isle of Arran' (personal communication).

Travelling was clearly important to Philla, and was not limited to the purpose of collecting baskets. Rather, with her interests in botany and wildlife, and her apparent ease in communicating with people she encountered, especially regarding craft technique, the collection could be seen simply as souvenirs of the tours and people she met, and need not serve another purpose.

Basketry and craftwork were an integral part of her life. She discussed techniques and processes whenever she had the opportunity. In Timbuktu she apparently taught a craftsman straw work techniques he did not know, derived from British corn dolly manufacture. A new piece of jewellery was fashioned, basketry drop earrings, which he could then make and sell. Years later in Indonesia, the arrival of this white-haired white woman on a pony and trap created quite a stir in a village: 'at that point, apparently, Philla spoke no Indonesian but, it is recalled, was "in no time" sitting on a verandah communicating with local women about craft techniques' (West, 1996, p. 125). Her travels around Great Britain and Ireland also brought her into contact with basket- and other craftmakers.

One unifying element to her collection is that it encompassed a range of styles and techniques. She did apparently collect for a purpose. In the 1950s Philla provided illustrations, photographs and jointly authored two books on straw work in Britain, especially looking at corn dollies and other traditional work. It is said that she travelled in North Africa looking for plaited work used in harvest festivals. Her second book (Sandford and Davis, 1964) included a photograph of a Balinese 'harvest figure' or rice goddess from the Horniman Museum; Philla was later to collect some five of these herself in Bali. The basketry formed by far the greater part of her collection.

It seems that Philla wanted to write a wide-ranging book on basketry. She had discussions with one publisher, who apparently wanted her to do a book on the 'isn't it sweet and rural aspects of straw work' while 'she wanted to do a scholarly one' (Dyer, personal communication). Part of her motivation for studying for a first degree and PhD in later life was that she thought she would not be taken seriously without the qualifications, and they would help her get published. Yet her studies centred on ecology and botany, which indicate her further dimensions: her intended book could probably have covered basketry materials, techniques, products and their uses, and where they are to be found. Her death represents a great loss.

Basketry

Basketry studies have frequently been the province of makers, illustrating a range of methods, styles and shapes, sometimes with intricate technical descriptions and classifications (see for example, LaPlantz, 1993; Rossbach, 1974; Wright, 1959 and 1977). Yet there does not appear to be a work of the type Philla seems to have envisaged that might contain the range of illustrations as to indicate the variety and complexity across a region. Paradoxically, her own collection shows the need for such a book. In terms of the identification of her collection, many baskets are troublesome. When shown to frequent visitors to Southeast Asia different origins are suggested for baskets decorated, for example, in what appear to be distinct coloured patterns. These are the type of baskets likely to appeal to tourists as casual purchases, apparently distinctive and representative of the place visited. Some modern slipcases now include the name (e.g., Lombok), perhaps because the popularity of this type of basket has made its manufacture and sale so widespread that its origins need to be distinguished. These changes which, it would appear, are poorly if at all documented, also mean that it is harder to ascribe older baskets to particular places: they no longer have a distinct or precise identity.

In West Malaysia, for example, some shops now specialize in the sale of 'indigenous' basketry and other handicrafts. These are often the only places where 'traditional' baskets can be found for sale in towns: there are basketry shops which sell a variety of Chinese basketry manufactured in different styles. The few specialist shops sell material from across East and West Malaysia, and can be seen as part of a promotion of a distinct Malaysian national identity. But their wares seem principally aimed at tourists. In these shops it is possible to buy a range of baskets which look similar to those collected by Philla Davis across the region. Association with place has become association with a shop.

This shift of identity in Malaysia, often utilizing material culture, away from culture and place to nation might be contrasted with the movement in recent decades to identify artists of the past in the third or fourth worlds (see Graburn, 1976). This is accomplished through analysis of carving styles and more recently through recording the makers at work (see, for example, MacNair, Hoover, Neary, 1990). The identity is of an individual – this can be seen in North America in particular for some time, as many anthropologists photographed basketmakers and recorded their name – in contrast to others who were largely interested in technique and artefact (see, for example Mowat, Morphy and Dransart, 1992). A recent work on twill basketry is careful to include the name of the maker in the caption to every photograph, and to record 'anonymous' where this is not known: the frequent use of 'anonymous' for most non-American baskets would seem to be because the piece has probably been bought from a tourist shop, and is in the author's collection (LaPlantz, 1993). This book illustrates modern basketmakers seeking inspiration for form and technique from other craft workers. Philla Davis clearly did this herself on her travels, making a collection as a three dimensional note and recollection. But through travelling she also shared her own knowledge and craft skill, and influenced others (as indicated above at Timbuktu). Her tours and life show how material culture is not static and how makers change and adapt their production.

Conclusion

There is still much to be learnt about Philla Davis before an assessment of her life can properly be made. But asking 'how are we to regard her' prompts many other questions. She does not fall into any convenient professional category, and her primary occupation of craftworker is, or was, not of high status. She was interested in worldwide material culture studies at a time in Britain when they were rather unfashionable among anthropologists and when many smaller regional museums were disposing of their ethnographic collections. Domestic rural craftwork was being rescued and studied; Philla played a part in this, but had broader interests. Her travels might perhaps be properly recognized as her 'fieldwork': she is believed to have kept notes and photographs, which have been destroyed or lost. Perhaps Philla should be seen as an amateur, as have many anthropologists and ethnographers in the past (see West, 1994). In this context it is pertinent to note a recent call to 'promote the values of the amateur (care and affection, freed and an aversion to specialization)' (*Prickly Pear Pamphlets*, quoted by Rapport, 1998).

Philla left a collection which serves and has served many functions. She used it as a record of her travels to illustrate lectures and talks. The collection also demonstrated practical techniques, forms and uses of basketry around the world. Interrogation of the collection is bound up with questions of the identities of the people who are associated with it. Such associations are multiple, of maker and users, how the object is 'consumed', by whom, when and where? It poses problems with regard to firm identification and challenges the associated categories that are dependent on the social or cultural identity of the owner. We do not know that Philla Davis intended her collection for a museum: in Hull the collection is used for teaching and students' research and this may have pleased her. But Philla herself may not have been particularly interested in this work on her collection or her life. Correspondents who knew her are pleased to hear that her collection has been saved and her work appreciated, but another summing up of her character and life is perhaps useful and indicative: 'she followed her own star, regardless of her own or other people's comfort, and without expecting praise or reverence, which is why she was so well liked and respected round here.'

Notes

1   The collection was rescued from Philla Davis' house after her unexpected death by Dr Ian Glover and Dr Jan Christie. Dr Glover had met Philla Davis in Indonesia and also knew her in Shropshire.

2   The material which came to Hull was based on a preliminary identification by Dr Glover and Dr Christie (see note 1) as originating in Southeast Asia.

3   The other museums were Hereford Museum, the Pitt Rivers Museum, Oxford and Birmingham City Museum and Art Gallery.

4   Lewis Hill and I were primarily involved in identifying and cataloguing the collection, building on the initial lists of Ian Glover and Jan Christie (note 1), Mike Hitchcock's use of some of the textiles in his 1991 book, and other colleagues at the Centre for Southeast Asian Studies.

5   The assessment of an object, for the purposes of the museum or auction house is usually done by a professional, or a person regarded as expert with some credentials to match. This professionalization of the evaluation of an object utilizes a set of categories that may be

very different from those of the collector or souvenir hunter, especially when there are no specific indications of that person's evaluation.

6 Identification of some of the textiles and baskets was done by Mrs Alit Veldhuisen-Djajasoebrata of the Rotterdam Museum, who knew Philla well from the 1970s.

7 This short sketch of Philla Davis life and travels is part of a longer biographical project (see also West, 1996). The material is drawn from correspondence and interviews with various of her colleagues and friends. It is incomplete and further work is ongoing, in order to prepare as full a biography as possible.

Many people have helped and provided information in building up this abbreviated picture of Philla Davis' life. I wish to thank in particular: Miss Gillian Bulmer; Mrs Alit Velduisen-Djajsoebrata; Rita Bolland; Dr Ian Glover; Esta Poole-Hughes; Mrs Kate Mason; Miss Anne Dyer; Mr Jack Callow; Mr Jeremy Sandford; the Girl Guide Association; the Registry at Wolverhampton University and Liverpool University. I have corresponded and spoken with many others, too many to list here, all of whom have provided useful information, and who will be acknowledged when a full biography is prepared.

References

Allcock, J.B. and Young, A. (eds) (1991), *Black Lambs and Grey Falcons: women travellers in the Balkans*, Bradford: Bradford University Press.

Graburn, N. (1976), 'Introduction: the arts of the Fourth World', in N. Graburn (ed.), *Ethnic and Tourist Arts: cultural expressions from the Fourth World*, Los Angeles: University of California Press.

Hitchcock, M. (1991), *Indonesian Textiles*, London: British Museum Press.

Keay, J. (1994), *With Passport and Parasol: the Adventures of Seven Victorian Ladies*, BBC London: Books and Penguin Books.

LaPlantz, S. (1993), *Twill Basketry: a handbook of designs, techniques, and styles*, Asheville, North Carolina: Lark Books.

Layton, R. (1992), 'Traditional and Contemporary Art of Aboriginal Australia: Two Case Studies', in J. Coote and A. Shelton (eds), *Anthropology, Art and Aesthetics*, Oxford: Clarendon Press.

MacNair, P.L., Hoover, A.L. and Neary, K. (1990), *The Legacy: Continuing Traditions of Canadian Northwest Coast Indian Art*, Victoria, British Columbia: British Columbia Provincial Museum.

Mills, S. (1991), *Discourses of Difference: an analysis of women's travel writing and colonialism*, London: Routledge.

Mowat, L., Morphy, H. and Dransart, P. (eds) (1992), *Basketmakers: Meaning and Form in Native American Baskets*, Monograph 5, Pitt Rivers Museum, University of Oxford, Oxford.

Oxfam (1990), *Christmas Gifts from Around the World*, Oxford: Oxfam.

Oxfam (1991), *Spring/Summer Sale*, leaflet, Oxford: Oxfam.

Rapport, N. (1998), 'Review of Prickly Pear Pamphlets Nos 1–9', *Critique of Anthropology*, 18 (1), pp. 97–102.

Robinson, J. (1990), *Wayward Women: a guide to women travellers*, Oxford: Oxford University Press.

Rossbach, E. (1974), *Baskets as Textile Art*, Studio Vista, London (first published 1973, by Van Nostrand Reinhold Company, USA).

Russell, M. (1986), *The Blessings of a Good Thick Skirt: Women Travellers and Their World*, London: Collins.

Sandford, J. (1991), *Figures and Landscapes: the art of Lettice Sandford*, London: Roc Sandford at the Soho Book Company Ltd.

Sandford, L. and Davis, P. (1958), *Corn Dollies and How to Make Them*, Hereford: Herefordshire Federation of Women's Institutes.

Sandford, L. and Davis, P. (1964), *Decorative Straw Work*, London: B.T. Batsford Ltd.

Teague, K. (1995), 'Tourism, Anthropology and Museums: Representations of Nepalese Reality', *Journal of Museum Ethnography*, 7, pp. 41–62.

Traidcraft (1991/92), *Catalogue*, Gateshead: Traidcraft plc.

West, A. (1994), 'Writing the Nagas: A British Officer's ethnographic tradition', *History and Anthropology*, 8, pp. 55–88.

West, A. (1996), 'Philla Davis – traveller, collector, and craftworker', *Indonesia Circle*, 69, pp. 122–40.

Wright, D. (1959), *Baskets and Basketry*, London: B.T. Batsford Ltd.

Wright, D. (1977), *The Complete Book of Baskets and Basketry*, Newton Abbot: David & Charles.

10 Contemporary Crafts as Souvenirs, Artefacts and Functional Goods and their Role in Local Economic Diversification and Cultural Development

GRAEME EVANS

Introduction

The development of an international craft market and industry, reviving lost or declining practices and styles, now renders the label *tourist arts* (Graburn, 1976; Cohen, 1993) inadequate, or at best misleading. The explosion in demand for original craft pieces – functional and decorative – has reached beyond the tourist-exposure which has fuelled the ethnic art trade. Over 10 years ago handcrafts were estimated to be the second largest source of income, after agriculture in the developing world (Pye, 1986); in Latin America the estimated 40 million persons engaged in handcraft production are most often found in the 40 per cent of the population living below the poverty line (Tadmore, 1994). They therefore provide an important source of self-sustaining employment: for instance over 20 million people earn their living in the crafts in India for everyday, decorative and ritual use, and for sale/export.

This paper assesses the role and relationship between small crafts enterprises and cultural tourism, based on field research firstly in Greater Mexico (Meosamerica): Mexico – Tonala, Jalisco; Teotitlan del Valle, Oaxaca; San Miguel D'Allende, Guanajato; San Cristobal, Chiapas and in New Mexico (USA): pueblos, museum galleries and trade centres of Santa Fe, Taos and secondly in the Indonesian island of Lombok, specifically the 'Sasak Women

Potters'. These case studies present both a contrast and comparative example of local crafts-based economic development at mature and developing stages of evolution. Heritage sites, public and private museum and gallery collections and trading posts were visited and interviews were held at village/studios ('folk data' – Gottlieb, 1982) with craft producers, families, cooperatives, and with intermediaries. They were based upon the development of commissions and purchase of contemporary art and craft works for export to England and the USA, and included repeat liaison with craft-producers in Mexico and Lombok between 1990 and 1997.

Crafts Markets and Distribution

Outlets for contemporary and 'authentic' replicas are found in European cities, through mail order networks (including via aid and fair trade agencies) and through direct commissioning activity between entrepreneurs (gallery, shop owners) and indigenous artist-producers and village studios. These dealings take place in trade and art centres, alongside tourist visits in third world tourist locations and at places of production – at 'source' in studios and workshops in villages and towns (Popelka and Littrell, 1991). They do not presuppose tourism or tourist interaction, but in the absence of local or even national promotional and distribution agencies and 'owing to the geographical and cultural hiatus that often separates the producers from the consumers ... their production is significantly influenced by intermediaries' (Cohen, 1993, p. 2).

The range, and importantly the development and quality control of aboriginal and 'ethnic' art (sic) and crafts, are increasingly influenced by these factors; tourists, often unwittingly, are the beneficiaries of this cultural interaction and trade. The growth of ethnic art and crafts shops/centres and retailing in museums and galleries in 'generator' countries (as well as urban and regional cities and 'hubs' in receiving countries themselves), provides the 'leisure-shopping' experience:

> The immediate gratification felt by the department store customer in the act of purchase, and the experience of handling objects and learning more about them, which was the joy of the fair-goer, are united in the museum store, and seal the museum-going experience for many visitors. Appropriately enough in our culture, it is the commercial setting which legitimises as aesthetic setting (Harris, 1990, p. 80).

The role of the marketplace is fundamental in local economic development, including tourist management. Markets are often the prime source of souvenir and artefact, the closest many tourists get to local interaction beyond the hospitality industry. They do offer a compromise, a meeting ground between both tourist, broker and host community, that is both authentic and staged, since they can be located and housed in strategic sites, away from sensitive and private areas. This is also a trend in urban tourism in western cities, where street markets have become major visitor attractions in their own right. Natural and local markets, which occur regularly in towns and rural areas, also provide a genuine experience of local produce and cultural interaction. Their exploitation, however, risks the destruction of a local amenity and focus of exchange that would not easily be recreated.

Primitive Art and Crafts

The aesthetic ideas of the largely non-Western peoples studied by the putative founders of anthropology were largely ignored at a time (eighteenth–nineteenth centuries) when this could have still been the subject of fieldwork among the native populations of developing countries. Designs, for example, were featured in debates about diffusion and independent invention, but before the First World War anthropological interest was limited.[1] By the time of Boas' general reveil, *Primitive Art* (1927), large numbers of masks, figurines and exotic carvings had passed via the studios of the post-Impressionists into the hands of renowned collectors such as Paul Guillaume and Baron Eduord con der Heydt (Firth, 1992, pp. 20–1). With acculturation progressing at an ever-increasing pace, many of the traditional functions performed by certain objects vanished, or were served by industrially manufactured products. A large proportion of the now 'meaningless' artefacts ended up in museums, and with this final harvest the traditional collecting activity more or less came to an end. To their producers the 'museumification' of these objects removed them from both their meaning (symbolic, sacred) and function. Clifford's concept of the museum as 'contact zone', views the nineteenth century museum-as-collection as a frontier, structuring the itinerary of ethnological objects as a passage from colonial periphery to metropolitan centre and characterized by a relationship of 'uneven reciprocity' (1997, p. 13). Clifford (p. 209) argues that contemporary museum curators will have to 'reckon with the fact that the objects and interpretations they display "belong" to others as well as to the museum'.

While only a limited number of objects continued to be produced for tribal use, the production of crafts for an outside market grew in importance. These 'ethnic' arts, which employed native technologies to satisfy foreign tastes, have a history almost as long as the history of the encounter of Western civilization with the tribal world. Depending on the structure of the market, there was a tremendous variation in the quality of what is offered for sale. Neither producers nor buyers considered these wares works of art; for their makers they were a source of cash income on the basis of traditional skills; for the tourists they were curios and mementos.

Typologies

Feest (1992) lists four kinds of 'art', differing in terms of the artists' self-evaluation, their producer-consumer relationship and their function and meaning. Some social scientists and art historians may have reservations about the terminology (e.g., tribal) and general applicability of the typologies, but they provide a useful starting point for this discussion.

1 *Tribal art* – as produced by members of tribal societies primarily for their own use. As a rule there was no professional specialization beyond the gender division of labour (Van den Berghe, 1992), although specialist producers existed such as Asmat woodcarvers, Ashanti weavers and Eskimo mask-makers. Functionality was the overriding criterion for a product – the aesthetic component was not seen in isolation from the whole.

2 *Ethnic art* – as produced by members of tribal societies primarily for the use of members of *other* groups; in the case of Mexico/New Mexico, for the use of White Americans and Ladinos (mixed Spanish and 'white' blood)[2] and in Lombok, for other racial groups and recently for white tourists and traders. These artefacts are not thought of as 'art' by their makers. The technology of production is largely traditional, although new materials and treatments are introduced from buyers/intermediaries, in some cases substantially changing the form the art takes. Specialization is increasingly encouraged, although Indian craftsmen often do not know why their products are brought – for producer they are a source of income, but in the long run may become a symbol of the makers' ethnic (but not necessarily *tribal*) identity.

3 *Pan-Indian art* – as produced by indigenous natives, who feel themselves

no longer exclusively bound to the values and customs of their *original* tribal societies. They work for the art market of the dominant White society and consequently regard themselves as artists. While still drawing on the experience of their specific cultural background, their style is no longer unique to the tribe, but is largely shaped by White expectations about 'Indian style'. The first government-funded Indian Art School ('The Studio') was opened in Sante Fe in 1932, following the 1931 Exposition of Indian Tribal Art in New York. In other aboriginal societies, such as Maori, North Australian (*Aratjara*) and Inuit, contemporary artists straddle both 'pan-Indian' and 'ethnic' art categories.

4   *Indian mainstream art* – as produced by artists who happen to be Indians. Each has their individual influences which may or may not find expression in their art. The subject matter of their art may be related to their ancestry or ethnic heritage, their style is not:

> My artistic energy has been devoted to exploring the social and psychological facets of the North American Indian's relationship with European settlers. As an artist, I see a mutual strength in the marriage I have with the land, flora, fauna and the ways of the native culture. *My personal struggle is to maintain my native identity and heritage while drawing from the best of all other cultures* (Plains Cree Artist, Indigena Fine Art Publishers, Arizona 1992, my emphasis).

The significance of craft/artefact production (including the most significant: textiles, jewellery and ceramics) is their object-nature and commodification potential (Litrell, 1990). This separation and 'reification' in the West (Evans Pritchard, 1989, p. 92) has made the commodification of artworks possible, the unique nature of works of art and museum pieces ('treasures') is the basis of our art trade and collections (Clifford, 1990), and this exchange and rarity-value has encompassed 'primitive' and 'ethnic' arts, from commissions to acquisitions:

> Crafts may well gain competitive advantage as Western countries develop post-modern economies ... the so-called 'narrow cast market' should stimulate demand ... homogeneity in tastes are now being reversed with increasing fragmentation within the mass market' (Hillman-Chartrand, 1988).

Markets for such products are not limited to tourist exposure, although clearly tourist-art is particularly adapted to the transient visitor (by size/weight/ price). In terms of tourist interaction and trade, ethnic and pan-Indian art are now the established form of Amerindians and in the case of Lombok, indigenous crafts have recently evolved, with the help of intermediaries, to the ethnic art stage. Whilst the demise of tribal 'art' may be regretted, as such societies were destroyed and alternative materials and technologies superseded functional objects (e.g. metal for clay, wool for cotton), the development of a tourist and art and craft market has effectively revitalised indigenous art, and local economies, albeit in Western terms and tastes (Popelka and Litrell, 1991).

Graburn (1976, p. 8, adapted here, see Evans, 1994b) analyses art and craft forms for intended audiences within minority 'Fourth World' communities and external civilization's (consumers – including tourists and home-imports).

The traditional art-souvenir cycle often ends in imported mass-production, and tourism can revive lost or fading craft skills, such as the Kuna women of Aayara Island, Panama, 'who had to be taught to make the traditional mola blouse' (Christie Mill, 1990, p. 169). The *mola* was also used as symbol of ethnic reassertion by this group (Swain, 1993). Native Mexican replicas can be found in British craft shops, manufactured in *Indonesia* – post-Fordism has arrived as one indigenous group undercuts another, to the benefit of Western buyers. (This may have arisen due to historic links between Indonesia/ Philippines and Mexico, or more prosaically, be just a labour/market exploitation.) The 'delegation' of production can also be seen in the rug weavers from Zapotec/Mixtec tribes, who work in the Navajo-style; the authentic versions are too highly priced, having been adopted by the US art market. The impact of transport and tourism was also evident in the first wave of Mexican tourism. Up until the 1950s, *sarapes* were produced for indigenous use and trade in Oaxaca and Chiapas; however, following the arrival of the Pan-American Highway and tourism development, tourists were targeted for the *sarapes*, produced by weavers in Teotitlan del Valle. Initially the sarapes had functional, poncholike neck-slits. By the late 1950s, this had disappeared, and the *sarapes* were designed for use as interior decoration, as wall hangings – functionality transformed into tourist art (Popelka and Litrell, 1991).

Put another way, as colonial and postcolonial intervention has removed tribal society and culture from its roots; from land use to sacred ritual, another form of economic development – tourist and export culture – has stimulated creativity and acculturation, not only through commodification (notwith-standing museum/ancient 'fakes'), but also as a pragmatic form of cultural change. As with all 'culture', perpetual ownership is not an option, given a dynamic society only varying by the rate, degree and violence of change and cultural hybridity is increasingly the normal state of affairs (Hall, 1990), but eclecticism combined with consumerism is not without its dangers:

Aesthetic-formal sources and traditions

	Minority society	Novel/synthetic	Dominant society
Minority *Fourth World* **External civilizations**	*Functional traditional* e.g. Lega, Maori *marae*, some Pueblo and *Lombok* pottery	*Reintegrated* e.g. Kuna *molas*, pueblo *kachinas*	*Popular* e.g. Navajo jewellery
	Commercial fine e.g. Maori woodcarving, New Guinea shields	*Souvenir/novelty* e.g. Seri, Makonde carving, Xalitla *amate*	*Assimilated fine* e.g. Sante Fe Indian painting, Namatjira watercolours, Eskimo prints, Navajo rugs

Source: Graburn, 1976, p. 8 (adapted by author).

Cultural cross-pollination is healthily creative, and works organically to find its own way. The danger is that fashionability can ... create a consumer society in which ethnic phenomena are drained of their meaning, and reasserted as little more than infinitely transferable badges of a wholly superficial allegiance to different cultures (Bracewell, 1994, p. 3).

Whilst the fate of the Native Indian and Sasak (below) has been both violent and continuing,

there has been both continuity and change in the history of the native arts under White influence ... the changes seem to outweigh the continuity, but they must be regarded as the price paid for the survival of the arts (Feest, 1992).

As an economic development option and value-added aspect (and in certain circumstances, an alternative) to tourism development, indigenous production, of which artefacts and cultural production are growth areas, warrants greater attention and investigation of successful models of producer-control:

The Study of Fourth World arts is, par excellence, the study of *changing* arts – of emerging ethnicities, modifying identities, and commercial and colonial stimuli and repressive actions (Graburn, 1976).

Village Studio and Cooperative Distribution

The development of village-based studio workshops in remoter areas of

Mexico, has been enabled by the creation of cooperative distribution and marketplaces, as controlled outlets for crafts products, and the collaboration with intermediaries and fair trade organizations in Europe and the USA. Weavers and potters are traditionally family-organized, with both men and women in the role of craftmaker and entrepreneur. A critical mass of crafts activity, even in small villages, provides both stimulation and a diversity of production and skills, which produces cross-fertilization and cross-trading, as well as economies of scale in production. This also improves the trade and commissioning links with intermediaries and strengthens cooperative distribution and transportation efforts. In some cases, dealings also occur at places of production, such as at Teotitlan del Valle, Oaxaca state (hand-dyed/ woven textiles, and see Popelka and Littrell, 1991); Tonala (recycled glassware), San Miguel d'Allende (recycled aluminium) and Tlaquepaque (a Sante Fe-style art gallery 'suburb' of Guadalajara) and also at Mexican cultural heritage sites, such as Monte Alban and Mitla. The latter, however, presents the weakest form of local trade and the most inequitable and deleterious 'meeting ground' between producer and purchaser (i.e. 'tourist/street art' – Cohen, 1993, and see MacCannell, 1991).

Examples of sustainable crafts-based activity are represented by a range of media and craft forms, often using recycled materials and organic ingredients and production techniques. Individual and family crafts enterprises are identified with particular craft development and commissioning with fair trading and cultural tourism operators in generator/consumer countries, such as the following.

Glass

Gabriel Nuno has been recycling old Pepsi bottles and other discarded glass in a small workshop in Tonala, Jalisco, for over 30 years. This waste material is hand crafted into finely blown glass bowls, jugs and goblets, using methods that date back millennia. The style and shape of each piece is slightly different, as all the glass is finished by hand and eye. Most of Gabriel's family, which includes seven daughters, are actively involved in producing and selling the glass. The commissioning process with external trade companies has also produced a wider range of shapes and colour combinations than traditional glassware. This includes the design and production of 'branded' tequila glasses for the Jose Cueva drinks company in the UK.

Ceramics

Probably the greatest of all pre-Columbian handicrafts. Potters are still found extensively in Mexico with a diversity of form and decoration produced by these accomplished craft people. Work includes delicate figurative pieces fired in wooden pyres, coil pots fired in pit kilns and turned or mould-made pottery, fired in modern electric and oiled fired kilns. The Spaniards brought to Mexico tin glazed earthenware, known as Maiolica or Talavera, which has been adapted by potters in Puebla and Dolores Hidalgo. Talavera typically combines Islamic, Spanish, Italian and Chinese styles with local folk influences. The Amora pottery from Dolores Hidalgo, particularly draws on this tradition. Stoneware from Tonala, Jalisco is made from finely graded clay and fired in higher temperature kilns, which gives a more durable and functional ceramic. All the ceramics produced for fair trade export and tourist acquisition are hand painted and attempt to offer pieces which represent an evolution of traditional designs deeply rooted in local culture. Perhaps the highest volume production is in tiles – ceramic, terracotta, glass mosaic which have become fashionable in the USA and Europe. Here the greatest range of styles and colours is available, with two-way influence in terms of colours and finishes, as with glassware. Local crafts producers however still maintain the handcraft production techniques which maintains the unique quality of tiles and other products, resisting mass production which Western retailers impose, requiring product uniformity and 'perfection' (i.e. homogeneity).

Rugs

In Teotitlan del Valle, Oaxaca, pre-Columbian traditions of weaving are still practised, though the technology has changed. Almost every house boasts its own wooden treadle (shaft) loom, a Spanish introduction that replaced the indigenous body tension loom. Two village families have specialised in tourism and export trade, and who use natural dyed handspun wool to produce bold geometric designs in vibrant colours. Dyes are extracted from locally found flora and fauna. Greens and yellows are derived from mosses and other plants, browns and blacks from beans, and reds from the Cochineal beetle which is found on cactus plants. The weavers are continually experimenting with new colours and combinations. Design influences come from the nearby Mixtec ruins of Mitla and the much valued weavings of North American Navajo Indians. Again rug design is influenced by commissioning processes, sometimes mixing Western with Mayan symbols, and weavers resist 'cheaper' machine production, which does create pricing difficulties against mass-produced rugs sold in the West, generally made in India and Indonesia.

Aluminium

In San Miguel de Allende, Jose Maria Fuentes produces chunky but elegant cast aluminium bowls, platters, candlesticks and picture surrounds amongst other fascinating objects. Jose is a picador by trade, however the foundry, which he opened in the 1980s as a sideline, has now become his major occupation. Old aluminium beer and soft drink cans and hub caps are melted down using a low technology smelting process, involving a gas burner in an oil drum and cast in fine sand moulds. To recover the finished piece it is necessary to destroy the mould, which means that each product has a unique character. After polishing, the final result is a beautifully burnished metal finish, with a lustre somewhere between silver and pewter.

Most of these crafts producers are located in rural or semi-rural locations outside of large towns and cities. A hub-and-spoke system with marketplaces and retail distribution centres located in central towns and tourist gateways, such as San Miguel D'Allende, Guanajuato, Morelia – central Mexico and in the south, Oaxaca and San Cristobal, as well as Mexico City itself, supports a network of outlying village-producers, who are guaranteed sale quantities and income, with maximum value-added and minimum disturbance to fragile village socio-cultures, including authentic markets and sacred sites. The role of intermediaries is therefore crucial in this process, particularly where tourist and export trade is featured.

Intermediaries

The role of intermediaries in the economic development of local communities in developing countries, particularly the impact on indigenous communities, has been at best, paternalistic, and at worst, exploitative, whether led by dominant societies represented by state governments, or western agencies and industry (Goodland, 1982). In most cases, the need for skills-exchange and in some instances protection from short-term profit maximization is pivotal to local economic and sustainable development. The case of village-studio based craft production by indigenous communities in Mexico and Lombok provide examples of both *fair trade*, and the sensitive use of intermediaries, as well as a degree of self-management by craft-producers themselves.

An atypical example of ethnic art and craft tourism is evident in San Cristobal, an ex-colonial town in the Mayan highlands of Chiapas in the southeastern border region with Guatamela (see also Van den Berghe, 1992, and with Colby, 1991; Vogt, 1978 and 1990). Here Ladinos act as middlemen between participating Indian groups and effectively operate as buffers between tourists and Indians. They

> mediate, facilitate and benefit from the tourist-touree interaction, occupy all the niches of the hospitality industry, but they also use their knowledge of the local situation to bring tourists and tourees together (Van den Berghe, 1992, p. 236).

This internal colonial role is confirmed by their

> membership of the dominant ethnic group in the polity and economy of the country … They are at ease in the market place and are firmly planted in the 'modern' sector of the local economy. In effect they exploit their position at the intersection of modernity and authenticity (ibid.).

Intervention in Indian affairs is not confined to Ladino middlemen; the Instituto Nacional Indigenista (INI) run cooperatives to display and sell Indian crafts to tourists and organise 100–300 Indian women weavers and piece-rate workers. State intervention in this case is paternalistic and lacks the producer control and local economic benefits evident from the village networks outlined above. The institutionalization (and commodification) of crafts production also serves to separate producer from consumer, and with the role of middlemen: 'many tourists do not even go to the Indian villages. As thousands of Indians come to the San Cristobal market daily, tourees are widely available for viewing without leaving town' (op. cit.).

The reaction and impact on local communities is varied, however, beyond the unavoidable points of contact (road, town periphery), because between the two Indian communities, *Zinacantecos* and *Chamulas*, the former have little interest and do not welcome tourists, seeing this as undignified – photography is not accepted and there is little direct craft trade. Their neighbouring tribe have 'embraced' tourism and are the active craft seller-producers, despite the fact that the Zinacantecos designs are more attractive to many tourists. Ladinos or Chamulas Indians in fact sell the Zinacantecos' handicrafts. Craft production has also adapted to the market segments – tourist art: smaller pieces and items made of cheaper materials and more quickly produced are sold alongside higher quality and priced ethnic art, for more discerning (and well-off) tourists and traders, cases, respectively, of 'encroaching' and 'complementary commercialisation' in tourist arts (Cohen, 1993, p. 3 and see 1989).

The purchase of ethnic art by a tourist at home may also respond to a former visit, where they can still be: 'among their most valued possessions' (Wallendorf and Arnould, 1988, p. 532). In practice, the choice of craft items will represent a wider range and quality of products than available whilst on 'tour', and without the hassle. The price of Western-import mark-up may be worth it. Such availability may also stimulate a first visit at a later date, and serve as a source of information on ethnic art forms. It may just serve as part of an eclectic goods market which we take for granted. A developed craft market does, however, present a positive opportunity for indigenous production, beyond the constraints, culture-clash and other deleterious effects of tourist trade. Three models of producer exhibition, commission and distribution can be extracted.

1   Craft producer – broker – outlets (national and for export).
    Direct commissioning from *source*, producer guaranteed sale, buyer influences style and quantities, subject to market (consumer) demand/ assessment and feedback.

2   Craft producer – market/exhibition – consumer (trade and tourist).
    Specialist art and craft markets (e.g. Oaxaca, Santa Fe, Taos), located in central and destination-locations. Range of products from basic to quality, possibly fake-authentic (Messenger, 1989).

3   Craft producer(s) – cooperative – controlled retail/exhibitions.
    Collective production (village or studio-based) is sold via special trade centres in regional towns, 'gateways' and resorts. A wide range and 'best quality/examples' stocked.

These are obviously not exclusive and could be complementary. They do offer a degree of control and where desired, distance between producer and consumer, as well as greater opportunity for economic development. As experience and confidence is gained, the broker's role may be taken over by national and potentially indigenous representatives, thus cutting out the middleman and reducing monetary leakage. In Mexico this would require support in the form of capital and greater recognition for indigenous production by regional and national government and by institutional finance bodies.

New Mexico (USA)

In contrast to Mexico, where tourism originated in the 1950s (international tourists totalled only165,000 in 1945, but by 1963 reched one million), New Mexico tourism developed in the late 1800s and was well-established by 1920. The encroaching railroad was the main factor of change and promotion of settler immigration and relocation. Native Indians were allowed to ride for free on trains as romantic exotica and the Sante Fe railway company used Indian symbols in their promotional literature and encouraged Indians to set-up craft stalls outside stations. An enterprising 'tour operator', Fred Harvey Corporation (a 'US Thomas Cook') even devised 'Indian Detours' which offered passengers a few days off the train and excursions to Indian villages and sites. During this period, Indian groups began to see tourists as sources of income (Sweet, 1989).

Today, some Amerindians, such as the Mescaleros (Apache), promote tourism more so than other groups. This includes the management of a luxury ski-resort ('Ski Apache', 'Inn of the Mountain of the Gods', 'Apache Haven Motel') and game hunting tours. More recently, exploiting state legislation, reservations have opened popular gambling centres, much to the chagrin of non-Indian Americans, some of whom are spuriously claiming Indian ancestry, in order to receive Reservation status (Wright, 1993)! Amongst Pueblo settlements, some are more 'open' than others; over two thirds do not allow cameras or videorecorders (Laxson, 1991) – a degree of choice and destiny-control is evident, therefore, unlike their equivalents in Mexico. In New Mexico, dealings take place in trade and art centres, alongside tourist attractions, in Sante Fe, Taos (Kemper 1978 and 1979) and the capital Albuquerque (host of the Indian Pueble Cultural Centre, State History Museum and Maxwell Museum of Anthropology). Cultural quarters, such as Sante Fe and Taos are the focus for intense tourist art and craft business (Sante Fe, $134 million turnover: Eichztaedt, 1988) and craft production takes place elsewhere; studio and housing rents also create a 'gentrification effect' and a non-indigenous, professional art gallery 'class'. In Mexico, Tlaquepaque, outside of Guadalajara, has followed these New Mexican models and is dominated by US art trade and gallery-owners, although some local production and ownership continues, mostly family-based, such as at Tonala, nearby (e.g. coloured glass, volcanic stone and recycled tin products).

New Mexican pueblo crafts have also incorporated imported and imposed technology. Their influences include the Spanish, such as silver-making, wool-weaving and looms, as well as modern and traditional farming, oil and mineral production and forestry and more recently, tourism development and management, from skiing to gambling . An example of modern materials and treatment in ethnic art is the distinctive black pottery produced in Teotitlan', Mexico, which is worked with car aerials to produce a burnished finish, and the use of recycled glass (coke bottles) and aluminium, from cans and wheel hubs, melted down and recast into bowls, cups and cutlery – above.

Island of Lombok, Indonesia

The island of Lombok is due east of Bali, with a population of two million and a minority but formerly dominant Balinese culture. The Balinese-ruled from the 1600s to the mid-nineteenth century, from when it was part of the Dutch east Indies until World War II. Eighty per cent of the population are Sasak Muslims, the remainder being Balinese and Chinese: however, this majority are the poorest group, effectively 'Fourth World minorities' as with the actual minority Indian communities of Mexico. The Sasak Muslims are divided into the *Waktu Lima*, those who have accepted the full teaching of Islam, and the *Waktu Telu*, a small minority, who adhere to many pre-Islamic customs and beliefs. Parallels may be drawn with the Mexican Indians who were converted to Catholicism by invaders; the Sasaks have adapted the new religion with symbols and traditions from the past, mixing Hindu-Buddhism and other pre-Islamic customs with Islam.

Tourism in Lombok has until recently been relatively undeveloped, and could be compared with Bali 25 years ago. Luxury hotel and apartment developments on the northwest coast (Sengigi) feature in long-haul package tours, and as 'overspill' for Australian and New Zealand tourists. The south coast is still touted as unspoilt; however, further tourist development is under way, and pressure will intensify as Bali reaches saturation point and destination-fatigue sets in. Indeed, twin island holidays are already promoted (20 minute plane journey), with Lombok as the 'unspoilt haven' that previously was afforded Bali. Lombok's proximity to Bali's tourist market has created specialist craft communities in villages such as Gunung Sari, Beleka, Senanti and Sukaraja. Gamelan ceremonies and staged performances can be seen here, but away from Bali's 'madding crowds'. The host Sasak community, outside of the few hotel areas, has yet to 'act' for the tourist – 'Westerners are such a rarity that children run away in fear, an *orang bulan* (moon person)[3] is a sensation, with people crowding round to touch the pale skin' (Wheeler et al., 1992).

Sasak Women Potters

Throughout Indonesia, earthenware pottery (*tembikar*) is produced by village potters for local domestic use. Sasak pottery is widely acknowledged both inside Indonesia and abroad for its rich variety and beauty. The pots are from three major pottery producing villages of Lombok; Benyumulek, Penujak and Masbagijik Timur, which formerly supplied most of the island's population with their cooking, storage and serving vessels. These traditional pots have specific functions in domestic and ritual life. They are handmade, using paddle and anvil and coiling methods with home-made tools of wood, bamboo, metal blades, shell and stone, and even obsidian river pebbles that have been handed down through generations. Firing is carried out in hollow mounds (clamp kilns) and more recently with handmade kilns.

The Sasak women potters are recognised within their communities as 'masters' of their craft and are looked up to as teachers, yet they see their work primarily as the only means of making a living available to them, and with encroaching tourist development, a viable alternative to servile hospitality work away from their homes. Starting at an early age, the skills of the potters are passed from generation to generation, from mother to daughter (Van den Berghe, 1992). Pottery provides the main source of income for over 1,500 potter families in the three villages, and although the women are the actual potters, the overall production is a family enterprise. Most potters are assisted by their husbands, children and other relatives in the various tasks involved, including clay gathering, processing, finishing and decorating, gathering fuel and firing to childcare. Lombok's landscape is dominated by Indonesia's second highest volcano, Gunung Rinjani, surrounded by hills of greyish-brown clay, the source material.

Living on one of the most densely populated islands of Indonesia, the Sasaks are one of the poorest, and least educated cultural groups in the country. Potter families are mostly landless, or own land that is less than sufficient to meet their food needs: the island is acid by Indonesian standards and the more verdant western half is settled by Balinese farmers. Wage labour in the villages is limited to sharecropping and day-labour at planting, weeding at harvest times, many villagers run small businesses and increasingly seek work outside of the village. The production and sale of pottery in local markets is therefore of vital importance to survival, but where the majority of customers are equally poor, prices are inevitably low.

Since 1988 the Lombok Crafts Project has been assisting the women potters of three villages to improve the standard of living through technical and marketing assistance (Evans, 1994b). A bilateral agreement between Indonesian and New Zealand governments, has funded the building of work shelters and showrooms. Technical, quality and design skills have been improved through advice on marketing, finance and distribution, and export of pottery is now developing with independent trade organizations ('ethnic art'). One of the most important technical changes introduced by the project is the open topped kiln used in Penujak village. In choosing this kind of kiln over more advanced designs, the potters have met the needs of greater fuel efficiency and productivity, as well as satisfying their wish to work together as they always have. Through this bilateral assistance programme, quality, durability and marketability of the pottery has improved significantly, without loss of integrity or intrinsic values of the creative process and ritual experience. This has helped to increase the income of the potters substantially, and all surplus profits from sales are used by the potters to improve living and working conditions in the villages. It is likely, however, that a two-tier production may develop, ensuring protection of tribal quality and significance, similar to the San Cristobal and Oaxaca, Mexico and Pueblo, NM experience. Since the collaborative phase of this project has been completed however, there is evidence that the Sasak community have reverted to some of their previous practices and in some respects the quality and robustness of the pottery ware has deteriorated, particularly limiting its scope for export trade. Why this has occurred is not clear, but the 'dependency' created by external intervention in the form of technical 'assistance' has evidently not been replaced by either 'technology-transfer' or self-sufficiency in improved production techniques. The Sasaks' isolated position socially, culturally and economically, and therefore politically, means that infrastructure support is lacking, and the government focus continues to be towards commercial tourism development on the island.

Conclusion

Christie Mill (1990) poses the conundrum: 'Does tourism force people to remain artisans at the expense of attempts to achieve economic growth and independence?' The encouragement of cultural *involution* through staged authenticity (Graburn, 1976; MacCannell, 1984 and 1991) and tourists seeking the 'old ways' and customs, *may* be justified where control over their destiny is effectively denied local communities: control over land ownership and use; protection from economic 'dumping' from first world producers and dominant cultural invasion. James Wong, Sarawak Environment and Tourism Minister, 'timber concessionnaire, golfer and poet', epitomises the dialectic over the impact of cultural interaction and exchange, writing in his third volume of poetry (Vidal, 1994, pp. 7–8): 'Oh Penan – jungle warriors of the Tree – What would the future hold for Thee? Would you choose to carry on with Primitive Traditions – Or cast that aside and join our Civilization?'

The degree of self-sufficiency apparent, but under threat (i.e. employment, land use/ownership) within these local and indigenous communities (Goodland, 1982) does however offer an opportunity through the interaction between tourism, related production and producer services (e.g. crafts, agriculture, cultural) and consumer-based fair trade (Evans, 1994b; Evans and Cleverdon, 1999). When combined with the experience of local economic development in response to globalization, particularly in urban areas, fair trading relationships between northern consumers and intermediaries, and between tourist destinations in the south, present particular advantages over the free market system prevalent in international tour operation and mass craft production, where market failure through the unsustainable life-cycle, short-term contract and trading horizons and small profit margins is perpetuated (Josephides, 1993).

The environmental impact of production is also an important aspect of fair trading in crafts and cultural tourism. An obvious facet of this is the use of recycled raw materials (glass, aluminium, natural-dyes in Mexico and natural tools and fuel in Lombok). Perhaps less well acknowledged are the ways in which Third World trading can affect the actual structure of a community. Small businesses and workshops run by families, such as in Lombok and Teotitlan, Oaxaca, provide work for members of isolated villages. Their ability to maintain a sustainable trade may often continue the life of these communities, arresting the drift of people towards the cities and resorts, and help keep vital craft skills and cultural expression alive, for the benefit of those people, and as an externality, for the public good. Writing in England in 1933, Ethel Mairet echoed the sentiment that: 'Village industries should be started again but not on the old basis at all. They should be an integral part of the whole country development, not arty crafty revival of badly done crafts' (*Rural Industries Magazine*).

The opportunities for craft enterprise, cultural industry and producer-control are evident from the New Mexico Pueblo art and craft markets, and also from cooperative studios and distribution initiatives in Mexico. These act, not only as buffer and quality-control, but as an alternative to the commercialization by the American art and gallery trade and super-profits of some intermediaries (cf. lessons from the Taos, Sante Fe, NM and Bali experiences). In Lombok, the prospect of tourist-led development and influx threatens the social fabric, and acculturation may be inescapable, unless development and transport routes are restricted (the 'closed' Pueblo model may offer an alternative). The revitalized craft industry will also continue to offer an export trade to village communities, as well as an opportunity for trade at tourist markets and resort sites. As a diversification-strategy and value-added element of tourism (Barratt Brown, 1993), craft demand and development is therefore a major opportunity for indigenous communities and producers.

Notes

1   Augustus Hamilton compiled a study of the 'art workmanship' of the Maori, which was published in 1896. A.C. Haddon (1894) published on the decorative art of New Guinea and Franz Boas analysed the art of the Native Americans of the northwest coast (1897).
2   *Ladinos* is a 'non-Indian' person of mixed Spanish/Italian and white (European) blood/ culture. In this context a Hispanic or Spanish Mexican today is not 'white' since this is also a politico-cultural term (like 'black') referring to anyone rejecting Mayan Indian values and heritage, as well as being of 'mixed blood'. A person of mixed Spanish/Indian extraction is referred to as a *Mestizo*.
3   The term *orang bulan* is Malay-Indonesian and not Sasak and it remains unclear how it came to be used in this context. The term may be either a local version of *orang bulai* – albino or white person – or a misrecording.

References

Barratt Brown, M. (1993), *Fair Trade: Reform and Realities in the International Trading System*, London: Zed Books.
Boas, F. (1897), 'The Decorative Art of the Indians of the North Pacific Coast', *Bulletin of the American Museum of Natural History*, 9, Art. 19, pp. 123–76.
Boas, F. (1927), *Primitive Art*, Oslo, Aschehoug, Instituttet for Sammenlingnende Kulturforskning (paperback (1955), New York: Dover).
Bracewell, M. (1994), 'A Question of Ethnics', *The Guardian*, 8 January, pp. 14–15.
Bronstein, A. (1982), *A Triple Struggle: Latin American Peasant Women*, London: Inter-Action Inprint/War on Want.
Christie Mill, R. (1990), *Tourism: The International Business*, Englewood Cliffs, NJ: Prentice-Hall International.
Clifford, J. (1990), 'On Collecting Arts and Culture', in R. Ferguson (ed.), *Out There: Marginalisation and Contemporary Culture*, 4, M.I.T. Press.

Clifford, J. (1997), 'Museums as Contact Zones', in *Travel and Translation in the Late Twentieth Century*, New Haven: Harvard University Press.

Cohen, E. (1988), 'Authenticity and Commoditization in Tourism', *Annals of Tourism Research*, 15, pp. 371–86.

Cohen, E. (1993), 'Introduction: Investigating Tourist Arts', *Annals of Tourism Research*, 20, 1, pp. 1–8.

Coote, J. and Shelton, A. (1992), *Anthropology, Art and Aesthetics*, Oxford: Clarendon Press.

Daly, H.E. and Cobb, J.B. (1989), *For the Common Good: Redirecting the Economy towards Community, the Environment and a Sustainable Future*, London: Merlin Press.

Eichztaedt, P. (1988), 'Indian Arts: Heritage affects legal standing', *The New Mexican Newspaper*, Alberquerque, 21 August, p. 131.

Evans, G.L. (1994a), 'Fair Trade: Crafts Production and Cultural Tourism in the Third World', in A. Seaton (ed.), *Tourism: State of the Art*, London: Wiley Press.

Evans, G.L. (1994b), 'Whose Culture is it Anyway? Tourism in Greater Mexico and the Indigena in Mexico', in A. Seaton (ed.), *Tourism: State of the Art*, London: Wiley Press.

Evans, G.L. (1996), 'Tourism and Indigenous Cultural Heritage in New and Old Mexico: A Comparative', in P. Burns (ed.), *Tourism and Minorities' Heritage: Impacts and Prospects*, PILTS No. 6, London: University of North London Press.

Evans, G.L. and Cleverdon, R. (1999), 'Fair Trade in Tourism – Community Development or Marketing Tool?', in G. Richards and D. Hall (eds), *Tourism and Sustainable Community Development*, London: Routledge.

Evans-Pritchard, D. (1989), 'How "They" See "Us": Native American Images of Tourism', *Annals of Tourism Research*, 16, pp. 89–105.

Evans-Pritchard, D. (1993), 'Ancient Art in Modern Context', *Annals of Tourism Research*, 20, 1, pp. 9–31.

Feest, C.F. (1992), *Native Arts of North America*, London: Thames and Hudson.

Firth, R. (1992), 'Art and Anthropology', in J. Coote and A. Shelton (eds), *Anthropology, Art and Aesthetics*, Oxford: Clarendon Press.

Goodland, R. (1982), *Tribal Peoples and Economic Development – Human Ecological Considerations*, Washington: World Bank.

Gottlieb, A. (1982), 'American's Vacations', *Annals of Tourism Research*, 9, 1, pp. 165–87.

Graburn, N.H. (ed.) (1976), *Ethnic and Tourist Arts: Cultural Expressions from the Fourth World*, Berkeley: University California Press.

Haddon, A.C. (1894), *The Decorative Art of British New Guinea*, Cunningham Memoir 10, Dublin: Royal Irish Academy.

Hall, S. (1990), 'Cultural Identity and Diaspora', in J. Rutherford (ed.), *Identity*, London: Lawrence and Wishart.

Hamilton, A. (1896), *The Art Workmanship of the Maori Race in New Zealand*, Wellington: New Zealand Institute.

Harris, N. (1990), *Cultural Expressions: Marketing Appetites and Cultural Tastes in Modern America*, Chicago: University of Chicago Press.

Hillman-Chartrand, H. (1988), 'Crafts in the Post-modern Economy', *Journal of Cultural Economics*, 12 (2).

Josephides, N. (1993), *Proceedings of Sustainable Tourism Conference*, London: English Tourist Board.

Kemper, R.V. (1978), 'Tourism and Regional Development in Taos', *Studies in Third World Societies*, 6, pp. 89–103.

Kemper, R.V. (1979), 'Tourism in Taos and Patzcuaro', *Annals of Tourism Research*, 6, 1, pp. 91–110.

Laxson, J.D. (1991), 'How "We" See "Them": Tourism and Native Americans', *Annals of Tourism Research*, 18 (1), pp. 365–91.

Leong, W.-T. (1989), 'Culture and the State: Manufacturing Traditions for Tourism', *Critical Studies in Mass Communication*, 6, pp. 355–75.

Litrell, M.A. (1990), 'Symbolic Significance of Textile Crafts for Tourists', *Annals of Tourism Research*, 17, pp. 228–45.

Litrell, M. A., Anderson, L.F. and Brown, P.J. (1993), 'What Makes a Craft Souvenir Authentic?' *Annals of Tourism Research*, 11, pp. 197–215.

MacCannell, D. (1976), *The Tourist: A new theory of the leisure class*, New York: Schaken Books.

MacCanell, D. (1984), 'Reconstructed Ethnicity: Tourism and Cultural Identity in Third World Communities', *Annals of Tourism Research*, 11, 1, pp. 375–91.

MacCanell, D. (1991), *Empty Meeting Grounds: The tourist papers*, London and New York: Routledge.

Messenger, P. (1989), *The Ethics of Collecting Cultural Property: Whose Culture? Whose Property?*, Albequerque: University of New Mexico Press.

Popelka, C.A. and Litrell, M.A. (1991), 'Influence of Tourism on Handcraft Evolution', *Annals of Tourism Research*, 18, pp. 392–413.

Pye, E. (1986), 'Crafting the Future', *Craft International*, 4, 1, January–March, pp. 27–35.

Sayer, A. (1992), *The Arts and Crafts of Mexico*, London: Thames and Hudson.

Swain, M.B. (1993), 'Women Producers of Ethnic Arts', *Annals of Tourism Research*, 20, 1, pp. 32–51.

Sweet, J.D. (1989), 'Burlesquing the "Other" in Pueblo Performance", *Annals of Tourism Research*, 16, 1, pp. 62–75.

Tadmore, M. (1984), 'Developing Crafts in Developing Countries', *Craft International*, 1, 4, p. 10.

Van den Berghe, P.L. (1992), 'Tourism and the Ethnic Division of Labour', *Annals of Tourism Research*, 19, 1, pp. 234–49.

Van den Berghe, P.L. and Colby, B.N. (1961), 'Ladino-Indian Relations in the Highlands of Chiapas, Mexico', *Social Forces*, 40, 1, pp. 63–71.

Van der Kraan, A. (1980), *Lombok: Conquest, Colonization and Underdevelopment 1870–1940*, London, Heinemann.

Vogt, E.Z. (1978), *Bibliography of the Harvard Chiapas Project, the First Twenty Years, 1957–1977*, Cambridge, Mass.: Peabody Museum of Archaeology and Ethnology, Harvard University.

Vogt, E.Z. (1990), *The Zincantecos of Mexico, A Modern Maya of Life*, Fort Worth, TX, Holt, Rinehart and Winston.

Wallendourf, M. and Arnould, E. (1988), '"My Favourite Things": A Cross-Cultural Inquiry into Object Attachments, Possessiveness, and Social Linkage', *Journal of Consumer Research*, 14, pp. 531–47.

Wheeler, T. et al. (1992), *Indonesia: Travel Survival Kit*, Hawthorn, Australia: Lonely Planet Publications.

Wright, R. (1992), *Stolen Continents: The Indian story*, London: Pimlico.

11 Tourism and Ainu Identity, Hokkaido, Northern Japan

JANE WILKINSON

Hokkaido, the most northern island of Japan, has been a desired destination for tourists from Japan and other countries for over a century. In this respect the Ainu, an indigenous people of Hokkaido, have been making curiosities for a tourist market since the latter quarter of the nineteenth century. Distinctive Ainu design is both appealing and adaptable.

The Ainu also lived in northeast Honshu, Sakhalin and the Kuril Islands. They are probably related to peoples driven north by the invading Yamato just before the beginning of the Christian era.

The National Museums of Scotland have an important collection of Ainu material mainly acquired at the end of the nineteenth century when their rituals and customs were disappearing. Our main donor, a Scottish doctor, Gordon Munro, spent most of his life in Japan. Later in his life he crusaded on behalf of the Ainu. His wish was that they could retain their ethnic identity and it was to this purpose that he spent the later part of his life recording their rituals (Munro, 1966).

The earliest item in the collections which can be identified as being made directly for visitors to Hokkaido, came from Mrs Isabella Bird-Bishop. It is an Ainu *attush* (woven elm bark) coat, one of seven Ainu objects she donated to the Museum in 1882 (Reg. nos 1882.22.1–5). Her journey through Hokkaido in August and September 1878 and her impressions of the Ainu are described in her book *Unbeaten Tracks in Japan* (Bird, 1880, pp.216–321).

The coat is especially interesting as it has straight kimono-type sleeves rather than the more typical Ainu type, which have a triangular section. Made of bark cloth with a regular dark blue single warp cotton stripe, it has neither appliqué nor embroidery decoration. The woven nettle patches at the back of the neck and the hem are still very white, indicating that it has not been worn.

The Ainu in Biratori were making items to barter with the Japanese living on the southern coast of Hokkaido in the 1880s. Isabella Bird mentions women making clothes for their families and extra to sell (ibid., p. 248). It is likely that this coat was made to sell or give to visitors rather than as an item for the Ainu themselves to wear. Bird mentions buying a bark cloth dress with some knives and arrows.

The Ainu suffered discrimination and prejudice from the Japanese, whose government have encouraged miscegenation since the beginning of the nineteenth century leading to a loss of Ainu identity through their superficial immersion in the lowest strata of Japanese society. Ainu disguised their ethnic background to avoid discrimination. Today this is changing and Ainu descendants are reclaiming their cultural heritage. The re-emergence or rediscovery of hitherto suppressed and concealed ethnic identities is a recurring theme in the literature on tourism. What would be worth ingestigating are the circumstances under which those of mixed descent choose to emphasize their Ainu credentials.

This chapter will examine the expression of Ainu identity, the representation of Ainu culture, and discuss how they are utilizing a growing interest in their heritage. Ainu culture is a saleable product. Dances are performed and craft objects made for tourists. New museums have been built which exhibit past lifestyles using objects, video, music and the Ainu voice.

My research is based largely on two visits to Japan, made in 1987 and 1992 and described in my thesis (Wilkinson, 1994). Whilst the political aspects of Ainu identity play an ever-increasing role, they comprise too large a subject to be dealt with adequately here, and so will only be mentioned where they impinge directly.

Expressions of Ainu Identity

One of the richest sources of Ainu heritage is the oral literature. Today, Ainu wishing to learn their language often learn to recite *yukar*, or epic poems, which is a way of approaching the Ainu language in context. As these are often learnt with recitation in mind it can become a useful way of announcing publicly the reciter's newly-found identity with his or her Ainu forebears.

Recitation to music was common. Toyooka Masanori today has made one of the most successful uses of this material. His contemporary Ainu music arises from the ideal ancient world of the Ainu people where gods, humans and animals lived in interdependent harmony expressed in the oral literature. His Ainu name, Atuy, means the sea and he has formed a group called Moshiri, the old Ainu name for Hokkaido, who brought out an album with Sakata Akira, a well-known Japanese jazz player (Yaresu, 1991).

Regional Ainu dances are being preserved and taught to the younger generation within regional Ainu associations. These are branches of the *Utari Kyokai* which is the largest political and cultural organization of Ainu.[1] The Ainu Centre at Sapporo, run by this organization, has a library, display area and classroom to promote a deeper understanding of Ainu history and culture. Apart from Ainu language classes and the teaching of various ceremonies and crafts, such as embroidery, old dances are also researched and reworked.

A focus for all this activity is a recently invented Ainu festival held in February when the dances are performed. Regional identity is also reinforced as Ainu kimono worn for the occasion are introduced as representing the traditional patterns of the region.

Dance has always been an important part of Ainu festivals, expressing the associated feelings of pleasure and enjoyment which the Ainu believed they shared with their gods on such occasions. Dance is therefore an excellent vehicle for expressing and cementing Ainu identity and group solidarity today as long as it remains more than just performance. Groups meet to dance together and learn new dances, motivated by a shared interest in their heritage. These dance groups also perform for tourists. Ainu culture has become a saleable product. This is particularly true of the arts and crafts of the Ainu which are sold as souvenirs. Wooden bowls and Ainu kimono are copied from examples in museums.

A more popular souvenir, the realistically carved bear with a salmon in his mouth, originated in the post war period when US servicemen were stationed on Hokkaido. They asked rural Ainu to carve them figures of bears as souvenirs (Graburn, 1976, p. 220). Ohnuki Tierney tells us that the idea of realistic bear carving was introduced to the Ainu at Asashikawa, Hokkaido, around 1920 by a Japanese to encourage the use of their skill in carving to earn extra money. She also says that her informant was very clear about the taboo against that the realistic representation of Ainu gods (Ohnuki-Tierney, 1974, pp. 37, 38).

Ainu carve characteristic, mainly two-dimensional and sometimes symbolic patterns on utilitarian or ritual objects, including designs representing an empty bear skin, and bear's face. Bears' heads have been carved on libation sticks and head dresses worn by elders for the bear ceremony since the mid-nineteenth century. The NMS collection has several libation sticks with bears and fish realistically carved in three dimensions as part of the design (Reg. nos. 1909.309.38, 40). Ainu, in southwestern Hokkaido, had longer contact with Japanese and foreign missionaries such as Batchelor. It is possible that they no longer revered taboos against the realistic carving of their most sacred deity On the northwest coast of Sakhalin, where Ohnuki-Tierney was doing her fieldwork, relations between the Ainu and their deities were perhaps preserved more as a part of everyday life.

The realistic carving of a bear with a salmon is therefore a departure from, rather than an expression of, Ainu heritage. However it is not the subject matter so much as the skill of carving itself, which is significant. Woodcarving was always an occupation of the Ainu male, and continuing this craft is a way of reaffirming ethnic identity. In the same way, women who use appliqué and embroidery designs on woven or imported cloth are continuing Ainu skills. Manufacturing new items, such as matchbox covers and bookmarks, using Ainu design as decoration, does not detract from reinforcing their cultural identity by carrying on the craft.

However, in arguing for these tourist activities as an expression of ethnic identity, care must be taken to examine who controls the pricing, marketing and distribution of the goods, and the motivation of these people, be they Japanese or Ainu. Just as dances performed 15 times a day at Shiraoi Museum for groups of Japanese tourists could lead to a loss of the original meaning of the dance, and enjoyment in its performance, so carving three or four poor quality bears a day may diminish the carver's sense of pride in his traditional skills.

The diminished product could become a representation of Ainu heritage, not only in the eyes of the visitor but also of the younger Ainu population. The need for a sense of pride in these representations should not be underestimated. Ainu today live in houses of a similar design to their Japanese neighbours and shop at local markets for their food. Living within Japanese society without the need to manufacture their own material culture the younger generation may lose the sense of identity and pride associated with traditional forms of Ainu culture. The motivation of those involved in tourism must include a sensitivity to the culture which is being marketed or there is a danger of diminishing the product. The future could depend on how Ainu youth view their heritage.

Education is no longer segregated for Ainu and Japanese though even when it was, Ainu were taught in Japanese. Now private schools such as that run by Shigeru Kayano in Nibutani teach Ainu language to Ainu children. He has also made videos for the teaching of the Ainu language and culture.

This series of videos includes material in which Kayano is seen directly involved with teaching children about their past. In one he takes a group of children into the countryside surrounding the Saru River for 24 hours and teaches them how to live off the land, using Ainu technology. They make bows and barbed arrows which double as fishing spears, catch their dinner and cook it outside a night shelter, also made earlier in the day. All through the video, natural woodland resources such as forked branches, specially shaped leaves, twisted vines or grasses are found and used (Kayano, 1978).

Pure enjoyment for both children and Kayano is obvious, but so is the value of what they are being taught in terms of using Ainu skills and knowledge to survive. Instead of being made to look at pictures in books or objects in a museum, these children receive direct experience of why these objects were made and the important part they played in Ainu life.

Representations of Ainu Culture

Videos as representations of Ainu culture bring us to our second main area of discussion. How are the Ainu represented in Hokkaido and the outside world today? Again political representation is an important issue, but is only mentioned here in direct relation to the main subject.

The Ainu and their past lifestyles are considered as tourist attractions. Several museums are either dedicated to Ainu culture or include their history within thematic displays about the history of Hokkaido and colonization. These different displays and how they changed between 1987 and 1992 have been described elsewhere (Wilkinson, 1994, pp. 134–45).

The Biratori Municipal Museum at Nibutani, built in 1991, illustrates several important aspects of Ainu representation. It is an imposing building in a delightful setting by the Saru River. Behind it and slightly up-river, a park is being developed which borders the lake formed by a new dam. The Museum was part of a local government-funded operation which also has national government support.

The dam was the cause of much controversy. Shigeru Kayano, now the first Ainu member of the Japanese National Diet, initially refused to sell his land to the government, so the project was delayed. The new lake has drowned important plants still used by the Ainu, who enjoy collecting them for traditional crafts or medicine. Kayano is reported to have made the government raise fishing quotas as part of the negotiation (Paxton, 1992).

It is important to understand the background of the new development, which includes a new school, because it is seen by some people as a government hand out to appease opposition to the dam. Although the museum is part of this project intended to attract more tourists to Nibutani, Hideki Yoneda, the curator is concerned with educating the younger generation about objects used in the old Ainu way of life. Particular attention is given to the Ainu language, which had no written form. Every object displayed has its Ainu name written in Katakana, a Japanese syllabary for foreign words. Nibutani has a large Ainu community.

Two video booths enable the visitor to watch the Kayano videos, which often devote over 30 minutes to one aspect of Ainu culture. There are no life-size figures or dioramas. The Ainu people are represented on video, or are often the visitors. I saw several mothers visiting with children after school.

The architecture of the museum looks towards the future with a soaring roof giving the entrance hall a sacred atmosphere, 'calming the mind ready for instruction'. However, this could be interpreted as enshrining Ainu culture. The imposing architecture probably attracts tourists passing through Nibutani.

The Kayano family made most of the objects on display in Nibutani over the last 30 years. The open display inviting examination includes examples of plants used for food and in producing Ainu material culture. It also increases the visitors' knowledge of the habitat surrounding the Saru River.

Contemporary craftsmen are represented with their photographs and a short biography beside the objects they have made. The curator uses the music of Moshiri in the high entrance hall. When the museum is silent strains of this beautiful contemporary music can be heard everywhere, giving a somewhat ethereal atmosphere but also a feeling of life and hope.

Ainu cultural heritage has a much higher profile in Hokkaido now than it did even six years ago when I carried out my research and had changed greatly then from my first visit in 1987. For instance, greater coverage on television included the funeral of an Ainu leader and a programme about an Ainu girl searching for her roots and trying to learn the Ainu language. Moshiri also did a televised concert on the shore of Lake Akan. Television provides an immediacy and directness not provided by other forms of representation.

Film has played an important part in the documentation of Ainu culture since the end of the nineteenth century. In 1915 Gordon Munro made his film of the bear festival, which is one of the earliest known ethnographic films (Munro, 1931).

At the Ethnological Museum in Osaka there are 12 short videos of Ainu life filmed over the last 20 years.[2] Obviously shot with Ainu cooperation, but Japanese direction, they can encourage the illusion that the Ainu still live off the land and practice their festivals as in the past. If it were not for the motivation of the video some of these events would not have taken place.

Severe editing of the Kayano videos to the 12–18 minutes of the versions available at the Osaka Ethnological Museum not only prevents the detailed record of an event but also overrides Kayano's commentary, which in itself gives the unedited version, available at Nibutani Ainu authenticity. The compromises are however necessary for educating schoolchildren, the main users of the videotheque at Osaka Museum.

An important temporary exhibition took place at the Osaka Ethnological Museum in 1993. The catalogue (Ohtsuka, 1993) states that the exhibition recognizes the existence of the Ainu people as an indigenous people of Japan supporting the 'International Year for the World's Indigenous Peoples, 1993' (ibid., p. 124). The 'Foreword' by Komei Sasaki, Director General of the museum, and the 'Message from Ainu Moshir', by Shigeru Kayano on behalf of the Ainu people, are printed in both Ainu and Japanese.

Ainu Livelihood and Tourism Today

In the final section of the displays at the Hokkaido Historical Museum, Sapporo a series of screens show images of Hokkaido today. Images of the Ainu are restricted to their dances and crafts, both seen as Hokkaido tourist attractions.

The Ainu Museum in Shiraoi is run by the Shiraoi Institute for the Preservation of Ainu Culture, a self-styled group led by Ainu, now more interested in the commercial exploitation of their heritage as a tourist attraction than in the preservation of Ainu culture for its own sake. When I first visited in 1987 museum staff were carrying out important research with a small group of surviving Ainu elders. The museum and large souvenir shop are now run as a commercial enterprise, by a reduced staff.

The display takes the visitor through various aspects of the Ainu life cycle and subsistence economy, using dioramas and large numbers of objects grouped by function representing Ainu history from the end of the eighteenth century. The importance of trade to their original prosperity is ignored. The museum guide (n.d., p. 3) states that the 'lifestyle of the Ainu, handed down unchanged from the distant past, no longer exists and the folk arts on display are an attempt to reproduce that life style'. The exhibition makes no real effort to explore that past except in an idealized view of the hunter-gatherer.

The present is represented outside the main museum in the form of Ainu dances performed 15 times a day for groups of Japanese tourists, and women sewing and weaving in the Ainu houses built in the extensive grounds. A large shop full of 'craft' souvenirs forms the entrance and exit of the museum. The main object is to attract tourists and make money.

Here a small group of Ainu is utilizing the growing interest in their heritage to earn their livelihood. They also provide work for other Ainu: making and selling souvenirs, demonstrating crafts and dances and in the museum itself. The role of the museum staff no longer includes research as there is little time to do more than keep the museum open for its many visitors, a high proportion of which are Japanese groups. It remains unclear how visitors drawn predominantly from the majority community view the Ainu minority after visiting the museum. A potential area of research might be to investigate whether or not an enhanced understanding of Ainu life is achieved.

Many Ainu are involved in seasonal occupations such as commercial farming, the fishing industry, construction, truck driving, forestry and tourism. Ainu who suffer from a lack of education and technical skills find it difficult to obtain steady work. A supplementary income for men can be obtained from carving for the tourist industry, and for women from weaving, embroidery and appliqué. The division of the crafts between men and women still exists.

Even small places such as Nibutani have several shops selling souvenirs. Rock cutting is becoming more popular. Several shops in Nibutani have a workshop in the corner where a carver can be seen working for at least some of the day. Although the bear with a salmon in his mouth is still a popular subject more horses are carved now. Breeding racehorses is increasingly important to the economy. A Japanese friend reflected that horses were more important than people in Hokkaido today! The horse is certainly taking over from the bear as a symbol of Hokkaido.

Does this also reflect a loss in centrality of the bear to Ainu life? Perhaps young Ainu men find it easier to relate to a racehorse seen in the fields, representing wealth and success, than they do to a bear. Though an important part of their past bears are no longer pivotal to Ainu life.

The carved horses could be seen as a way, whether conscious or unconscious, of replacing the bear with a saleable product which has no Ainu overtones. It moves the carver away from the debasement of a central icon of Ainu culture. As already noted lifelike carving of bears, as an isolated ornament was not part of Ainu material culture until this century when they were made for outsiders.

Pride in their heritage may prevent Ainu carvers from wishing to mass-produce poor quality carved bears. The bear is being re-established as an important figure in Ainu nostalgia for their past and is now perhaps too precious a subject for such commercial purposes. Horses are popular with Japanese and American tourists but are not associated with Ainu culture. Perhaps this is how the Ainu can exploit, develop and market their traditional craftsmanship without compromising their icons.

Ainu women are able to find a market for their embroidery. Dancers need costumes, Ainu coats are sold to tourists and several women are adapting their embroidery to new uses such as hangings, tablecloths and covers. Mrs Kayano has made coats for the Osaka Ethnological Museum, the new museum at Nibutani and Kayano's museum.

The future for the Ainu is not reduced to the images left on the multiple screens at the end of the Hokkaido Historical Museum exhibit. The Ainu will be represented by their crafts and dances, but these are seen by Hiroshi Shoji, in his article in the catalogue to *Ainu Moshir*, as a positive force originating from the same source as the present movement of indigenous peoples (Ohtsuka, 1993, p. 124). They are, however, not the only reaffirmation of Ainu heritage.

Apart from a renewal in their music with which the young can identify and the renewed interest in the Ainu language, the Ainu are also reclaiming their cultural heritage, reworking their dances and crafts and taking a new pride in their ethnic identity. The best use must be made of the new fund to educate and train young Ainu, enabling them to face the future with new skills, grafted onto their Ainu heritage wherein lies a respect for and knowledge of their environment.

To conclude, tourism can be an important stimulus for education and indigenous cultural regeneration. Involving local communities at all levels will facilitate the representation and appropriation of an indigenous culture for commercial purposes.

Notes

1 *Utari Kyokai* has its headquarters in Sapporo, with a membership of around 25,000.
2 A list of videos can be acquired from the National Museum of Ethnology, Osaka.

References

Ainu Association of Hokkaido (1992), statement submitted to the Tenth Session of the Working Group on Indigenous Peoples, Geneva, July.

Akira, S. (1991), *Yayresu (Disciplining Myself)*, pamphlet accompanying CD recording.

Bird, I.L. (1880), *Unbeaten Tracks in Japan*, New York (1978 reprint, Tokyo).

De Vos et al. (1983), *Japan's Minorities, Burakumin, Koreans, Ainu and Okinawans Minority rights Group*, Report No. 3.

Graburn, N.H.H. (ed.) (1976), *Ethnic and Tourist Arts: Cultural Expressions from the Fourth World*, Berkeley: University of California Press.

Kayano, S. (1978), *Children's Play*, video.

Munro N.G. (1931), *The Bear Festival*, film.
Munro N.G. (1962), *Ainu Creed and Cult*, B.Z. Seligman (ed.), London.
National Museum of Ethnology Osaka (1991), *Guide to the National Museum of Ethnology*.
Ohnuki-Tierney, E. (1974), *The Ainu of the Northwest Coast of Southern Sakhalin*, New York.
Ohtsuka, K. (1993), *Ainu Moshir-World of the Ainu through their design motifs*, Osaka.
Paxton, M. (1992), 'Profile, Ethnic Ainu's First Diet Candidate', *The Japan Times Weekly, International Edition*, 20–26 April.
Wilkinson, J. (1994), 'A Study of the Ainu, Inspired by the Collections at the National Museums of Scotland, Edinburgh', MLitt. thesis, University of Stirling.

For bibliographies on the Ainu see:

Adami, N.R. (1991), *Bibliography of Materials on the Ainu in European Languages*, Sapporo.
Gusinde, M. and Sano, C. (1962), *An Annotated Bibliography of Ainu Studies By Japanese Scholars Collectanea Universitatis Catholicae Nanzan*, Series 3, Tokyo.
Taguchi, K.Y. (1974), 'An Annotated Catalogue of Ainu Material in the East Asian Institute of Aarhus University', *Scandinavian Institute of Asian Studies Monograph Series*, No. 20.

12 Awaji Ningyo: Its Changing Role Within a Local, National and International Community

JENNIFER VERLINI

In the summer of 1997, I spent a month in the Kansai area of Japan, around Osaka and the island of Awaji, making a comparative study of the Bunraku and Awaji puppetry traditions of that area. This chapter has developed out of the research which was conducted at the Awaji Ningyo Shibai, the only official puppet theatre on the island of Awaji. The present Awaji theatre troupe consists of around 35 full-time paid performers, who have, since 1987, occupied a purpose built theatre, on the southernmost tip of the island, with views out over the famous Naruto channel. The theatre is part of a small tourist complex, with a shop, restaurant, and large coach and car park. The troupe has been designated as an 'Important Intangible Folk-cultural Property' and as such, receives support at local government level.

This troupe is the most recent manifestation of a tradition which stretches back four centuries, and the current performers are keen to stress the continuity between their puppetry style and that of the past. In reality, however, the current theatre is the culmination of a 40 year struggle to save the tradition from extinction. During this struggle, the outward appearance of the puppetry style has been radically adapted in order to attract support and funding in order to ensure the survival of the tradition.

The focus of this chapter will be an examination of the choices which the theatre has been forced to make in recent years, in order to survive. Furthermore, I will look at the role of the puppet theatre on the island of Awaji in an attempt to gauge the extent to which it still plays a meaningful role for the islanders, or whether is has become merely a contrived recreation of an extinct historical tradition.

Awaji is a small island, lying between the two larger islands of Honshu and Shikoku. It is joined to Shikoku at its southernmost end by a bridge, which spans the Naruto Straits and is a short ferry ride from Osaka and Kobe

157

at its most northern end. Awaji is significant because it is reputed to be the birthplace of Japanese puppetry. According to tradition, a specific shrine on the island marks the place where, in the sixteenth century, an individual named Hyakudayu travelled from Nishinomiya, an important shrine centre between Osaka and Kobe, to Awaji, in order to teach the islanders to manipulate mannequins to entertain the local gods and to ensure safety at sea, good harvests and general prosperity. Although there has been much academic discussion as to the veracity of this claim, the tradition is widely accepted both on Awaji and throughout Japan, and this fact has greatly strengthened the island's close identity with, and pride in, its puppetry.

At first glance, Awaji Ningyo seems to be very similar to Bunraku, the better known puppetry style which developed in Osaka in the eighteenth century. Both traditions consist of three elements: puppet manipulation by three manipulators; a text narrated by a chanter and musical accompaniment by a lute-like instrument called a *shamisen*. The term Bunraku, however, is never used to describe Awaji puppetry. Instead, it is referred to as 'Awaji Ningyo' or 'Awaji Ningyo Joruri'.

'Ningyo' is one of the many words used in Japanese to describe puppets and puppetry. It is formed from two Chinese characters which mean 'person' and 'shape'. The word can mean puppet, doll and effigy, however, when used in the context of 'Awaji Ningyo', it is widely understood, both within Awaji, and elsewhere in Japan, to refer to the island's long-established puppet tradition. The word 'Joruri' refers to the style of narration with musical accompaniment, typical of both Awaji Ningyo and Bunraku. The word is taken from the name of a character in a well known sixteenth century tale, *Joruri Junidan Soshi*, a story about the love between the warlord Yoshitsune Minamoto and the Princess Joruri. This tale was so popular at the time, that the word 'Joruri' became synonymous with all accompanied storytelling of this genre.

History of Awaji Ningyo up to World War II

Awaji Ningyo originally developed as part of a religious ritual, conducted by itinerant puppeteers, who performed at annual festivals throughout the year, and especially at new year. They travelled around established circuits on Awaji and throughout large areas of Japan, performing in each home a cleansing ceremony designed to bring good luck to the household in the coming year. Nowadays, many puppet troupes throughout Japan claim direct descent from these itinerant Awaji performers, and such claims are regarded as proof of the modern troupe's authenticity.

Over time, however, the puppetry tradition on Awaji evolved and changed. The focus shifted from that of ritual appeasement of the gods and spirits, to secular entertainment of the human audience. Indeed, the current director of the Awaji Theatre, Umazume Masaru can remember the profusion of puppet troupes who performed around the countryside of Awaji until just before the second world war. Archive photographs show these performances taking place by torchlight, on ready made stages, in front of an audience sprawled on the grass. The repertoire of these puppet troupes was allegedly over 800 plays; more, the current Awaji Theatre troupe is quick to point out, than that of the professional Bunraku Theatre in Osaka. Before the advent of television, puppetry was one of the most popular forms of entertainment on Awaji. Many islanders were amateur puppeteers, chanters or carvers, and the social aspects of performance and entertainment played a key role in establishing and defining social interaction on the island.

History of Awaji Ningyo in the Post-World War II Period

During and immediately after World War II, however, Awaji Ningyo went into serious decline. With extreme poverty, and, in some cases, near starvation, on the island, puppetry was one of the first activities to be sacrificed.

One of the elderly residents of the island remembers this time saying:

> I was about 10 when the war started. I remember that time clearly. Like so many other people in Japan, we were soon starving as Japan moved further into the war. Things were really tough ... So one day, to feed the family, Grandfather decided to sell his puppets. No sooner had he made the decision, it seemed than several men from Osaka showed up in the courtyard to look them over ...
>
> ... The men from Osaka paid my grandfather a small amount of money, packed the puppets into the car, and drove away ...
>
> ... I was only a kid, but I felt really sad. I don't know what made me sad then. But thinking back on it now, I guess I felt like a part of Awaji had been packed into the back of a car and stolen away to Osaka. Or maybe I felt something had died ... (Law, 1997, p. 3).

It is clear that by the end of World War II, Awaji Ningyo was in crisis and had action not been taken in the 1950s, there was a very real danger that the tradition could have died out altogether. The initial impetus for the revival of the tradition did not come from within the island, but from abroad. In 1957 the USSR extended an invitation to the island's puppeteers to conduct a tour of the Soviet Union. This invitation spurred the current director, Umazume Masaru, then in his late twenties, to single-handedly revive interest in the tradition, organize a small troupe of performers, and successfully undertake the tour. This event marked the beginning of the recreation of the puppet theatre on the island. The process of resurrecting a troupe as a showcase of island culture for a foreign audience is, I believe significant. From the start of this new phase, Awaji Ningyo was set up as an art form, not *for* the people of Awaji, but *about* them. From the 1950s onward, a main reason for the survival of Awaji Ningyo joruri was to be its appeal to outsiders wishing to glimpse the 'exotic', or the 'historical' Japan. Although now well established and fairly secure, this motivation is still what shapes and directs the activities of the theatre.

Contemporary Awaji Ningyo

Contemporary Awaji Ningyo has defined itself around one particular play, *Keisei Awa no Naruto*, or *Family Tragedy*, which tells the story of a mother who is, by chance, temporarily reunited with her child, whom she was forced to abandon in infancy, only to lose her again, when the child is murdered by her father, unaware of the child's identity. This play is famous throughout Japan for its pathos and emotion. The scene in which mother and child first meet is particularly famous, and it is this scene which forms the centrepiece of the Awaji theatre troupe's repertoire.

The particular choice of this play, and this scene from the play, as the centrepiece of the Awaji theatre is interesting, since there is no evidence that it had a particular historical significance for the puppeteers of the island in the past. Certainly, it is a local play, in the sense that the places named are recognisably linked to, or close to Awaji. The title, *Keisei Awa no Naruto* refers to 'Awa', an ancient name for the island of Shikoku, and it is the Naruto channel which separates Awaji from Shikoku. The theatre complex, looking out onto both the Naruto channel, and Shikoku, is therefore strategically placed to reinforce the connection of the story to the local area. In addition, the play is, in many ways, the perfect choice for a fairly small theatre group, since the entire scene can be performed with only five puppeteers, and, because both protagonists are female, it is a scene which does not make huge demands on an inexperienced chanter. However, the very fame and pathos of the piece have, in many ways created a problem for the theatre. As Umazume Masaru, has said:

> When we first started to present the plays ... we wanted something people liked. Although many people were familiar with both the larger piece from which this scene is taken and also the larger repertoire of joruri pieces, this was a favourite, and a regional piece referring to lower Awaji and Tokushima. But eventually, it got to the point where people would only come to see that piece. It is the only piece of theatre they associate with Awaji Ningyo ... If a tour bus calls to book a showing, they request that piece. Whenever I suggest that perhaps the performance might change, the tourist industry becomes uncomfortable (Law, 1997, p. 225).

Here then, the complex tensions inherent within the revival of this so-called 'traditional' theatre can be seen. Dependent on a largely tourist industry, the theatre has been forced to concentrate its entire identity on one play, and perform it in a way which accommodates the short attention span of holidaymakers to the island. This scene is performed on the hour, eight times daily, seven days a week, and has been performed in this way for the past 12 years. Moreover, the theatre markets itself within a highly effective island-wide advertising campaign which promotes Awaji as the perfect holiday destination and an all-round escape from the demands of everyday Japanese life. Within the framework of a highly fast-paced society, Awaji has managed to retain its image of a traditional island, untouched by time. I was told many times, both by people from Awaji, and elsewhere in Japan, that Awaji is noted for its fresh food – fish, beef and onions; for its unique coastlines, and mountainous central regions; for its whirlpools, and, of course for its unique puppet theatre. The island is marketed as a package, and is indeed the perfect size for a visit of even one day. Whilst visiting a contact in Kobe, a short ferry ride from Awaji, I was indeed taken to Awaji for a day trip. We had lunch in one of the many famous restaurants, drove around the island to the southernmost tip to view the whirlpools, stopping in the theatre complex for tea, to view the puppet theatre and to purchase some onions from the shop. The Awaji theatre is a success precisely because it has managed to harness this tourist market and present a bite size piece of traditional folk art which can be sampled along with the island's other delights.

In the past Awaji Ningyo was an outdoor tradition, performed by travelling amateurs for a largely local community. Nowadays, precisely the reverse is true. The puppet theatre is a highly professional organization, housed in a purpose built theatre, fulfilling the expectations of a constantly changing tourist audience. What I was curious to discover during my own visit to the island, was the way in which the people of Awaji reconciled these contradictions in the survival of modern Awaji Ningyo. Did they see a continuity between the old and new forms? Did the work of the present theatre represent for them, the essence of Awaji Ningyo, or was it merely an empty performance of interest only to tourists?

Within the theatre itself, there is a genuine commitment to professional standards and the preservation of Awaji Ningyo. The theatre's chanters and *shamisen* players are taught twice weekly by Tsurusawa Tomoji San, reputed to be one of the best *shamisen* players in Japan. So, although the tourist market restricts the troupe's repertoire, they have a commitment to the learning and revival of old pieces, which they are able to perform intermittently. Indeed, while I was there, they were preparing a piece for a special performance later that year. The members also have a close relationship with several school puppetry, chanting and *shamisen* clubs in the islands, and many of the younger members of the troupe have entered the theatre as a result of the skills which they gained whilst at school. One of the troupe members conducts a weekly master class for the children of Mihara Junior High Puppetry Club. The quality of puppetry and the dedication of the children is remarkable, especially when you realize that they the meet for six hours every week after school, to perfect this craft.

The art of *kashira* (puppet head) carving is also being kept alive in the form of a weekly carving class which meets in a local community hall each Sunday afternoon. There are many individuals of all ages, who have spent a lifetime carving Awaji *kashira* as a hobby. Awaji *kashira* differ from Bunraku in several fundamental ways, and, without fail, all of the carvers who I spoke to were careful to point out these differences and to stress that is was the Awaji *kashira* which they were making.

In recent years Umazume Masaru has also been responsible for encouraging the regeneration of puppet groups outwith Awaji. Understanding at first hand the perils facing small puppet theatres striving to survive in isolation, he inaugurated in 1991 the first *All Japan Puppetry Summit*. These conferences, now an annual event at the Awaji theatre offer a coming together of diverse puppetry traditions throughout Japan. As in the past, Awaji places itself at the centre of the growth of the puppetry tradition in Japan, but, whereas previously Awaji puppeteers travelled outwith Awaji to teach and establish new traditions, now it is these struggling traditions who make the annual pilgrimage to Awaji to be renewed and encouraged.

Historically, Awaji Ningyo has been noted for the strong association of its adherents to the island of Awaji, together with its ability to reach out to a larger community. During my short visit to the island, I was particularly struck by the attachment and pride which people of all ages felt towards the folk art. From the dedication of the children in the high schools, to the skill of the carvers who I met, it was clear that the revival of Awaji Ningyo on the island is filling more than just an economic gap. Awaji Ningyo appears to be used by many of the islanders in a very direct way to cement their sense of belonging to the island, and to be seen to belong to the island.

This strong identity has, I suspect, grown in tandem with the growth in prestige and recognition of Awaji Ningyo's greatest rival, Bunraku. It was very obvious, both on Awaji, and in Osaka, that both traditions eyed the other with disdain and contempt. The members of the Bunraku theatre openly expressed amazement that I could spend time with 'amateurs', when there were their performances to watch. The Awaji performers, on the other hand, fel that although internationally recognized, the Bunraku performers had not suffered for their art in the way that the Awaji troupe had had to. The elderly Awaji resident quoted at the beginning of this chapter clearly linked the demise of Awaji Ningyo in the past to its appropriation by Osaka. It is unclear the extent to which this is actually true, but it would appear that his remark underscores the importance which the tension between Awaji Ningyo and Bunraku has played in the rediscovery of puppetry on the island of Awaji.

It could be argued that the Awaji theatre places a greater emphasis on making *ningyo joruri* accessible than does the Bunraku theatre. Marketed largely on its high culture, high quality and exclusivity, Bunraku performances are expensive, and do not have a wide appeal to a mass audience. The Awaji theatre has always had a much closer link with its audience and I believe that the fact that the modern theatre actively seeks to reach as wide an audience as possible, through training of youngsters, through workshops, through tourist performances, and through annual puppetry summits is an element of continuity which links the pre- and postwar traditions.

In addition, the Awaji Theatre has had admirable success at reaching an international audience. Just as it was at the request of the USSR that the postwar revival took place, much of Awaji Ningyo's current recognition within Japan has developed as a result of interest shown in the tradition by foreign audiences. The Awaji Ningyo Shibai has, in the recent years undertaken several international tours, making successful trips to Australia, the USA, Eastern Europe, and much of Western Europe. As well as touring, the theatre has combined forces with Mihara Junior High School to produce a video in English explaining the history of Awaji Ningyo, which is available from the theatre box office, and furthermore, the school has also produced an informative Web page. They have thus recognized the appeal which Awaji Ningyo and Awaji itself has for an international audience, and have been prepared to grasp the latest technology to present and widen the audience base of the tradition.

Conclusion

In conclusion, the complex mix of tradition, tourism and innovation which was evident at the Awaji Ningyo Shibai is not an easy one to untangle. The current theatre tradition is a modern creation, resurrected largely through the dedication and determination of the current director. However, I believe that it can be read as far more than a recreated art form performed for tourists. It is possible to trace elements of continuity within Awaji Ningyo from its development in the sixteenth century, to the present, even though the outward appearance of the puppetry style has changed almost beyond recognition. In her recent book on the subject, *Puppets of Nostalgia*, Jane Marie Law argues that in its most essential form, Awaji Ningyo has been concerned with mediation between communities: between the secular and sacred, between the neighbour and the foreigner, between insider and outsider. In this way, puppetry has served a strong and important role in the creation and definition of identity for the islanders of Awaji.

The current renaissance of puppetry on Awaji has both sparked and been fuelled by the islander's own love for, and pride in, their unique heritage. Historically, the craft has served an important function at the level of the local community, but has also been representative of the culture of the island at a more national level, as puppeteers performed throughout Japan. What I discovered during my short stay on the island was that although in appearance very different to its historical counterpart, in essence Awaji Ningyo was still fulfilling these two roles.[1]

Note

1   This chapter has developed out of a four week fieldwork project to Japan, conducted on behalf of the Horniman Museum & Gardens in July/August 1997. The project was made possible through the generous financial support of the Great Britain Sasakawa Foundation

and the Horniman Museum. I am especially grateful to the members of the Awaji Puppet troupe, and in particular to Umasume Masaru-san, Matsuyama Mitsuyo-san and Chiaki Bando-san for their patience, cooperation and kindness. Thanks are also due to Chika Tanimoto-san for providing me with accommodation, acting as interpreter, and teaching me to dance! The final word of thanks must go to Giovanni Verlini, for his duties as proofreader and chief tea-maker during the writing of this paper, and for all of his support and help throughout the development of this research.

References

Adachi, B. (1985), *Backstage at Bunraku*, Tokyo.

Hironaga, S. (1976), *The Bunraku Handbook*, Tokyo: Maison des Arts Inc.

Law, J.M. (1997), *Puppets of Nostalgia: The Life, Death & Rebirth of the Japanese Awaji Ningyo Tradition*, Princeton, New Jersey: Princeton University Press.

Mayer, F. and Immoos, T. (1977), *Japanese Theatre*, London: Studio Vista.

13 Stealing Souls for Souvenirs: Or Why Tourists Want 'the Real Thing'

STEPHANIE BUNN

Introduction

This chapter sets out to explore the question 'Can there be authenticity in tourist art?'. The chapter is based on field work among pastoral nomads in Kyrgyzstan, a small Central Asian state of the CIS. The Kyrgyz are traditionally high mountain pastoralists, and among other skills, they are particularly known for their great expertise and the richness of their feltmaking tradition. Felt is a textile known to have been used and made by nomads in Central Asia for at least 2000 years.

Now, in Kyrgyzstan, there is a small growing industry in making tourist goods, based on the former Soviet institution, the *beriozka* or Intourist shop. Felt is a particularly popular medium which is being translated into use for tourist goods. This has been developed and supported by an influx of World Bank microfinance and aid agency funding. None of the aid bodies seem to take account of the role of Kyrgyz material culture in the traditional economy, and their aid actively directs Kyrgyz material productivity away from those tasks which we might label 'traditional' or useful, towards those aimed at satisfying the demands of the wealthier participants in the global economy.

Few of the debates about the appropriate targeting of such aid address deeper questions such as 'What is tradition?', or ask why tourists want what they do. And anthropologists seem unsure of how to deal with the question of tradition and falter when trying to decide whether tourist goods are authentic or not, torn between avoiding the romantic notion that tradition is in the past, and embracing the more post-modern view that 'anything goes'.

As an anthropologist who makes her living as an artist, I consider the question of authenticity to be particularly important, which is why I chose to write about the subject. I dashed off the proposal for this chapter with great

166

ease, but when I came to write it, found that by looking more deeply into 'authenticity', my sense of what it was dissolved, and I have ended up by asking far more questions than I have answered.

Much of my field research has been among feltmakers in Kyrgyzstan. I want to begin the chapter with an examination of four pieces of Kyrgyz felt and to ask whether, in the light of the context in which each piece was made, it is possible to say if any one piece is 'authentic' or not.

Are all four pieces 'authentic'? Is only one – perhaps the classic piece? Is the new-style traditional piece equally authentic because it is part of an ongoing process and shows a dynamic synthesis of the old with the new? How about the Umetov piece – surely the only felt which is 'art' rather than artifact? Should we even consider the tourist piece?

Let us consider the context within which each piece was made.

Figure 13.1 is a classical Kyrgyz *shyrdak* felt. This means it was made by Juzumbubu *apa* for her wedding. It is a mosaic felt. It was made by cutting identical felt patterns from two colours of felt (in this case red and blue) and interchanging them. Both in construction and design the pattern in the felt shyrdak uses principles of positive and negative. The motif and the background are equally balanced. The leftover felt will have been used to make a second shyrdak the mirror opposite of the first – probably for Juzumbubu *apa's* sister's wedding, or if small size pieces had been used, the positive and negative mosaics would all have been incorporated into one whole felt piece. Only certain colours will be used and everything has been made by hand, even the sewing thread. From my understanding, people take their meanings of the felt both from the patterns and motifs, *and* from the making process. The understanding of symbolism is not the kind we might assume, in that the names of the motifs in the patterns do not necessarily indicate significant meanings in terms of the felt as a whole. Rather it seems to be the arrangement of the pattern that is most important.

For example, I have heard people say, about meaning – 'The beginnings of pattern is life. The central *tabak* or diamond is the family, the home, life', and at the same time, 'The old Kara Kyrgyz send their ideas from the past through to the future through the pattern'. And at the same time, when sewing and quilting the *shyrdak*, a woman sews in all her hopes and wishes for her future marriage and family – from her happiness with her husband to the number of children she may have. These felts are not made for sale. Women will make other *shyrdaks* after their weddings and these too will not be sold, but made for the home, to give to relatives or for their own children's wedding. The wedding *shyrdak* is always particularly special. The act of making it for

Figure 13.1 Photograph of a traditional classic blue and red wedding felt *shyrdak* made by Juzumbubu Ayanbyekova[1]

this purpose is in some way tied up with its meaning. The function is not economic.

Figure 13.2 is made by a woman who is recognized as a 'master' or *usta* in the times of the Soviet Union – Jangyl Alibyekova, of the Naryn region. It was made after her marriage. Jangyl *eje* has made many, many felts and received medals and awards for her skills from the Soviet Authorities. She makes felt for her own use, for gifts, for sale in tourist shops and is especially known for a kind of felt called '*Kopolok Shyrdak*' – literally 'butterfly shyrdak' which are the only kind of Kyrgyz felts I have seen used as wall hangings.

I first came across Jangyl Alibyekova because I was interested to visit the area in Naryn where she lived which was said to be the centre of production of the *Kopolok* or butterfly *shyrdaks* influenced by the close proximity of Chinese neighbours When I went there, I found that the *Kopolok shyrdak* was not so much a regional tradition, but that Jangyl *eje* was the originator of all the designs. They all came from her. She was the master or *usta* who, as all *ustas* do in feltmaking, drew the *shyrdak* designs for all the other women to make up.

And when I asked Jangyl *eje* where she had learned the patterns, she showed me some embroidery of flowers done by her mother in the 'Bulgarski' style. This is a Russian-influenced type of embroidery which was very common in Kyrgyzstan during the Soviet period. She said she had simply wanted to put them onto felt and so she began to do so.

Those designs are quite different from classic Kyrgyz patterns, being far more literal and naturalistic – featuring leaves, flowers, butterflies and birds – as opposed to more abstract patterns indicating ram's horns, swan's necks, dog's tails, mountain or the water of life, and so on. However, in both cases, the patterns link the importance of nature to the Kyrgyz into the designs. Aside from the use of visual imagery, her work technically is the highest quality I have seen. Her quilting is perfect, the quilted patterns match the cut outs and the back of her work is of as good a finish as the front.

Figure 13.3 is the work of Jumabeg Umetov, a Kyrgyz artist who went to art school in Moscow and St Petersburg and became the first artist of applied art with a higher education in Kyrgyzstan. His childhood was spent in the villages, surrounded by men and women practising traditional handicrafts. He, with his wife's help, made felt in the traditional way. However, Umetov approached the subject matter of his work very much as fine artist. His work also shows the influence of Matisse cut-outs, which he has synthesized with traditional design to create a style which is still very popular today in Kyrgyzstan.

Figure 13.2 Photograph of a 'traditional' felt *shyrdak* made using non-traditional motifs by Jangyl Alibyekova

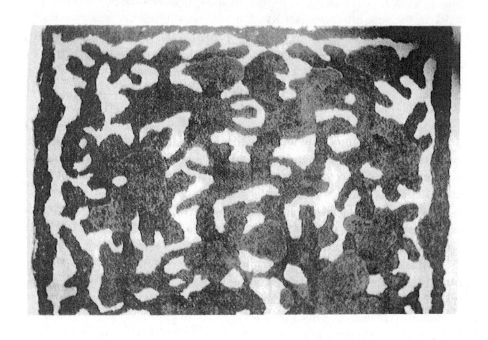

**Figure 13.3   Photograph of an 'art piece' made by the Kyrgyz artist
Jumabay Umetov**

Figure 13.4 shows typical examples of Kyrgyz tourist art, made for the tourist market. The history of tourist art in Kyrgyzstan has it's roots in the work of the folk art enthusiast Ryndin, who set up folk art factory-schools before the second world war (the Great Patriotic War) in Kyrgyzstan. Masters were encouraged to develop their art to sell in the *beriozkas* or Intourist shops. The *Kyal* or Artist's Union, formed in the 1960s, also has a shop for selling handmade goods to tourists and foreigners. This was all really very small scale, reflecting the lack of enthusiasm the Soviets had for entrepreneurialism. But it did reflect a Soviet vision of Kyrgyz Art and represented a change in function and design of previous work, introducing the practice of making work for sale. These changes in the feltmaking tradition were much compounded by the effects sedentarization had on the need for traditional nomadic textile artifacts. Once settle, there was far less need for many tent textiles, such as felt carrying bags, felt tent covers or decorative tend bands. Felt carpets are, however, still very much a part of life, made for weddings as before, and until recently were used almost as much in houses as they were in tents.

With Independence in 1991, the Kyrgyz economy changed almost overnight and went into crisis. One way world aid agencies decided to help was through giving 'aid', usually loans, to promote the development of handicraft businesses. This was directed towards the production of tourist textile goods and aimed to satisfy the call for souvenirs which the new influx of foreign visitors and tourists demanded.

This development has been fraught with problems. Not the least of these is that a three tier economic structure has grown up where none existed before in this area. Much of the aid is subject to almost auto consumption by the aid agencies and consultants. Very little money filters down to the artisans who are now told what to make for the market by middle men – ignoring the traditional expertise and lived experience they have themselves. Expertise is being diverted to make goods to sell and mechanization and use of ready made materials is far more frequently used for this kind of work.

So where does this leave us in terms of 'authenticity'? And what are the meanings bound up in our Western understanding of the word?

One Western notion of authenticity, especially applied by museums to material culture, is that traditional authentic goods are made by the members of a society, using materials produced by that society, made for the people of that society and used by them. On these terms, artifacts not falling into these categories may be termed 'fakes'. By this token, tourist goods most certainly do not fit the bill. Graburn (1976) distinguished 'inwardly directed' from 'outwardly directed' arts, but without the associated value judgments.

**Figure 13.4   A piece of tourist felt (reproduced from Sorokin and
               Maksimov, 1986)**

Figure 13.5 Photograph of Guljan Arakieva's *tabak* felt

Figure 13.6   Photograph of Jangyl *eje* at work

Figure 13.7 Photograph of *shyrdaks* made for sale and home

Figure 13.8   Photograph of a *Kopolok shyrdak*

Figure 13.9   *Kopolok shyrdak* in Jer Kochku, Kochkor region

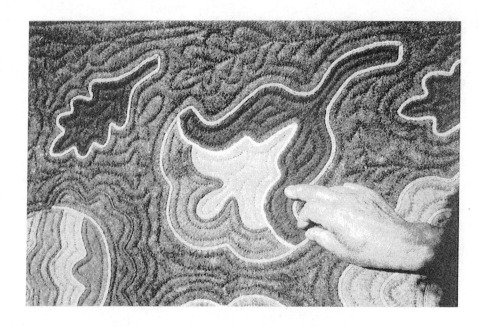

Figure 13.10 Photograph of quilting

Figure 13.11 Photograph of back of work

Figure 13.12 Photograph of *dorozhka* felt for house

But there is also the approach that authenticity lies in making work which tries to recreate the past. One group which has recentlyformed to produce felt is Altyn Oymok (Golden Thimble). Their philosophy is actively to recreate tradition through researching traditional natural dyes used a century ago and using traditional patterns taken from books.

Both the above approaches to 'authenticity' imply an assumption that culture is unchanging, closed or frozen. As if real tradition existed in an untouchable past. They eliminate the dynamism in culture. Such ideals patently are not the case in everyday Kyrgyz feltmaking, where traditional developments over the last 50 years are very marked in terms of an introduction of increasingly brighter colours, new forms of layout, and are characterized by women swopping designs, imitating each other's work and improvising.

Designs are passed down, but also brought in by newly married incoming wives, and every felt is made anew and is unique. The Kyrgyz women feltmakers I worked with tended to be particularly proud of 'the new' – in terms of new designs, or recently made work. As a felt wore out it might be used to keep a tractor engine warm, cut up to use for slippers or a doormat, and so on. The Western fascination with the old as that which is more authentic and somehow more valuable does not apply here. No-one could understand me as an anthropologist being interested in the older felts and they were quite ashamed to sell them to a museum.

I think that our Western conception of 'authenticity' in the crafts and material culture has been very much influenced by the Arts and Crafts movement at the end of the nineteenth century – by the writings of people like Ruskin and William Morris. Both looked with nostalgia back to a 'so-called' historically perfect time for the crafts as exemplified by medieval craftsmanship – rejecting the alienating effects of mechanization and the damage it had done to hand labour. But they tended to ignore the role of domesticity in the production of handicrafts (as opposed to technology and design) and the fact that medieval art and craft was extremely dynamic, a fascinating meeting point between the sensual and the intellectual, and full of innovation.

Up to this point I have emphasized that traditional art is dynamic and am asking whether it is not possible to say that if this is so, then all forms of Kyrgyz feltmaking are a part of this process.

I now want to point to a second series of illustrations which challenge the open-ended nature of this perspective.

My first period of fieldwork was in a village called Tam Chi, on Lake Issyk-Kul, learning feltmaking with local women. I quickly became a focus

Figure 13.13 Altyn Oymok's work

**Figure 13.14 Photo of Sabira *eje*'s work influenced by Alpymysh her
husband in passing**

for aid agencies and the like. In one very busy two week period, I had visitors from the World Bank, the UNDP, GTZ (German Agency for Technical Cooperation) as well as a textile study tour from the Washington Textile Museum. Thankfully things became a little quieter after that.

As a response to the visit from the Washington Textile Museum, local women were being encouraged to make felts to sell to the visitors. In one house, I was requested by a friend to show the women what designs to make for the visitors. I resisted. The women themselves asked me. I tried to explain that visitors from a specialist textile tour would like best the work that the women had made themselves. (Thereby adding my own notion of what was authentic to the situation.)

I was wrong, I was told. Foreign visitors wanted felt a certain size, to carry on the plane, but most Kyrgyz felts are very large, four metres or more. Tourists didn't like bright colours, and so on. I would not be moved. The woman of the house had previously made some very beautiful felts and embroideries. A Kyrgyz friend from the city drew the design.

At another house where women were also making work for this visit, I was invited to comment. Another guest remarked in passing, 'Is it a bird, or is it a cow?' 'I don't know, it's for money', was the reply.

I find it difficult in the light of the above experiences and others like them not to intuitively say that work made for tourists is usually qualitatively lacking compared to work made within the context of the traditional Kyrgyz lifestyle. I am faced by the contradiction between a gut feeling that fundamental damage has been done to traditional skills and culture by aid incentives to small businesses which are transforming something of high quality, full of implicit meaning, not made for sale, into a low quality, meaningless commodity – and the knowledge that tradition is dynamic and that the latest developments could possibly be the only future outlet for the Kyrgyz feltmaking tradition.

Neither perspective gives a complete answer to the question of authenticity. Perhaps the problem lies in the fact that when considering authenticity we tend to focus on the object itself, asking whether it and the activities associated with it are authentic. It might be more helpful to look at the maker and the making process itself – what goes on during the creative act of making. Secondly, we should also consider the desires of the tourist. All these factors come into play in the question of authenticity.

In terms of the maker, to a certain extent the making process will be different for a group of women making felt in Kyrgyzstan, or a bark painter as described in Howard Morphy's seminal article 'From Dull to Brilliant' (where the aesthetic intention is not to produce individualistic work) or a surrealist

Figure 13.15 Photograph of a felt cut up as a door mat

Figure 13.16 Photo of felt made from samplers cut up

Figure 13.17 Kymbat Apa's wedding *tush kiiz*

Figure 13.18 Kymbat Apa's traditional felt

Figure 13.19 Kymbat Apa with laid out 'tourist' felt

Figure 13.20 Guljakis *eje*'s tourist felt

sculptor or a late twentieth century British woodcarver. While there will be intercultural differences between these processes, they all have one thing in common, which is that they all come out of a creative act of making. As times change, work and artists adapt and evolve according to contemporary needs, or they cease to exist. The artist's intent may vary across cultures but there are also, surely some aspects of artistic engagement which are common to all, regardless of whether the work is channelled towards a collective need, individual expression, the desire for the new or to bring into being the old. Different arts bring into focus different faces of art. There may be times when the maker is forced to compromise his or her artistic intent, and if that compromise is too strong then the work becomes inauthentic. But the artist is still engaging. It may also be the case that human collective creativity constantly seeks ways to be expressed through the act of making and if blocked it will usually find new ways to do so. Hence, for example, the exciting new developments in recycled art in India and Africa, and the growth of Aboriginal fine art in Australia, none of which could be described as inauthentic.

Where does this leave the tourist? Or is he or she simply irrelevant? Before we simply consign the tourist souvenir into the realms of consumption and memory, I think we have to ask some important questions about this part of the relationship – because memory and consumption are only half the story. The questions include 'What is a tourist?', 'What is a holiday?', 'What is collecting?', 'Why do we pick things up off the beach?', 'What is a talisman?' and 'Why is it important to give things which are handmade?'

In Kyrgyzstan, life is not easy for the tourist. When I first went there after independence, there were no bazaars, or tourist shops. Kyrgyzstan may have been on the Silk Road, but it wasn't easy to travel there in the early post-Soviet period, and it certainly wasn't easy to find souvenirs. I truly did hear a visitor say, 'But where's the shop, I want to buy something and I will buy'.

If the attitude of many contemporary tourists is one of consuming souvenirs, buying keepsakes for the memory, this act is also about collecting, and the essential human practice of engaging and exchanging with other cultures. When tourists want 'the real thing', it is not as simple as trying to buy it though this may be what it has become. We also have to ask *why* they want it. Why is it that embodied handcrafted work, integrity, beautiful and functional aspects of work, and collecting are important. We must ask not just 'What is authenticity?' – but, 'Why is authenticity important?'.[2]

Notes

1 All photographs, with the exception of Figure 13.4, by the author, who holds the copyright.
2 I am indebted to Jane Blackburn for several enlightening conversations about this subject.

References

Blackburn, J.M. (1995), 'Finders Keepers', dissertation submission No. C.R. 3991, Lancaster University.
Bunn, S.J. (1995), 'Kyrgyz Shyrdak', *Textile Museum Journal 1995–1996*, Washington, pp. 74–91.
Cerny, C. and Seriff, S. (eds) (1996), *Recycled, Reseen*, Museum of New Mexico.
Dormer, P. (ed.) (1997), *The Culture of Craft*, Manchester: Manchester University Press.
Graburn, N.H.H. (ed.) (1976), *Ethnic and Tourist Arts: Cultural Expressions from the Fourth World*, Berkeley: University of California Press.
Morphy, H. (1989), 'From Dull to Brilliant', *Man*, 24, pp. 21–40.
Paolozzi, E. (1985), *The Lost Magic Kingdoms*, London: British Museum Publication.
Rhodes, C. (1994), *Primitivism and Modern Art*, London: Thames and Hudson.
Sorokin, U. and Maksimov, V. (1986), *The Kyrgyz Pattern*, Biskek: Kyrgyzstan Press.

14 Tourist Markets and Himalayan Craftsmen

KEN TEAGUE

For centuries, Nepalese metalwares have been made to meet local and foreign markets, most recently those resulting from mass tourism. During this historical process of social and cultural change some artifacts have remained relatively constant in form whilst being changed in their decorative elements and methods of manufacture, and others have been added to the range of available artifacts. These changes raise questions about tradition and the authenticity of artifacts. After considering these questions as they relate to museological issues involved in selecting and collecting material, I outline the techniques referred to in the context of their production for tourist consumption in the Himalayas as a means to challenge assumptions about authenticity in material culture.

From 1881 to 1925, the period when most museum collections of Nepalese artifacts were started in Britain, Nepal had only 153 European visitors, listed by name, and was perhaps more effectively closed to Westerners than Tibet (Cole, 1972, p. 94; Landon, 1928, pp. 298–305). After 1951 when Nepal was opened to foreign visitors, mass tourism developed so that by the late 1980s over a quarter of a million foreign visitors were entering the country each year (Acharya, 1991, p. 3; CBS, 1990, p. 145).[1] The craftsmen of Nepal responded to the influx of tourists by expanding their production of various objects, including metalwares, in volume and range.

Museological Issues and Turistica

'Souvenirs' or objects kept to recall occasions, places or people, etc., along with samples and tokens, by definition form the main part of museum collections. In my view one of the primary functions of museums is to serve, in this way, as material and cultural memory banks. The authenticity and typicality of collections is inevitably in question, and is especially raised when objects made for the tourist market, turistica are incorporated in these collections. Museum staff and their public in general tend to prefer 'genuine' objects, and often regard turistica, along with replicas as somehow 'inauthentic'. This issue has preoccupied the museums profession in Britain, with varying degrees of intensity, since the formation of the Museums Association over a century ago. Further issues relate to the ethics of collecting, and the development of collections.

Turistica is obviously produced and made available for collecting. Apparently it should be ethical and legal to collect it. However, this is often qualified. For example in Nepal, wooden objects such as backstrap looms, and what would appear to be obvious tourist items, may be refused exit by Customs officers who view such objects as 'antiques'. Here I am thinking of a particular line – a goat's or sheep's skull inlaid with base metal plates which became popular among tourists (but was regarded with a certain amount of sardonic levity by Nepalis themselves) on the streets of Kathmandu in recent years. Metal images of modern manufacture also require a seal of approval that they are not of antique status from the Department of Archaeology.

The local definition of 'authenticity' is obviously variable and must equally obviously be taken into account in defining 'authenticity' in museum terms. Does quality or ethnicity (Graburn, 1976) make objects authentic? Whose definition are we to apply? Is 'authentic' what people actually do, or is it a category imposed either by a foreigner, or perhaps another local group such as a different caste group from the producers?

Is turistica a clearly defined class of objects made for the tourist market, as opposed to 'real' objects which local people use and export as part of their own 'traditional' economy? Again, this is not so easy to disentangle. How long is a tradition? At least a generation perhaps, so that the techniques of production of objects is handed down, or is it a shorter time span than this? Turistica may be part of a corpus of real objects made for use within a particular society, for example decorative masks or utensils, or may be exported for resale to tourists elsewhere, for example Nepalese-made religious images are sold as Tibetan images to tourists in Tibet. In Nepal, as in many other countries, tourists are increasingly buying objects such as domestic utensils as souvenirs. Turistica represents what people do, it indicates what their circumstances and relationships are, that is it represents aspects of modern culture. Turistica may thus provide new categories of collectable material, to extend existing museum collections.

Part of the authenticity problem and the uncertainty about the educational value of turistica in museums is due to the lack of documentation. This can only be accommodated by the investment of fieldwork to study the manufacture of turistica, and its systematic collection and acquisition, rather than by the casual purchase of 'souvenirs' and their deposit in museums as passive collecting. Pro-active collecting obviously gives more data for research and its relation to existing literature. This could be extended by collaborative collecting between museum curators. I would argue that one could grade the educational value of objects in museum collections, as well as display them, in terms of the hard and soft information attached to them, as with any other types of evidence.

As ethnographic curators we are concerned to interpret the collections – to dispense meanings about 'the other', and ourselves. Where a museum's brief is clear, for example to deal with 'peoples and their environments on a universal basis'; and their public audience, both current and proposed, is clearly defined, then turistica may be readily incorporated into the collections for exhibitions and as formal teaching material. I would suggest that the issue of authenticity is primarily a problem for fine art collections. Whilst one may describe objects in terms of typical attributes (Pearce, 1992, pp. 86–7), this mode of thinking does not apply to people. Logically it is an unscientific quest for certainty, and might even be said to have racist elements – these things or attributes characterize these people. This approach has been discredited in terms of physical anthropology, and is even less tenable in cultural terms. For ethnographic purposes all artifacts are authentic and may be used to represent a society or culture. Turistica, as part of a corpus of material culture, has equal existential status with ploughs and pots and pans. I would argue further, that turistica is especially valuable by serving as linking objects which render 'us' and 'them' an increasingly less valid distinction.

Tourism and Himalayan Craftsmen

In this section I consider three types of artefacts made for the tourist market in Nepal: religious figures, and two types of jewellery – one made in gold, the other in base metals. These artifacts each have differing timespans of production, which raises the question of 'tradition'. By placing them in their historical and social contexts I try to support the critique outlined above.

Nepal, a Hindu kingdom situated between India and Tibet, has been renowned for the production of metalwares from the sixth and seventh centuries AD, although the legendary origins of production are said to date from the time of Sakyamuni Buddha (Pal, 1978, p. 39). The modern population, mostly consisting of subsistence farmers, is diverse and comprises 40 linguistic groups.

The Newars are perhaps the original population of the Kathmandu Valley, which was synonymous with 'Nepal' itself until recently. For centuries Patan, one of the three largest cities of the Kathmandu Valley located a few miles south of Kathmandu, has been the metalworking centre of the entire country, with some caste groups or subsections of the Newars, such as the Sakyas, providing the preeminent nonferrous metalworkers of the country, both in antiquity and today.

The Newars have been termed an 'interface' society since their religion consists of a mixture of Hinduism and Mahayana Buddhism. Irrespective of religious belief, Newar craftsmen produced images for both Hindu and Buddhist purposes. Essentially these depict stereotypical, idealized images of a 'universal monarch', a religious ruler who might be represented as a Buddha or a Hindu god such as Vishnu; and the Goddess. These images largely differed only in their attributes (Kar, 1952, pp. 12–13, 15; Pal, 1978, pp. 39, 43 and 1985).

The antecedents of modern tourism in Nepal lie in a complex of religious diffusion, pilgrimage, trade and political events. Images were made for the domestic market, that is for use in temples and shrines within Nepal, as well as for Buddhist and Hindu pilgrims to Nepal, and for export to neighbouring countries such as Tibet and India. Icons were both inward and outward in nature, and were instrumental in the diffusion of Buddhism.

Between the seventh and eighteenth centuries, Newari craftsmen took their metalworking skills and settled along the Himalayan chain as well as to China in the thirteenth century. From about the eleventh and twelfth centuries onwards Hindu refugees from the Muslim invasions of India, high caste Brahmins and Chetris (Kshatriyas) and low caste Kamis and Lohars, settled and established petty kingdoms in the hills of what is now Nepal. The low castes manufactured ironwares including ploughs and weapons which added to the corpus of metalworking skills in the Himalayas.

In 1769 the ruler of Gorkha in west central Nepal conquered the Kathmandu Valley kingdoms and began to establish an empire which eventually stretched along the Himalayas from around Simla in the west to Darjeeling in western Sikkim. The Gorkhas came into conflict both with Tibet and the British East India Company in India. Internally the Gorkha regime restructured the government of Nepal by establishing provincial governors who took their own courtly establishments including metalcraftsmen into the hill regions. Newar and Kami craftsmen thus became more widely dispersed (Sill & Kirby, 1991, p. 103). The dispersal of Buddhist Newar craftsmen was also a further consequence of the withdrawal of patronage from Buddhist temples and craftsmen by the new Hindu elite.[2]

In the later nineteenth century a number of factors, including the imposition of heavy taxes within Nepal, and the demand for labour in the development of tea cultivation in India, led to a further dispersal of Nepalese farmers and craftsmen, especially eastwards to Sikkim, Bhutan and British India. The British encouraged Nepalese peoples as well as other ethnic groups to settle around newly developing hill stations such as Darjeeling, in order to counteract Tibetan and Bhutanese influence in Sikkim (Singh, 1988, pp. 181, 204).[3]

The Indian hill stations such as Darjeeling (ceded to the British in 1835) were developed to serve the purposes of the British in India, particularly those in Calcutta and Bengal from the 1830s onwards. For several months each year government employees and their families regularly moved residence from the plains to the hills, as did soldiers who used Darjeeling as a centre for leave, convalescence, and as a garrison town and training centre for mountain warfare. Tourism followed on from these social changes.[4]

Darjeeling commanded one of the easiest routes into Tibet and so further into central Asia. By 1860 Darjeeling was a centre of commerce and western influence among the hill states, and, after a branch line of the East Bengal railway was built from Siliguri to Darjeeling in 1881, became a primary centre of commerce and western influence both among the hill states and a primary market for Indo-Tibetan trade by the end of the nineteenth century (Lamb, 1986, pp. 71, 79–80, 181). This overall development in western Sikkim ended the Nepalese monopoly control of Indo-Tibetan trade.

The development of Darjeeling and the trade route through the Chumbi Valley to Tibet attracted craftsmen such as Newari Sakyas to settle in the Darjeeling district. Here they could supply several markets. One of the particular demands which they met was to supply traditional types of jewellery to the Ghurkha troops stationed at Ghum, a major recruitment centre for Gurkha regiments now serving in the British Army. Gurkha soldiers enjoyed relatively high pay and pensions and were usually eager to invest in jewellery for the women. Until recently Gurkhas serving in Hong Kong were legally entitled to import into Nepal a few kilograms of bullion duty free. The practice in Nepal is to provide a jeweller with precious metal so that he may make objects according to customer requirements and take a percentage as his payment. This same pattern remains in operation around modern army camps in Nepal.

Metalworkers also supplied European families resident around Darjeeling, and for European markets in Calcutta especially. Newar craftsmen were adept at manufacturing 'Tibetan' jewellery and other Himalayan arts and crafts which flooded into Calcutta in the winter season to meet the growing tourist demand

(Byron, 1930, pp. 161–2, 169). When Frederick John Horniman visited Darjeeling in 1895 he made a point of visiting, 'the well-known local depot of Tibetan Curios' (probably Paul Mowis's shop in the bazaar), which:

> enabled him to have his fling amongst the Buddist [sic] Images, Temple Vessels, Bells, Gongs, Trumpets, Bones and Skulls, Pictures, Dresses and Masks of the Devil Dancers, Musical Instruments, Wearing Apparel, Swords and Knives of the Tibetans, Lepchas, Bhutias and Nepalese, as well as jewelry worn by their women.

His purchases prompted a telegraph instruction to Quick, his curator at the Horniman Museum, to 'build another room' to house this new collection.[5]

New Techniques for Tourists

The commonest, and characteristically Nepalese, method of image production for centuries, is by the lost-wax method of casting, where an original wax model is melted out of its clay investment and replaced with molten metal, to produce a unique figure. The quality and price of such figures then depends in large part on its finishing by chasing, engraving and polishing. This method is supplemented by repousse work on sheet metal, for example to manufacture the nimbus (halo) and mandorla found on some figures. Today, mass production methods and machinery are also used to make images.

The family of Chini Kaji Sakya were among those who were displaced in the search for new markets for their products. About 1900 this family of Newari gold and silver smiths left the Kathmandu Valley and settled in Darjeeling and Kalimpong where they made jewellery for the tourist market. They had no tradition of figure-making in the family. About 1965 Chini's brother learned techniques of deep undercutting and the imitation of applique work which he applied to manufacture metal figures. He taught the combination of these techniques to Chini, and the two brothers, attracted by the developing mass tourist market in Kathmandu, returned and settled there. Chini refined these new techniques and taught them to his three sons (Figure 14.1). These are now the only figure makers in Kathmandu. In brief their method of manufacture is as follows: copper sheet is formed into a topless cone, the lower third of the cone is belled out; the cone is shaped crudely into the form of a figure and is filled with solder; the figure is then carved against the solder cushion, and the solder is melted out; the figure is then cleaned and finished. The figure may then be filled with a mastic, *laha,* and the base sealed with a metal plate

Figure 14.1 Chini Kaji Sakya's method of manufacturing religious figures

inscribed with crossed thunderbolts, to sanctify it. Chini Kaji has tried to teach other people this technique but has not succeeded since the spoilage rate is extremely high. The family's figures command high prices, and manufacture is mostly for the local Buddhist market, that is figures and religious apparatus are made for temples rather than domestic use (local people cannot afford their prices). Some items are made for tourist shops and large hotels, but they make little jewellery since 'there are goldsmiths everywhere in Kathmandu now' and the market is very competitive. Devendra, the eldest son, has been invited to go to Japan to make Buddhist figures in gold there.

This technique is essentially the same as that employed by jewellers in making objects such as gold *tilari/tilahari*, the marriage necklace tied around the bride's neck by the groom. Traditional jewellery, made primarily for dowry goods for the domestic market, is made in a very different way from lost-wax figure manufacture. The two main techniques are as follows: 1) seven gold rings, four with a flower motif, three with an arrow motif, are mounted on a silver cylinder and joined with lac (Domingo-Barker and Barker, 1984, p. 113); 2) a gold ingot is beaten into a sheet, and is then worked by chiselling techniques against a cushion of lac or mastic (Figure 14.2).

Some examples of modern Newari jewellery demonstrate an antiquity of original forms comparable with the continuity found in image production, but since the *tilari* works in conjunction with glass beads, which are primarily produced by Muslim craftsmen, only present in Nepal from the sixteenth century onwards, it is probable that this artifact has a shorter tradition than images in the Nepalese corpus of metalwares.

During the 1980s another Newar metalcraftsman turned from making domestic utensils for the local market to making figures.[6] Brass and copper utensils are sold by weight in Nepal, and, with some exceptions, make very little profit. In 1984, Siddhi Raj Sakya (Figure 14.3), a member of a long-established family (13 or 14 generations) of Patan metalworkers turned to making traditional religious images. By 1990 he had become recognized as one of Nepal's leading craftsmen. His techniques include traditional lost-wax casting, and a technique of deep chiselling. His work is signed, illustrated and described in international journals and books, including the Kathmandu *Handbook of Craftsmen*, and has been collected and displayed in museums in the USA and Canada (Gredzens, 1983; Greenwald, 1990). Siddhi Raj has won several prizes in Nepal and Germany; he made King Birendra's coronation crown, and a large bell for the Kamaladhi temple in Kathmandu. His figures now (1991) command the very highest prices, and are sold in top-quality retail outlets in Kathmandu and are made to commission from abroad.

Figure 14.2 Filling a gold *tilari* with mastic before carving

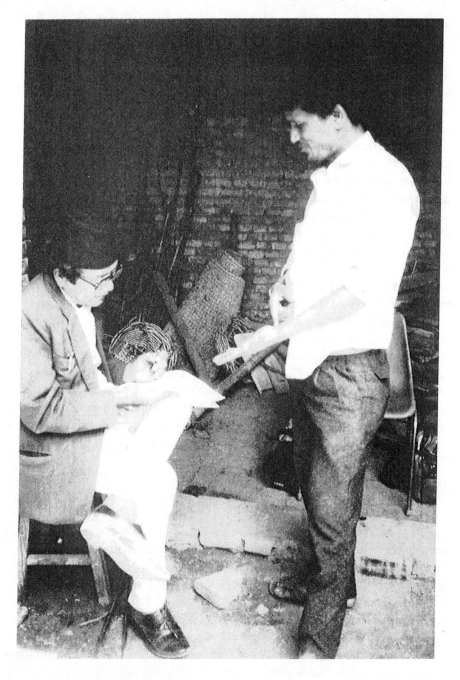

Figure 14.3 Siddhi Raj describing the proportions of religious figures

Base-metal Jewellery Production

Low caste Hindu ironworkers and peoples from the Nepal-Tibet borderland have also turned to manufacturing objects in silver and base metals in response to local and tourist markets. An example is provided by Pemba Lami and his family, originally from the Kirung area northwest of Kathmandu, and now settled in the western part of Kathmandu itself. Formerly the family used to make iron tools, hammers, beaters and shears, etc. for the carpet industry. In recent years they turned to making turistica, particularly bracelets to order. Businessmen buy their products, stockpile and then sell them, mostly from street stalls, to European and Indian tourists, and to some Nepalis. Pemba Lami makes a particular type of bracelet which has been on sale in Kathmandu from before 1981 when I first observed it. Copper, brass and white metal wire and plate is bought in Patan. The metal is heated on a hearth then left to cool naturally. The wire is then cold-worked by stretching and twisting it around two nails driven into the doorstep with pincers and hammers. The flattened twists are then fixed to a backing plate and the bracelet is cleaned in a solution of weak, commercially made nitric acid (Figure 14.4). Although they specialize for the sake of speed, each member of the family, including Pemba's wife, can perform all the processes involved in production. One person can make eight bracelets in one day. The family prefer to work for a fixed price, they do not stockpile, and do not sell their products on the open market. Although business is good they anticipate that they will eventually have to switch lines since, when something is selling well, the bigger firms start to make them by machine and drive smaller craftsmen out of business.

Conclusion

Contemporary Nepalese craftsmen now produce for several domestic markets including individuals and institutions such as temples and hotels; for the tourist market and developing Buddhist markets within Nepal; and for export to numerous other countries including Tibet, Mongolia, Thailand, Taiwan, Japan, as well as to North America and Europe. As always, the distinction between objects made for the pilgrim/tourist market and the export trade is blurred. 'There is nothing new about tourism in India and Nepal' (Fisher, 1991, p. 4), since pilgrimage has traditionally been organized and commercialized in the sale of tokens and souvenirs for centuries (Naqvi, 1968, p. 269).

Nepalese metalworkers have played and continue to play a major role in

Figure 14.4 Washing a base metal bracelet in nitric acid

producing artifacts which are critical in defining Nepalese culture, both to Nepalese themselves and to others – to foreigners who accept such artifacts as 'Nepalese'. The image of the 'universal monarch', essentially Sakyamuni Buddha is, to restrict discussion to the basic icon, a 'butterfly' (Leach, 1968, p. 2) or type specimens which has persisted in manufacture in Nepalese society for more than 1,000 years. There have been changes in decorative elements, and, in recent years, changes in methods of production, yet the stereotypical icon remains despite numerous contextual changes in social organization and structures, in political and economic systems and cultural shifts from city-state to empire, to oligarchy and closure, to contact with other societies which are themselves in process of major changes, and now to mass tourism. Perhaps this image represents 'authenticity' in form, despite changes in production methods and decoration? Jewellery presents different questions. The example of gold jewellery which I have given, the *tilari,* the typical indicator of marital status which is thus embedded in the social structure, has a much shorter time span, perhaps only a few centuries. Does this make it a less authentic Nepalese artifact than the image? Yet the *tilari*, which is made primarily for the domestic market, may be regarded as more traditional than the base metal bracelet which is made primarily for the tourist market. Even so, some Nepalese women also buy and wear the base metal bracelet, which has been manufactured for some 20 years or more. Who defines and sets the parameters of 'authenticity' in 'traditional' artifacts?

Cultural knowledge, like physical, technical and artistic skills, is not uniform in a given society, and even more so in a culture. This lack of uniformity renders the usage of terms such as typical and authentic open to question. Nepalese metalcraftsmen function as entrepreneurs and innovators in adapting technology to produce both traditional, authentic, as well as new products, to serve the contemporary tourist market – the latest in a series of differing patrons for their wares. In either case, the unskilled customers are obliged willy-nilly to recognize their products as genuine 'souvenirs' which define Nepalese culture today.[7]

Notes

1 These figures do not include Indian nationals who form the largest number of visitors to Nepal, for example, in 1988 72,000 visited by air alone. There are no figures for the many more thousands who enter Nepal by road, across the open border between the two countries. Indian nationals visit Nepal to make pilgrimages, shop, gamble at the casino, and simply relax in the hill environment (CBS, 1990, p. 143; Gurung, 1989, p. 153).

2   From an art historical viewpoint there is said to have been a decline in the quality of
    Nepalese crafts during the Rana period (1846–1950), yet a number of fine pieces were
    shown in international exhibitions at this time, such as the Great Exhibition in 1851, and
    the Colonial & Indian Exhibition (1886) (Gimlette, 1886 and 1890–1; Pal, 1985; Palikhe,
    1986, p. 4).

3   Nepalese migration continues today. There are some 2–6 million people of Nepalese origin
    resident in India, which also experiences an annual labour migration from Nepal. Bhutan
    has recently started to expel its former Nepalese population, who are now housed in refugee
    camps in eastern Nepal (Hall, 1996, pp. 132–4).

4   Although the Anglo-Nepalese Treaty of Sagauli (1816) limited Nepal's political boundary
    to the Mechi River, Nepalese peoples continued to migrate into Sikkim, Bhutan and Assam.
    When Darjeeling was ceded to the British in 1835, the village had a population of about
    100. By 1900 the town and its region had a population of 250,000; in 1996 the population
    of Darjeeling and its district was about one million, of whom 700,000 were ethnic Nepalese
    (Hall, ibid.).

5   It is assumed that Mr Horniman's tour of India was arranged through Thomas Cook & Son,
    who opened a branch office in Calcutta in 1883, and were General Passenger Agents to the
    Colonial & Indian Exhibition in London, from which Mr Horniman bought a number of
    artifacts for his collection. On returning from India Mr Horniman disembarked at Brindisi,
    where Cook's had an agency, from where he took a train back to London. Mr Horniman
    shared Thomas Cook's philanthropic, temperance and Christian interests (Brendon, 1991,
    pp. 142, 205). A subsequent curator of the Horniman Museum, Dr Otto Samson, also made
    a collecting trip to Darjeeling in the 1930s.

6   In the 1970s and 1980s there were several fluctuations in the number of tourists visiting
    Nepal, and the curio shops became overstocked. This affected many Newari jewellers who
    had switched to figure production. Some observers, both foreign and Nepali, anticipated
    the end of the lost-wax technique in Nepal (Michaels, 1988, pp. 16–17, 24–5; PIE Handicraft
    Section, verb. comm.). This pessimism appears to have been confounded on an individual
    level, the case of Siddhi Raj is a prime example, and on a general level by a shift in markets.
    In the early 1980s various craftsmen estimated (verb. comm.) that 60 per cent of metalware
    production in the Kathmandu Valley was for sale on the local tourist market. In 1991,
    similarly informed opinion held that export orders for metalwares were now earning more
    than sales on the local tourist market.

7   This paper is based on fieldwork carried out in Nepal between 1981 and 1994. I express
    my deepest gratitude for financial support from the Emslie Horniman Scholarship Fund,
    the Frederick Soddy Trust, the British Council, and the former Committee and present
    Trustees of the Horniman Museum and Gardens. And for personal support from Tsering
    Chodak and his family, John and Susi Dunsmore, Naresh Gurung and especially Louise
    Teague.

References

Acharya, N. (1991), 'Government and the Tourism Industry, Kathmandu', *The Image Nepal
    Newsview*, Vol. 10, No. 1, Jan./Feb. 1991.
Brendon, P. (1991), *Thomas Cook, 150 years of Popular Tourism*, London: Secker & Warburg.
Byron, R. (1933),*First Russia, then Tibet*, Penguin: Harmondsworth.

Central Bureau of Statistics (1990), *Statistical Pocket Book*, Kathmandu NHMG.

Crossette, B. (1995), *So Close to Heaven*, New York: Alfred Knopf.

Domingo-Barker, E. and Barker D.K. (1984), 'Ethnic Jewellery of Nepal', *Arts of Asia*, Vol. 114, No. 4, July–Aug., pp. 111–16.

Fisher, J.F. (1991), 'Has Success spoiled the Sherpas?', *Natural History*, 91 (2), pp. 39–45.

French, P. (1995), *Younghusband. The Last Great Imperial Adventurer*, London: Flamingo.

Gajurel, C.L. and Vaidya, K.K. (1984), *The Traditional Arts & Crafts of Nepal*, New Delhi: S. Chand.

Gimlette, G.H.D. (1886), 'Nepal', *Colonial & Indian Exhibition Catalogue*, London.

Gimlette, G.H.D. (1890–1), 'The Art Industries of Nepal', *Journal of Indian Art*, 3.

Graburn, N.H.H. (ed.) (1976), *Ethnic and Tourist Arts*, London: University of California Press.

Greenwald, J. (1990), *Shopping for Buddhas*, London: Harper & Row.

Gurung, H. (1989), *Nepal. Dimensions of Development*, Kathmandu: Awarta Press.

Hall, A. (1996), 'Himalayan Eodus: Nepalese Migrant Groups', *Asian Affairs*, Vol. XXVII, Pt II, June.

Holdich, Col. Sir Thomas (nd.), *India*, London: Henry Frowde.

Kar, C. (1952), *Indian Metal Sculpture*, London: Tiranti.

Lamb, A. (1986), *British India & Tibet 1766-1910*, London: RKP.

Landon, P. (1928), *Nepal*, London, Constable 2vv.

Leach, E.R. (1968), *Rethinking Anthropology*, London: The Athlone Press.

Naqvi, H.K. (1968), *Urban Centres and Industries in Upper India 1556–1803*, London: Asia Publishing House.

Nash, D. (1989), 'Tourism as a Form of Imperialism', in V.L. Smith (ed.), *Hosts and Guests. The Anthropology of Tourism*, Philadelphia: University of Pennsylvania Press.

Pal, P. (1978), *The Ideal Image*, New York: The Asia Society.

Pal, P. (1985), *The Art of Nepal*, London: University of California Press.

Palikhe, K.P. (1986), *Cottage Industries in Nepal*, Kathmandu: Sankalpa Press.

Sill, M. and Kirkby, J. (1991), *The Atlas of Nepal in the Modern World*, London: Earthscan Publications.

Singh, A.K. (1988), *Himalayan Triangle*, London: The British Library.

Singh, B.R. (1991), *Glimpses of Tourism, Airlines and Management in Nepal*, New Delhi: Nirala.

Smith, V.L. (ed.) (1989), *Hosts and Guests. The Anthropology of Tourism*, Philadelphia: University of Pennsylvania Press.

Teague, K. (1995), *From Tradition to Tourism in the Metalcrafts of Nepal*, unpublished PhD thesis, University of Hull.

Teague, K. (1997), 'Representations of Nepal', in S. Abram et al. (eds), *Tourists and Tourism*, Oxford: Berg.

Veblen, T. (1899), *The Theory of the Leisure Class*, New York: Macmillan.

15 Ceramic Arts of Peru and Ecuador: Echoes of the Prehispanic Past and Influences of the Tourist Present

GEORGE BANKES

The modern republics of Peru and Ecuador have a long tradition of making ceramics which stretches back to about 5,500 years ago on the coast of Ecuador (Kennedy Troya, 1987, p. 12; Marcos, 1984, p. 12) and about 3,500-4,000 years ago on the upper Marañon river in Peru (Bankes, 1989, p. 11). During the two millennia before the Spanish Conquest in the 1530s both regional and pan-Andean ceramic styles developed, using a range of techniques but not the European kick-wheel or glazes. The coast of what is now Peru was noted for the quality and quantity of its painted and modelled pottery which has been variously termed 'fancy ware' (Menzel, Rowe and Dawson, 1964, p. 1) and 'elaborate ceramics' (Donnan, 1992, p. 11) by US archaeologists. Many complete examples of this have been excavated from tombs and have found their way into public museums and private collections and have been published in the numerous books on pre-Columbian, now usually called prehispanic, art (Donnan, 1992; Marcos, 1984). Much time and effort has been devoted to deciphering the language and meaning of the designs on these pots (Berrin, 1998). Alongside this artistic tradition there was also one of producing the utility vessels needed for cooking, making *chicha* (maize beer) and storage. The two traditions were not mutually exclusive, especially in the time of the Inca Empire in the 80 years or so before the Spanish Conquest. Thus the Inca jar with two handles and a pointed base, originally termed aryballus by Hiram Bingham (1915, pp. 260–1) and more recently aryballoid jar (Bankes and Baquedano, 1992, p. 69, no. 65), was used for *chicha* but was often painted with geometric designs on the facing side of the chamber.

In prehispanic Peru there is evidence for archaism in pottery styles. John Rowe (1971, p. 101) has defined archaism as 'direct imitation by later craftsmen of objects decorated in an earlier style'. The examples he cites are incised and painted feline motifs on Moche III style jars and stirrup spout bottles from the north coast of Peru which are based on earlier Chavín style models. At lease 500 years separate the Moche III and Chavín styles. This tradition of archaism still survives in some tourist souvenirs and studio ceramics in Peru and Ecuador. Since mid-1970s the work of the *Sañoc Camayoc* potters of Chulucanas in the far north of Peru has been partly inspired by Vicús pottery, made between about 300 BC and AD 500 (Bankes, 1989, p. 62; Camino, 1987, pp. 228–9; Sosa, 1984, pp. 14–15). In Cuenca in southern Ecuador Eduardo Segovia has been inspired by motifs and shapes from Paracas textiles, Tiahuanaco felines and the Inca pottery aryballus which are all iconographic hallmarks of the prehispanic cultures of the Central Andes (Segovia, 1997).

However, the ceramic arts of modern Peru and Ecuador also show influences from Europe. When the Spaniards conquered Peru and Ecuador in the sixteenth century they brought European pottery technology such as the kick-wheel and lead glazes (Litto, 1976). In addition they imported new forms like jugs and large jars for olive oil and wine. Some of these forms and elements of the technology have been incorporated into modern pottery made as souvenirs for the tourist trade. For example the *chuas* or bowls from Pucará near Lake Titicaca in Peru (Litto, 1976, pp. 36–40), are not only made on the kick-wheel but employ lead glazes for the execution of Spanish designs, like the bull, and Peruvian ones, like the llama.

An important impetus to pottery produced for the tourist and 'ethnic arts' market both in and outside Peru and Ecuador has been the antiquities laws introduced since 1950. Even though there were antiquities laws before then (Bruhns, personal communication, 1998), it was relatively easy to remove antiquities, especially pottery, from Peru and this was done by foreigners who had either worked there or just gone as travellers. Since 1958 (O'Keefe and Prott,1989, p. 994) Peru has had a law in place about the export of any object of archaeological and historic value and Ecuador has had a Cultural Heritage Act since 1979 (ibid., p. 984). Under the antiquities laws of both countries it is illegal to export any pre-Columbian artefact and this point has been and still is emphasized in many of the tourist guide books to these countries (Brooks, 1980, p. 706; Brooks, 1984, p. 827; Rachowiecki, 1997, p. 50). This has meant a tourist market has grown up for reproductions of pre-Columbian ceramics (Perrottet,1991, p. 357) and for modern *artesanías* or handicrafts.

Since about 1970 Peru and Ecuador have come within the orbit of tourists of all ages and income groups from North America, Australasia, Europe and Japan and they have wanted souvenirs of their visits in the form of *artesanías*. Since almost all of these tourists have to fly to and from their destinations they have tended to purchase small items like little pots or textiles which can easily be packed into airline luggage (Bankes, 1995, p. 7). The growth of the 'ethnic arts' market, especially in North America and Europe, since about 1970 has prompted a demand for *artesanías* including larger examples of pottery which can be professionally packed and shipped by sea and air. Owners of shops which import *artesanías* like *Tumi* in Bath, England, have published books on South American arts and crafts (Davies and Fini, 1994) as well as catalogues of what their shops sell (*Tumi*, 1997).

In about 1972 Gerásimo Sosa Alache and a group of potters in Chulucanas in the province of Piura in north Peru made a study of the archaeological remains near them, namely in the area of a hill called Vicús (Camino, 1987, pp. 228–9). In the 1960s grave robbers or *huaqueros* looted tombs in this area and this produced a whole new pottery style which has been called Vicús. Gerásimo studied both the whole pots and also the potsherds left behind by the looters. In his book (Sosa, 1984, p. 25) he points out that 'I feel I have a foundation in my ancestors' and later on (ibid., p. 30) says 'Very few Vicús pieces seem to have been made with paddle and anvil, all seem hand made. The big vessels have marks of paddles. Also I think they used the mould' (my translations). Vicús potters used organic black pigment and the resist painting technique and also made whistling vessels, often with two chambers (Donnan, 1992, pp. 22–3).

Gerásimo had been trained by his father to make utility pottery using the paddle and anvil method. This involved beating on the outside of a vessel while holding a round stone inside. Therefore he could recognize the hallmarks of this technique on Vicús pottery. He had been making utility vessels like *tinajas* (jars) and *chicha ollas* (pots for cooking *chicha*) but found this work uncreative and boring. So he and his co-workers, especially his cousin Flavio Sosa Maza, started experimenting with production techniques of Vicús pottery, especially the modelling, colouring and firing. The negative technique involves two firings and before the second one the design would be covered with a thick clay slip, which would be removed after the second firing, leaving a lighter coloured design underneath.[1] They received assistance and encouragement from outsiders like Gloria Joyce, an American Catholic missionary sister and Lupe Camino, a Peruvian ceramics teacher and researcher on popular culture. Lupe Camino says in her introduction to Gerásimo's book

(Sosa, 1984, pp. 14–15) that she sees in him a direct manifestation of Vicús culture. In addition he received assistance from the Centro de Investigación y Promoción del Campesinado of Piura, a non-government organization run by Jesuit-trained staff with Peruvian employees, which helped him reconstruct his workshop after the heavy rains of 1983. Gerásimo, his cousin Flavio and his brother-in-law, Segundo Moncada, and others established a group of potters called *Sañoc Camayoc*, a hispanicized version of the Quechua for 'pottery specialist'. One reason for this was to help safeguard their supplies of clay.

Gerásimo and his co-workers often used local themes such as the *chichera*, the woman who sells *chicha*, as subjects for their pottery. Gerásimo specialized in making modelled tripartite vessels depicting a lady, the *chichera*, with two *tinajas* (jars) for *chicha* set in front of her. He usually employed negative painting for the design and polished the whole vessel after its 'negative' decoration had been finished after the second firing. His earlier *chicheras* tended to be holding a large stirring spoon set in one of the *tinajas* (Sosa, 1984, p. 64) but in 1986 he made a magnificent *chichera* for the Manchester Museum with a gourd set on top of one of the *tinajas* (Bankes, 1989, p. 67) and (Plate 15.1). His *chicheras* usually had their hair in two long tresses coming off their shoulders and down their chest. The *chichera* does not appear in Vicús pottery and seems to be an original creation of Gerásimo's. Sometimes she is shown surrounded by jars of varying sizes (Davies and Fini, 1994, p. 128). Up to about 1986 the Chulucanas potters tended to work in just two colours, a dark brown (the background) with lighter brown geometric negative designs. Besides local themes foreign ones could feature like 'The Man in the Moon' jar made in 1984 by Flavio Sosa (Plate 15.2). Both Gerásimo and his cousin Flavio incised their name, Chulucanas and dated their work on the base of the pot. In the 1980s the outlets for their work were partly to occasional local private collectors in Piura. Mostly they sold to a cooperative called *Antisuyu* in Lima where most of the customers were foreigners. *Antisuyu* has put on exhibitions of Chulucanas negative painted pottery in Lima.

In the second half of the 1980s and the 1990s the Chulucanas potters have branched out and more young potters have started production. A wider range of colours involving positive slips has been employed. Unfortunately the increase in production by younger potters in the late 1980s meant that the quality of their wares sometimes suffered with rather garish designs being used (Mike Young, personal communication, 1989). Gerásimo Sosa now no longer makes pottery but does design work and supervises the implementation of designs by young potters (Izumi Shimada, personal communication, 1997). Small pottery figures of dumpy women made in Chulucanas are now found in

Figure 15.1 Modelled *chichera* (female seller of maize beer). Negative
painted. The *chichera* has two *tinajas* (jars) in front, with a
poto (gourd) on top of one. Made as a special commission
for the Manchester Museum by Gerásimo Sosa of
Chulucanas in 1986. Height: 290 mm. Manchester
Museum, University of Manchester: 0.9726/39

Figure 15.2 'Man in the Moon' jar. Negative painted design of a 'man in the moon' on each side. Made by Flavio Sosa of Chulucanas in 1984. Height: 195 mm. Manchester Museum, University of Manchester: 0.9726/38

the *artesanía* shops that cater for tourists along and near Avenida Amazonas in Quito.

Chulucanas pottery is now being sold in Zurich, Switzerland, by Sylvia Stulz. According to her publicity sheet there are about 20 or so families making pottery in Chulucanas on a whole range of subjects including 'The Fisherman', 'Water woman', 'Maize seller', 'Fruit seller', 'Wood seller', etc. She mentions that many make *'Gordita'* or 'Fatties', which seem to be mainly women connected with *chicha*. One *'Gordita'* recently sold by her shows a *chichera* signed on the base by Teofilo Viera B., Chulucanas, Peru but with no date. This shows a woman with one pigtail over her left shoulder, holding a gourd for drinking *chicha* in her left hand and a jug (for *chicha*) in her right. The whole pot has a polished black background with a 'rosette' design in light brown done by the negative technique. Green slip has been applied to her two piece neck collar and two modelled representations of cloth folds on the front of her body. The whole vessel has been burnished and looks well alongside one of Gerásimo's negative painted 'ollas' made in 1984. Also although Peruvian *artesanías* are sold in shops in Madrid and Barcelona, including ceramics, the Chulucanas pottery has not been reported in these locations (Mervyn Samuel, personal communication, 1998).

The Chulucanas pottery does not feature in the current catalogue of *Tumi* which advertises brightly painted 'San Pedro de Cajas' style vases from Peru (*Tumi*, 1997, p. 3, D 1). The painted scenes on these vases show women with wide brimmed hats, often seated next to large pottery jars which seem to have come from textile designs made in San Pedro de Cajas in the central highlands of Peru. However Davies and Fini (1994, pp. 33, 138 and 130) illustrate two of Gerásimo Sosa's pots, as well as a brightly coloured jar by Santodio Paz of Chulucanas. Santadio Paz's jar with its yellow-orange long necked heron-like birds and foliage looks slightly oriental in style and may have been influenced by the demands of the Japanese tourist market. In the same book Davies and Fini also illustrate a brightly painted 'arybola and plate' in modern 'Inca' style from Cuzco painted by Maximo Quinto (ibid., p. 120). The painted designs on these two vessels are a mixture of pre-Inca, especially the Moche inspired figures on the inside of the plate, and Inca motifs but both reflect influences from prehispanic Peru. The Maximo Quinto pots illustrate how what were distinctive cultural styles in prehispanic Peru, namely Moche on the north coast in the first millennium AD and Inca based on Cuzco in the fourteenth–fifteenth century AD, have become merged into pan-Peruvian decorative styles adapted for the souvenir tourist trade. These contrast with the more original work of potters like Gerásimo Sosa and Teofilo Viera from

Chulucanas who have developed their own style, albeit one with its roots in the Vicús ceramic tradition.

The work of the Cuenca potter, Eduardo Segovia, in southern Ecuador is an example of a contemporary artist who has been much influenced by prehispanic pottery styles but who also has his own fine creations. His house and workshop is in the Corazon de Jesus barrio in Cuenca which used to house many potters but he told me (personal communication, July 1998) that there were only three artistic potters left there now. In part of his workshop he has a collection of negative painted prehispanic Ecuadorian pottery and he also has a library with books on pottery. He has held exhibitions of his work in major towns in Ecuador such as Cuenca and Guayaquil and also in Cali (Colombia) and in Toronto, Canada. His father was a potter and he had started at the age of six and by 1998 had been making pottery for some 50 years. He told me he felt very much a potter and that he sought inspiration from pre-Columbian designs. In the leaflet published to accompany his *Pasado y Presente* (*Past and Present*) exhibition at the Archaeological Museum of the Bank of the Pacific in Guaqaquil in May 1997 (Segovia, 1997) he says, 'Past because I have used something of all the prehispanic culture, trying to recreate the best of the designs of our ancestors. I am an indefatigable admirer of our cultural roots of yesterday. Today with modern technology we cannot do better than them' (my translation). He goes on to say 'Present because I try to shape something of my spirit in the works. I am a restless seeker of forms of wonderful clay. I have put a lot of care into creating new forms and colours in my style, which uses a mixture of techniques, slips and brilliant colours' (my translation).

In July of 1998 Eduardo Segovia kindly let me examine and photograph a number of his pieces and I bought two for the Manchester Museum. His polychrome stirrup spout bottles are based on the Moche/Chimu north coast Peruvian shape. The motifs on these and on some of his jar forms consist of his interpretation of the backward-bent figure with flowing hair often shown Paracas textiles of the first millennium BC from the south coast of Peru (Frame, 1995, p. 13). He makes a point of including the flowing hair but the eyes of his figures are round in contrast to the oval ones on the original Paracas textiles. Also one of his figures holds a double-headed snake while another clasps a Moche-style club rather than the type of staff and tumi held by the original Paracas figures. Eduardo Segovia's work can be seen in the Andean tradition of archaism. However, unlike the Moche potters who drew on Chavin designs, he has 'picked and mixed' from the whole field of prehispanic designs so that he uses the odd Moche element on one of his 'Paracas' figures.

Eduardo makes two main type of pottery. His larger and more expensive pieces shown in exhibitions, such as the stirrup spout bottles referred to above, are invariably signed E. Segovia and can be dated with the year. He also produces a range of smaller, cheaper, signed and unsigned works like little churches. One of his favourite large forms is the 'aribalo' (aryballus) which copies the form of the Inca aryballus, complete with pointed base, but includes his own decorative canons. One example now in the Manchester Museum has a different incised motif on each side, one geometric and the other a fish (Plate 15.3). The geometric motif includes elements such as triangles found on Inca ceramics but the fish set on the other side seems to be his own creation. His own favourite themes include frogs, which can be modelled and painted in green glaze (Plate 15.4), and tall thin figures of people and of monkeys. He is thus fully aware of both the higher quality and more expensive end of the tourist market for which he makes the signed and dated pieces and of the cheaper end for which he produces the smaller unsigned pots.

There is evidence from Amazonian Ecuador of ceramics being produced by the Canelos Quichua people specifically for the ethnic arts market. The exhibition *From Myth to Creation* held at the Krannert Art Museum, University of Illinois, in 1988 included examples of vessels specifically made with the ethnic arts market in mind. Dorothea and Norman Whitten, in their catalogue of this exhibition, illustrate an example of a storage jar made for the ethnic arts market by Alegria Canelos of Curaray while on the facing page is a traditional storage jar made by Faviola Vargas of Campo Alegre (Whitten and Whitten, 1988, pp. 4–5). The neck of the ethnic arts market jar is covered with geometric motifs while that of the traditional vessel is just painted in one colour with a simpler geometric design round the shoulder. The Whittens (ibid., p. 10) point out that the Canelos Quichua are 'becoming increasingly bicultural in national and counternational lifestyles' so they have presumably become aware of what pottery looks attractive in the apartments of rich North Americans.

Elsewhere in Latin America there is a realization that the ethnic/tourist art market is a valuable source of income. In 1997 a book of Puerto Rican Crafts was published and this has a section on traditional pottery, termed *alfareria tradicional*, and contemporary pottery, called *ceramica contemporanea*. In this book traditional pottery includes reproductions of ancient indigenous pots while the contemporary section includes the Three Kings and a modern shaped vessel with indigenous designs (Rosado, Robinson et al., 1997, pp. 26–7, 42–3). Also, Mexico's gross national product includes a high percentage, over 30 per cent, of income from tourism (Karen Bruhns,

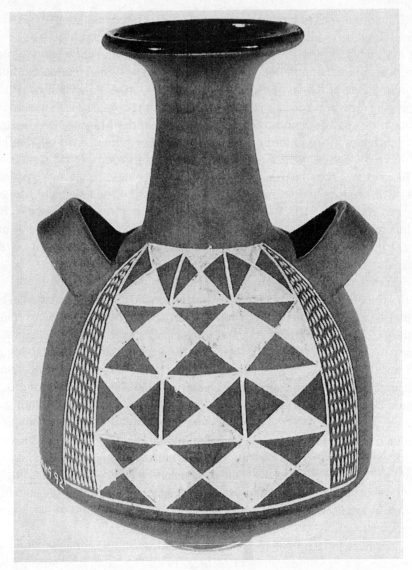

Figure 15.3 'Aribalo' (*aryballus*). Based on the Inca aryballoid jar but with the handles set high on the side instead of lower down as on Inca vessels. The incised geometric decoration shown here is derived from those found on some Inca ceramics. Made by Eduardo Segovia of Cuenca in 1992. Height: 240 mm. Manchester Museum, University of Manchester: 0.9814/10

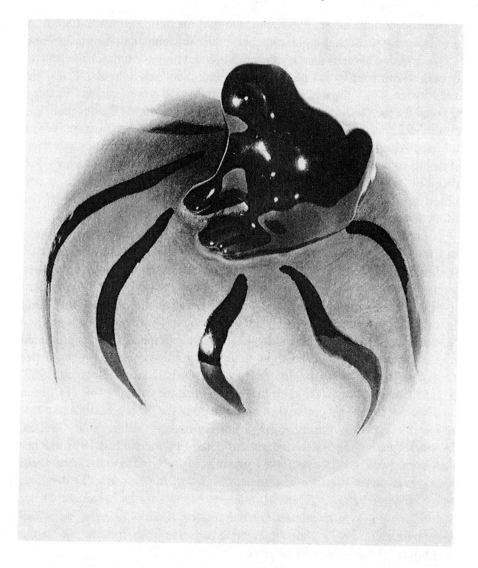

**Figure 15.4 Frog pot. A modelled frog in green glaze sitting on top of
an egg-shaped pot with black radiating lines. Made by
Eduardo Segovia of Cuenca, probably in the 1990s.
Height: 90 mm. Manchester Museum, University of
Manchester: 0.9814/11**

personal communication, 1998) and ceramics, including copies and fakes of prehispanic pots, form a significant part of the souvenirs that the tourists buy.

In addition there is also a substantial production of imitations and fakes of prehispanic pottery in Latin America, notably in Peru, Ecuador, Colombia and Mexico. The village of Pila de Montecristi on the coastal plain of Ecuador is noted for the production of copies of prehispanic pottery (Bruhns, personal communication, 1998 and Hosler, 1996), which is then sold on to unsuspecting tourists. Also polychrome slip-decorated ceramics in both Nasca and Wari styles have been falsified in Peru since the 1920s and have been studied in detail by Alan Sawyer (1982). Examples of 'Wari' style pieces made by one noted Peruvian forger, Servulo Gutiérrez, have been identified in the Manchester Museum (Bankes, 1989, pp. 58–60 and 1992, pp. 146–7).

Ceramics produced in the last 30 years in Peru and Ecuador, particularly in Chulucanas and Cuenca, do show influences of the prehispanic ceramic traditions of the Central Andes. However the potters in these areas have been well able to produce original high quality work for the top end of the collector/ tourist souvenir market while the cheaper, lower quality section, including fakes and copies, has also been taken into account. However it is not an easy life since pottery is breakable and takes up valuable space. Figures produced by the Grupo CIUU in 1983 show that pottery only accounted for 5.41 per cent of all the exports of *artesanias* from Peru (Albareda and Albareda, 1987, p. 217). Eduardo Segovia told me in July 1997 that the young people of Cuenca do not want to take up pottery but prefer to go in for the professions like law and architecture. In Jatumpamba, a pottery making village near Cuenca, Dolores Siguenza, one of the indigenous potters, told me in July 1997 that her daughters would not take up pottery making but preferred to make *sombreros*, the Panama hats of Ecuador. The Equatorial Gallery in Ashbourne, Derbyshire, which imports Eduardo Segovia's pottery, has to earn its bread and butter from Panama hats imported from Ecuador (Carry Somers, personal communication, 1997). Thus the Panama hat trade helps cross subsidize the pots imported from Eduardo Segovia.[2]

Notes

1   The first firing is up to 800°C, while the second is up to 400°C. The pot is polished after the first firing and the required design is drawn out using a thick clay slip which can be peeled off after the second firing.

2   I would like to thank Izumi Shimada for the information he gave me about Gerásimo Sosa's current work, Dolores Siguenza for her information and Eduardo Segovia for allowing

me access to his collection. Also I am grateful to Michael Chadwick for the information about the Chulucanas pottery being sold in Zurich and for the pot by Teofilo Viera B. In addition Mervyn Samuel has provided some helpful linguistic comments and information about Peruvian ceramics sold in Madrid and Barcelona. Also I would like to thank Karen Bruhns for her most helpful comments on and suggestions for this paper. Finally I wish to thank Carry Somers for her information about the Equatorial Gallery's import trade in Eduardo Segovia's pottery and Panama hats from Ecuador.

References

Albareda del Castillo, E. and Albareda del Castillo, F. (1987), 'Comercializacion y Exportacion de Artesanias', in J. Portacerrero Maisch (ed.), *Promoción de la Artesania y la Pequeña Industria en el Perú*, Ottawa: International Development Centre.

Bankes, G. (1989), *Peruvian Pottery*, Princes Risborough: Shire Publications.

Bankes, G. (1992), 'Authenticity and Restoration in the American Collections at the Manchester Museum', *Bulletin des Musées Royaux d'Art et d'Histoire*, Brussels: Musées Royaux d'Art et d'Histoire, Parc du Cinquantenaire.

Bankes, G. (1995), 'Peruvian Pots, Crafts and Foreigners', *Journal of Museum Ethnography*, No. 7, May, Oxford, pp. 1–16.

Bankes, G. and Baquedano, E. (1992), *Sañuq and Toltecatl Pre-Columbian Arts of Middle and South America*, Manchester Museum, University of Manchester.

Berrin, K. (ed.) (1997), *The Spirit of Ancient Peru Treasures from the Museo Arqueologico Rafael Larco Herrera*, New York and London: Thames & Hudson.

Bingham, H. (1915), 'Types of Machu Picchu Pottery', *American Anthropologist*, New Series, 17, pp. 25–271.

Brooks, J. (ed.) (1980 and 1984), *South American Handbook*, Bath: Trade and Travel Publications.

Camino, L. (1987), 'Las Artesanias en la Costa del Peru', in J. Portacerrero Maisch (ed.), *Promoción de la Artesania y la Pequeña Industria en el Perú*, Ottawa: International Development Centre.

Davies, L. and Fini, M. (1994), *Arts and Crafts of South America*, London: Thames & Hudson.

Donnan, C.B. (1992), *Ceramics of Ancient Peru*, Los Angeles: Fowler Museum of Cultural History, University of California.

Frame, M. (1995), *Ancient Peruvian Mantles, 300 B.C. – A.D. 200*, New York: Metropolitan Museum of Art.

Hosler, D. (1996), 'Technical Choices, Social Categories and Meaning among the Andean Potters of Las Animas', *Journal of Material Culture*, Vol. 1, No. 1, London, Thousand Oaks, California and New Delhi: Sage Publications.

Kennedy Troya, A. (1987), *La Ceramica en el Ecuador Proyecto para un Museo*, Cuenca: Fundacion Paul Rivet.

Litto, G. (1976), *South American Folk Pottery*, New York: Watson Guptill Publications.

Marcos, J.G., Zaldumbide, R.P. et al. (1984), *Tesoros del Ecuador Antiguo*, Barcelona: Museu Etnologic.

Menzel, D., Rowe, J.H. and Dawson, L.E. (1964), *The Paracas Pottery of Ica: A Study in Style and Time*, Vol. 50, Berkeley and Los Angeles: University of California Publications in American Archaeology and Ethnology.

Perrottet, T. (ed.) (1991), *Peru Insight Guide*, Hong Kong: APA Publications Ltd.
Prott, L.V. and O'Keefe, P.J. (1989), *Law and the Cultural Heritage Volume 3 Movement*, London and Edinburgh: Butterworths.
Rachowiecki, R. (1997), *Ecuador and the Galapágos Islands*, Hawthorn, Victoria, Australia: Lonely Planet Publications.
Rosado, R. et al. (1997), *Muestra de Artesanía de Puerto Rico de Boriquen para el Mundo: Sampler of Puerto Rican Crafts from Boriquen to the World*, San Juan, Puerto Rico.
Rowe, J.H. (1971), 'The Influence of Chavín on Later Styles', in E. Benson (ed.), *Dumbarton Oaks Conference on Chavín*, Dumbarton Oaks.
Sawyer, A. (1982), 'The Falsification of Ancient Peruvian Slip-decorated Ceramics', in E. Benson and E.H. Boone (eds), *Falsifications and Misreconstructions of Pre-Columbian Art*, Dumbarton Oaks, Washington DC.
Segovia, E. (1997), *Pasado y Presente*, Museo Arqueologico del Banco del Pacifico, Guayaquil, Ecuador, May.
Sosa, G. (1984), *El Barro nos Unió*, Piura: CIPCA.
Tumi Latin American Crafts (1997), Bath, England.
Whitten, D.S. and Whitten, N.E. (1988), *From Myth to Creation Art from Amazonian Ecuador*, Urbana and Chicago: University of Illinois Press.

16 Souvenirs from Kambot (Papua New Guinea): The Sacred Search for Authenticity

ROBERTA COLOMBO DOUGOUD

At the end of the last century Papua New Guinea was colonized by Germany and the United Kingdom. The arrival of colonial administrations, the introduction of other values as well as increasing mobility, exposed the local populations to strong and continuous external influences which caused a gradual breaking up of social and cultural structures. All these changes also had an effect on the artwork of the country and consequently, many traditional artistic forms, having lost their function and meaning, disappeared.

Nevertheless, over recent decades the search for new identity symbols and the demand for souvenirs on the part of the increasing tourist market have together renewed indigenous creativity, and new artistic forms have thus been created. These objects, described in anthropological literature as tourist arts, commercial arts, arts of acculturation, airport arts or pseudo-traditional arts, are often regarded with suspicion and disdain as, unlike traditional forms, they are created for consumption by outsiders. Yet, a more in-depth analysis enables us to understand that in spite of their predestination for the external market, these artefacts are also very important and meaningful for the producers. In the same way that traditional art embodied and expressed past values and identities, so the arts of acculturation express new values and identities as well as new relationships with the outside world (Graburn, 1976). They reflect a need in a population whose horizons have suddenly and dramatically widened and who have to find a way of expressing how they live, who they are and what they do. As Nelson Graburn (1976, p. 26) writes:

> The commercial arts of these small populations may be made for outsiders only ..., but they carry the message: 'We exist; we are different; we can do something we are proud of; we have something uniquely ours.'

Their art provides the means of communicating their separate identity, a

223

positive image of themselves and their most valued characteristics (Graburn, 1979). The study of these arts as systems of intercultural communication and of symbolic exchange, as was suggested by Jules-Rosette in her book *The Messages of Tourist Art. An African Semiotic System in Comparative Perspective*, shows not only the relationship between natives and tourists or art dealers but also their mutual preconceived ideas and expectations as well as the interaction between local and global.

It will be inside this theoretical work that I will present an artefact called a storyboard. Storyboards are carved and painted wooden boards which depict mythological stories or everyday scenes. These boards have been produced since the 1970s by artists of Kambot (Papua New Guinea, East Sepik Province) for sale to tourists and art dealers. This creation has been a very successful one and in the space of a few years they have gained importance in many senses for a number of different groups, including tourists, art dealers and institutions promoting Papua New Guinea not to mention the producers of the boards themselves. Storyboards are now a popular souvenir for visitors to Papua New Guinea and are mentioned in every travel guide as being amongst the most interesting objects to be found in the local artefact shops. Many hotel halls, public offices and banks are decorated with them. Furthermore these boards have been used overseas as a symbol of the Sepik river as well as of the country itself. A large storyboard was displayed at the Great Hall of the World Expo in Seville in 1992 and a number can be admired at the Commonwealth Institute in London together with masks, shields, potteries, and drums. Moreover, thanks to their great narrative capability and their easy readability, the representative scheme of the storyboards has also been used for other carvings, such as tables, doors, engraved bank walls (such as those of the AZN in Port Moresby).

In spite of the fact that storyboards are only made for the external market, they are very meaningful for the people who produce them and an analysis of them throws light on many aspects of the Kambots' lives, and on their attitude to their past and modernity. They strongly identify with the storyboards, which are a great source of pride. Furthermore, in the last few years they have started using the boards as visual support for the transmission of myths to younger generations.

My hypothesis is that the storyboards represent the ground where makers and consumers communicate their expectations, ideas, and desires to each other. With this contribution I aim to explore the consumer side and in particular will focus on the reasons why tourists like the storyboards and the message they convey. I will only slightly touch on the complex and relevant question of why the Kambots invented storyboards and continue to carve them. But before I get to the heart of the matter, let me give a brief description of the village of Kambot, its culture and traditional arts.

Cultural Setting

The village of Kambot lies on the banks of the river Keram, one of the lowest tributaries of the Sepik in the East Sepik Province, subdistrict of Angoram. The village has a population of about 700 people who subsist on hunting, fishing and cultivation. Their lives are marked by the alternation of the rainy season (from October to April) and the dry season (from May to September). As in many other villages on the river, the Kambots live on sago and fish, and during the dry season they work in their gardens until the arrival of the flood. In fact the village is flooded for a few months in the rainy season and the canoe is the only means of transport.

They speak a Papuan language belonging to the Grass family of the Grass stock which is a division of the Ramu super-stock (Laycock, 1973). It is estimated that it is spoken by 7,000 people. They themselves call it *bo-tin*[1] or *ap∂le-tin* where *ap∂le* means 'denial' and *tin* 'mouth'.[2] The use of the local language is becoming less frequent with the increased usage of Melanesian Pidgin.

In the past, ancestors of the Kambots lived along the Sepik from where, about 10 generations ago, they moved up the Keram in search of land abounding in sago, which together with fish constitutes their staple diet. They then settled near Kambot at Bosimbe. Their mythology tells us that from time to time a monster called Pand∂mo or Wotñana[3] would come to the settlement asking for a child. After several raids, they finally succeeded in freeing themselves of him. When they went down to his hole (*hul*[4]), they discovered some powerful objects and designs which they later put in the *haus boi* (men's house). That is how they acquired all their strength and might.[5] Wotñana disappeared but as they were never certain of having killed him, they fled to the river where Kambot now lies.

The traditional art was closely linked to the *haus boi* (Kelm, 1966). The *pangal*, paintings on the smooth inner surface of the midrib of the sago palm, were of great importance. These pieces of bark were smoothed, flattened and then put together in order to get a larger surface on which several designs were painted. The colours – red, white, black, reddish brown and yellow – were obtained by mixing water with earth pigments. On these *pangal* the artists used to draw animals – crocodiles, snakes, sharks, parrots, dogs, pigs, cassowaries, butterflies, frogs, etc. – mythological figures – not human but a few particular ancestors or spirits – and the sun, the moon, stars and decorations. The animals were represented both in profile and from above, whereas the mythological figures were always depicted from a frontal view. I believe that this is due both to the importance attributed to the nose, considered the centre of human beauty, and to the characteristic nose decoration which permits their identification. There was no representation of the vegetable kingdom.

Another important object connected with the *haus boi* was the ceremonial shield, **angop wai**, decorated with feathers that depicted animals and mythological figures. The artistic sensibility of the Kambots was also expressed through the carving of ceremonial and everyday objects such as masks, drums, shields, statues, canoes, paddles, tools, etc.

Exploration of the area dates back to the beginning of this century. The Catholic Missionaries (Divine Word Society) arrived in Kambot in the second decade of the century, but it was only in 1933 that they settled there. Thus Kambot became the site of the second permanent Catholic Mission on the Sepik after Marienberg which had been established in 1913. The arrival of the mission and its presence had a strong influence on the life of the village. The ceremonial houses, *haus boi* or *haus tambaran*, which in Kambot had the shape of a crocodile with its jaws wide open, were the centre of social and religious life. Soon, however, all the sacred objects which embodied their ancestors' force and power were removed. This also meant the interruption of the initiation rites. Many young boys were recruited to work on the plantations of Madang and Rabaul or for the Catholic Mission. A German administration followed by an Australian one, the arrival of the Catholic Mission, and recruitment for the plantations of Madang and Rabaul, all negatively influenced traditional life and as a consequence artistic production went into decline.

Creation of the Storyboards

At the end of the 1960s local art was stimulated and underwent a revival. This was due in part to increasing tourism in the region with its attendant demand for souvenirs. The political situation also played an important role: progress towards independence was rapid and it was formally achieved in 1975. Papua New Guinea enjoyed a cultural renaissance encouraged by the awareness of the significance and value of their cultural heritage.

It was in this scenario of artistic revival that, between the end of the 1960s and the beginning of the 1970s, a group of Kambot artists – Simon Ñowep, Akryas Pase, Zacharias Wepnang, Ignas Gingan and Sigmund Manua – began to be active. They progressively modified the traditional representative scheme until a new artistic form was created, namely the storyboard. In those years some Kambots were carving artefacts for tourists and art dealers. The *hap kanu*,[6] boards from broken canoes carved with mythological figures and animals used in the past in funerary rituals (Lupu, 1972), were particularly appreciated. The *hap kanu* were rather small and the carvers were asked for bigger boards. One day Zacharias Wepnang and Akryas Pase were in the bush looking for some wood when their attention was drawn to a tree called *lendǝma* whose roots stand partly above ground. These buttress roots, *le-nang*,[7] the number of which can vary depending on the tree's age and dimensions, look like boards with a thickness of 6–7 centimetres and a height of two metres. They tried carving them and discovered that the wood was particularly soft. For a certain period, despite the use of the new medium, the carvers continued to follow the same representative scheme. However, under the advice of Father John Kovač[8] (Divine Word Society) the shape of the boards changed from a rectangular to an elliptical one. The priest suggested that they should consider the boards as clouds in the sky.

At this point a change in both medium and form took place but these objects could still not be regarded as storyboards. In fact, it was the modification of the representative scheme which led to the creation of a new artefact and this happened only when a new element, that is, the canoe appeared on the boards, and is still reproduced in most cases. The presence of the canoe shows the carver's intention to represent the river, the principal element of his life, and thus to depict his daily life. The innovative character of the storyboards lies in their illustration of ordinary life. Even when a mythological scene is evoked, this is done in a more realistic way. A shift occurs from the conceptual concerns of traditional art to a new narrative one. The aim was no longer the representation of the essential elements of the story but the imaginative reconstruction of mythological events. Maybe wanting to underline the importance of the canoe, Zacharias Wepnang and Akryas Pase pronounced the word storyboard as 'storyboat', saying that it was the representation of a canoe within the framework of a story. Akryas Pase has even proposed a translation into the local language *ya-munduma*, where *munduma* means 'canoe' and *ya*, the abbreviation of *yandoma*, means 'story'. This could also be linked to the original practice of using the broken sides of canoes.

The change in the representative scheme also entailed the introduction of elements alien to traditional art but which facilitate the reproduction of daily life, such as men, women, children, houses, drums, tools, trees, and flowers. Just to give an idea of how the representative scheme changed, I shall show how the myth of Dowena and Lowena was illustrated in the past and how it is depicted today in the storyboards. Dowena and Lowena are two brothers who transform themselves into cockatoos and from the top of a tree kill several men, and then throw down their headless bodies. As they have previously chewed some betel nuts with a magic lime, they are invisible and they can fly off with the human heads in their claws without being seen. After several adventures they fall into the river where Dowena turns into a crocodile. Traditionally this myth was represented though the following designs which were carved in the posts of the *haus boi* or were painted on pieces of bark in the rooms of the ceremonial house or on its gable. In the first drawing[9] (Figure 16.1) we can see one of the brothers with a human body but the head of a cockatoo. The second drawing (Figure 16.2) depicts another variant, a cockatoo with a lime container in its claws. Another possibility is represented by Dowena whose body is part human and part crocodile (Figure 16.3). In the storyboard[10] (Figure 16.4) which narrates the same myth we can observe a canoe with some people paddling, and a village on a river with huts, trees, animals, people. We would say that we are looking at a scene of ordinary life in the village but if we look more closely at, for example the human heads under the coconut trees, or the cockatoos flying away with human heads in their claws, we realize that the carver has depicted the story of Dowena and Lowena.

Why do Tourists like Storyboards?

Shortly after their creation, the storyboards became very popular with tourists and, as mentioned, soon became one of their favourite souvenirs despite the abundance and variety of Papua New Guinean artefacts which were already present on the primitive art market. Starting from some intrinsic characteristics of this artefact, I would like to investigate the reasons for this rapid success.

First of all, they are made in a variety of sizes (ranging from 25–30 cm in length and 15–20 cm in height to 250 cm in length and 130–150 cm in height) and sold at different prices, ranging from 4 Kina for the smallest to 600 Kina[11] for the biggest, which are normally bought and displayed in hotel halls. The cost of the boards is determined by the size, quality of the carving (the deeper it is, the more expensive it is) and the type of story depicted: those illustrating

Figure 16.1 Dowena or Lowena with a human body but the head of a cockatoo

**Figure 16.2 Dowena or Lowena as a cockatoo with a lime container in
its claws**

Figure 16.3 Dowena whose body is part human and part crocodile

Figure 16.4 Storyboard narrating the myth of Dowena and Lowena

a traditional myth are more valued. Due to the type of wood from which they are made, they are light and this makes them easy to carry in suitcases or even in handbags. They have a practical use in the houses of their buyers as they can be hung on walls like paintings. Furthermore they display a rich variety of themes and motives, and thus present a low degree of standardization. The diversity in size, price and themes makes it possible for everybody to find the storyboard that he would like and at the same time assures him that he is buying a unique piece of work. If we observe a board, we discover a lot of irregularities and technical imperfections such as marks of the chisels used to carve it, colours running into each other, all of which prove that the artefact in question is handmade. Lack of perspective and lack of an exact representation of reality feed tourists' imagination who consider natives as 'primitives' in every aspect of their life included art.

Storyboards are accessible as their language is very basic and understandable. No aesthetical or anthropological knowledge is requested to understand them as is the case for other artefacts. Even though there are different levels of understanding, anyone can grasp at least the basic meaning. As the board illustrating the myth of Dowena and Lowena shows, it is not essential to know the traditional story depicted to enjoy the carving as there is always something that can be understood and told about it.

Storyboards are not objects which are simply supposed to be looked at, but also to be narrated. As is suggested by the name itself, they are boards telling a story and at the same time boards through which a story can be told. And if carvers tell about their life and myths, tourists tell about their journey. While travelling the sense which is stimulated the most is sight. But as this action can not be protracted, the tourist tries to 'fix' the moments he has lived and to give a sort of eternity to an experience which is condemned to vanish. That is what photos and slides are supposed to do, namely to catch and immortalize the fleeting instant in order to recall it back home and share it with relatives and friends. If we consider travel as a *rite de passage* (Van Gennep, 1909), subdivided into rites of separation, rites of transition and rites of incorporation, we realize that the journey does not end at the exact moment when the house door is closed and the luggage unpacked. It ends when, after sharing his memories with relatives and friends who in this way acknowledge his changes, the tourist is once again incorporated into ordinary life.

But let us go back to the storyboards. During the phase of incorporation following a journey slides, photos and souvenirs are shown to support descriptions of places, adventures and encounters. The function of souvenirs is suggested by the etymology of this word derived from the Latin *subvenire* which means 'to come to mind'. Well, tourists can also use the storyboards as a support to their own stories as well as material evidence of their travels and adventures as a kind of synthesis between a photo and an artefact. Moreover, as the storyboards reflect the most common images and stereotypes of the Sepik river in particular and of Papua New Guinea in general, outsiders recognize in them some of their ideas of the country: people living on the river, hunting and fishing, paddling their canoes, working in their gardens, fighting with spears, dancing whilst beating hand drums, sitting in the ceremonial house and so on. It is no coincidence that the storyboards are now used as a symbol of the country in the presentation of Papua New Guinea abroad.

Nevertheless I think that another important factor should be taken into account. In order to understand why tourists like storyboards, we should analyze their reasons for travelling and the expectations with which they undertake it. In their article 'Tourism and Anthropology in a Post-Modern World', Frederick Errington and Deborah Gewertz (1989) classified the visitors of the Sepik region into two categories: travellers and tourists. The first group is composed of young people mostly in their 20s, making long-term excursions on a low budget. Proud of travelling autonomously, they call themselves 'travellers', wishing to distinguish themselves from ordinary tourists. They intend to engage with the 'primitive' as a means of personal development, as a contribution to their individuality and are disappointed to see the changes or the 'spoiling' caused by the encounter with Western values. The second category corresponds to middle-aged professionals visiting the Sepik for a few days on board a luxury boat called the *Melanesian Explorer* which was recently replaced by a more de luxe one, the *Melanesian Discoverer*.[12] Conscious of the ineluctability of changes, tourists come to the Sepik in order to witness the 'primitive' before it becomes acculturated. As Errington and Gewertz (1989, p. 45) argue, 'they viewed the "primitive" as an increasingly rare prize to be witnessed and captured before it was too late. But since they wanted to be among the last to do this, they also wanted assurance that they had come in time'.

Anyway, both travellers and tourists visiting Papua New Guinea want to have an 'authentic' experience, or at least, they want to believe that they have had an 'authentic' experience. They know that they are supposed to buy some artefacts because in any publication on Papua New Guinea it is mentioned that the Sepik is famous for its rich artistic tradition. One of the most famous travel guides declares that:

Papua New Guinea's arts and handicrafts have been recognized as the most vital in the Pacific. The art is amazingly varied for the same reason as there are so many languages – lack of contact between different villages and groups of people. ... The Sepik is easily the best known area for artefacts (Wheeler, 1988, pp. 63–4).

But the souvenir they take back to their homes like a sort of trophy must correspond to their image of the country, that is to say it must look 'authentic', 'primitive' and 'traditional'. The authenticity of the artefact is a guarantee of the authenticity of their experience in Papua New Guinea.

So, renewing my initial question, I think that if we want to understand why the storyboards are highly appreciated, the most important characteristic to be taken into account is that they seem to be 'authentic'. They reassure the tourists that the 'primitive' as they conceived it before their arrival in the country still exists and they have just encountered it. That is why tourists would never buy a storyboard depicting Papua New Guineans dressed in T-shirts and trousers, listening to the radio, or driving motor canoes, even if this corresponds to the reality. Several times I myself saw tourists refusing to purchase a storyboard because a few details had been painted with a yellow ground which in their (wrong) opinion was not traditional. In fact '... what most occidentals still seem to seek in the "primitive" arts is a set of qualities that correspond to their idea of traditional "primitive" life. ... Any object that does not fit the standard notions is rejected as inauthentic' (Delange Fry, 1971–72, p. 96). Some decide not to purchase a storyboard when they discover that, even though this object is related to traditional art, it was created only around 30 years ago (Colombo Dougoud, 1997).

Conclusion

In recent years the Kambots have become aware of tourists' expectations as well as of the message, conveyed by them through their purchase of storyboards. As tourists do not appear to realize that their culture, as any other one, lives in a constant dynamism in which the elements coming from other societies are elaborated and integrated, evidence of any encounter with modernity is suppressed. The Western public tends to condemn other cultures to stagnation. It interprets any change as a sort of degradation and treats new types of objects as inauthentic. But the Kambots have understood this mechanism and message and they do what in French is called *faire avec*.

They have realized that if they want their own message which is conveyed through the storyboards to be heard, a message which declares their existence identity and pride, they have to make the boards seem 'authentically primitive'. And that is what they do.

Notes

1   Words in the local language are in italic and bold type.
2   François Lupu (1972), a French anthropologist who carried out field research in Kambot in the 1970s, uses the expression *tin dama* which means 'this mouth, this language'.
3   Wotñana means 'give me another one' and it refers to the request for children.
4   Words in Melanesian Pidgin are in italic type.
5   The myth of Wotñana would also justify Kambot superiority over other villages sharing the same language: their ancestors' courage permitted them to be the first to enter Wotñana's hole and hence to bring back the best and most powerful designs and objects.
6   *Hap kanu* – from the Pidgin *hap* 'piece' and *kanu* 'canoe' means piece of canoe.
7   This word is formed from *nang* which means 'root' and *le* the abbreviation of *lendɔma*.
8   Father John Kovač was priest at Kambot from 1971 to 1976.
9   The drawings representing the story of Dowena and Lowena were done by Akryas Pase whilst I was carrying out my piece of research in Kambot in 1987/88.
10   This storyboard was photographed in 1988 in Kambot but it was carved by a man of the village of Yamen Gatwa.
11   In September 1999 the value of 1 Kina was about US$ 0.339.
12   This ship was immortalized by Dennis O'Rourke in his extraordinary documentary film *Cannibal Tours*, which shows a group of Western European and North American tourists travelling up the Sepik river and stopping at villages to take pictures and buy artefacts.

References

Colombo Dougoud, R. (1997), 'Les Storyboards de Kambot. Art du Sepik entre tradition et modernité', *Tsantsa*, 2, pp. 124–8.

Delange Fry, J. (1971–72), 'Contemporary Arts in Non-Western Societies', *Artscanada*, 162/163, pp. 96–101.

Errington, F. and Gewertz, D. (1989), 'Tourism and Anthropology in a Post-Modern World', *Oceania*, 60, pp. 37–54.

Graburn, N.H.H. (1976), 'Introduction: Arts of the Fourth World', in N.H.H. Graburn (ed.), *Ethnic and Tourist Arts: Cultural Expressions from the Fourth World*, Berkeley: University of California Press.

Graburn, N.H.H. (1979), 'New Directions in Contemporary Arts', in S.M. Mead (ed.), *Exploring the Visual Art of Oceania*, Honolulu: University Press of Hawaii.

Jules-Rosette, B. (1984), *The Messages of Tourist Art. An African Semiotic System in Comparative Perspective*, New York and London: Plenum Press.

Kelm, H. (1966), *Kunst vom Sepik*, Berlin: Museum für Völkerkunde.

Laycock, D. (1971), *Sepik Languages: Checklist and Preliminary Classification*, Pacific Linguistics B 25, Canberra: Linguistic Circle of Canberra.

Lupu, F. (1972), 'La Mort des Femmes, la Mort des Hommes chez les Tin Dama (East Sepik Province)', in J. Guiart (ed.), *Rites de la mort*, Paris: Laboratoire d'Ethnologie et Muséum d'Histoire Naturelle.

Van Gennep, A. (1909), *Les Rites de Passage*, Paris: Nourry.

Wheeler, T. (1988), *Papua New Guinea. A travel survival kit*, South Yarra: Lonely Planet Publications.

17 Souvenirs, Ethics and Aesthetics: Some Contemporary Dilemmas in the South Pacific

NICK STANLEY

Three Types of Souvenir

I want to consider some of the problems that confront visitors to the South Pacific seeking souvenirs of their stay. On the one hand there is no dearth of historically important artefacts similar to and even of equal value to those held in major Western museums available from willing private sellers or from the back rooms of souvenir shops in the capitals of South Pacific states. Many of these examples are historic and no longer manufactured within living memory. Purchasing these items raises, in condensed form, the same range of issues that confront museums in accepting items for accession.

Interestingly, for many visitors to the same region, the same scruples do not seem to attach to collecting items from World War II that litter the region. Why is this? Perhaps, it is because the material items are not considered 'indigenous' artefacts. This in itself is an interesting reflection on the politics of ownership.

A third alternative, untainted by the above considerations, is to look for contemporary souvenirs. This proves difficult in a region not geared up for tourism, particularly as tourists arrive infrequently but in significant numbers from tour ships. One example of collectible items is provided in the pidgin collective term 'basket'. These provide, on the one hand, a range of examples that have good historic provenance, but on the other hand challenge the contemporary western collector to come to terms with technical and material transformations in the manufacture of 'baskets' which undermine Western notions of craft and 'appropriate materials' for indigenous manufacture.

This chapter argues that these three perspectives are not watertight, but interrelate. Souvenirs in the context of the South Pacific always involve questions of ethics and aesthetics, both in terms of the producer and purchaser. I hope that some of the considerations that I raise here have resonance for other geographic areas and contribute to the broader discussion about the ethics of souvenir hunting and gathering.

Indigenous Souvenirs

The sheer beauty and range of artefacts from the South Pacific lodged in the major ethnological museums of the northern hemisphere serves to draw our attention away from two facts. Firstly, these treasures are seldom to be seen in their original location, and almost never in local museums. Secondly, they were collected not so much for their aesthetic appeal but more for their souvenir characteristics. In speaking of ethnological collections, Dominguez (1986, p. 554) declares,

> But what I [then] conclude is not that the value of these ethnological collections – and perhaps ethnological collections in general – lies in their being representations of the other, but rather that they can fruitfully be read as referential indices of the self. Their concrete objects come from other societies, but everything about the collection itself – the way the objects were collected, and how and why they get displayed – points to us.

These items in historic collections are as much souvenirs as any contemporary purchase. They fit clearly into the category of the historic souvenir. Charles Woodford, the first Resident Commissioner in Solomon Islands in the 1890s regularly supplied the British Museum with artefacts that clearly had a biographic reference as his letter to the Keeper of Ethnology, testifies,

> I send you herewith a specimen of a native woman's hair from the island of Ysabel, in the hope that it may prove of interest. The unfortunate creature from whose head the hair was cut had been confined in a pen for over six years on a charge of witchcraft. Of course, as soon as we had heard of it she was liberated and is now at the government station at Gizo (Woodford, 1894).

This vignette fits perfectly Graburn's contention (1979, p. 2) that 'in many cases the agents of colonialist powers, after they had overcome some of their revulsion towards the subject peoples, collected arts and crafts as souvenirs of their sojourn in the service of empire'. Whilst we might feel ethically troubled today at this highly personal form of souvenir, it fits into both the tradition of relics that links us to a once living and significant individual as well as to what Clifford (1988, p. 220) calls 'salvage ethnography'.

These historic souvenirs are open to two interpretations. Woodford's example is that of a trophy of incivility. Many of the items in northern hemisphere museums come from collections formed by missionaries out of the pre-Christian ritual items discarded by their converts (Stanley, 1994, p. 29). But missionaries and government agents were often ambiguous in their relationship to indigenous people and their civilizations. Whilst some artefacts might be seen as talismans of primitivity, others might reflect an uncontaminated pre-contact purity of design. This ambiguity resides in the change from the eighteenth to the nineteenth century view of the inhabitant of the South Pacific from that of the noble to treacherous and deceitful savage (Smith, 1985, p. 147). But both views contributed to the programme of systematic collecting which eventuated in a major transfer of curios (a term that embraces both attitudes to souvenirs) to private collections and to major museums. In this process dealers and auction houses played a key role in turning private souvenirs into public exhibits. The juxtaposition of these items in museums of contemporary art from those made by the surrealists to the present-day Sainsbury Centre further enhance their scarcity value.

Museums and cultural centres in the Pacific are keenly aware of the lack of good examples of customary artefacts in their collections and regularly appeal to the public to donate family and clan heirlooms. Tourist visitors to these museums quickly come to appreciate the cultural and economic value of these items which they may have known nothing about prior to their museum visit. Even though historic objects are officially protected there are sources that can supply visitors with examples as their own souvenirs. South Pacific nations, like many elsewhere in the world, forbid export of such antiquities. But every Pacific state has souvenir shops, and many of these shops have back rooms that are accessible only to those who are judged by the shop keepers to be reliable purchasers. The contrast between the contents of the front and the back rooms of the shop is tantalizing. For many visitors the temptation is to ignore official policy and to acquire a 'genuine' souvenir whose authenticity is confirmed by its age and scarcity. The ethical dilemma becomes even greater when a private gift or sale is suggested by local persons to 'do them a good turn', especially when such sellers are apparently poor. What, of course, is in contention here is the right of the souvenir hunter to acquire an item that is of particular value precisely because it has specific cultural significance to those from whom he or she acquires it. At first this might suggest that I am contradicting Dominguez in her assertion that souvenirs point to us. But, I maintain that we, as tourists, replicate our colonial forbears in our attitudes and approaches to purchasing curios. The missionaries and traders valued their souvenirs because they were culturally significant, or, to put it another way, because the objects contributed to a tale they could retell about the society they had lived in. They also collected items because they felt that they were disappearing in the onslaught of Western intrusion (Slobodin, 1997, pp. 193–207). These motives continue to fuel tourist desire for significant souvenirs that provide them with an authentic memory of their stay.

Souvenirs from Afar: War Relics

The South Pacific is, however, rich with souvenirs of another kind that relate directly to the biographies of western visitors. The second world war has left the Solomon Islands in particular with spoils of war scattered across the whole archipelago but concentrated particularly near the capital, Honiara (itself a creation of war) on the island of Guadalcanal. The coastline is dotted with rotting hulks of American and Japanese warships and transporters. In 1975 an enterprising Solomon Islander named Fred Kona brought together artefacts of war such as aeroplanes, guns and armoured vehicles in his own private war museum at Vilu on the plain near Honiara. Here and in the national capital an inflationary spiral of war commemoration has led to a rash of memorials placed 50 years after the Pacific war both by Americans and by Japanese (White, 1995, pp. 534–9). Both the US and Japanese monuments are shrines put up by ex-servicemen. Their intended audience is other veterans and their children. The consequences of this locus for pilgrimage are paradoxical. The local context is almost incidental: this could be a battle site anywhere in the world. The location is only a colonial terrain and the history being commemorated has minimal reference to the inhabitants of these islands where this world conflict took part. The effect of this movement of memorialization has been the importation of not only fully finished materials but architects and monumental masons to erect these structures. These shrines bear little intrinsic significance to the local inhabitants but are standard elements in the iconography of memorials for war veterans' veneration.

A consequence of this commemoration is that war souvenirs become major objects of desire. But this in turn raises further ethical, and political issues. To whom do these spoils of war belong? At first sight the question seems easy to answer. The artefacts are to be found on the sovereign territory of the South Pacific states, in this case, Solomon Islands. But indigenous people do not seem to treat these objects with much reverence and slowly most of the items seem destined to disappear under the ravages of a harsh tropical climate and under the shroud of the rapidly growing bush. Inhabitants of the Pacific in general, it could be argued, although they have a keen interest in the preservation and development of customary culture, seem little taken with museological practices of conservation and display (White, 1996, p. 53; Stanley, 1998). Furthermore, precisely because such nationals have seldom, if ever, been incorporated into the standard histories of World War II, their attachment to the myriad objects littering their environment is likely to be slight; 'The war was not our war', as a prominent Solomon Island survivor put it (White, 1995, p. 532). In fact, the war could be seen as a cataclysmic event but nevertheless, essentially, a diversion from the task of nation-building. Under these circumstances it might readily be conceded that the spoils of war could be relegated to become the souvenirs of former combatants.

For a long time after the war, particularly during colonial rule which persisted until the late 1970s, and prior to any systematic planning for tourism, war souvenirs were accorded no special importance. But the growth of tourism has led to a rapid reconsideration of battle sites as visitor attractions. Consequently the Solomon Islands National Museum has now added war remains to its remit for preservation and interpretation. Similarly, the provincial authorities have come to take an interest in the activities of scuba divers plundering wrecks for souvenirs. What has changed? The answer involves the assertion of a local right to control the traffic and marketing of items that are enjoying an increasing international exchange value. Essentially, such a development enhances the claim by local brokers to become controllers over the market in souvenirs whether they be of traditional pre-colonial source, or proto-colonial. Although the manufacture of these rather peculiar souvenirs of war comes from outside the site of collection, the new constraints on casual expropriation serve to remind tourists and serious collectors of the moral rights of those on whose lands these items came to play such a significant role.

'Baskets' and Contemporary Souvenirs

Csikszentmihaly and Rochberg Halton (1981) define a souvenir as 'the memory of a place'. In the above discussion I have been closing down the possibilities for the ethically-minded tourist to acquire souvenirs: firstly in terms of the inalienability of antiquities with respect to the history and constitution of a culture; secondly in terms of the claim of a people or state to artefacts emanating from extrinsic sources but which have had a marked impact on their lives and development. What, if anything, remains ethically and aesthetically worth collecting as a memory for visitors to the South Pacific? The question breaks into two: on the one hand there are a few locations that have generated a tourist trade. Fiji (for Australia) and the Cook Islands (for New Zealand) have become significant tourist destinations and have developed a tourist art. But, where no continuous sale of tourist souvenirs occurs what is there to collect?

There is a range of tourist arts which is made with a specific eye to trade. At White River outside Honiara in an international resettlement camp set up by the Seventh Day Adventist Church and the South Seas Evangelical Church there are carvers sculpting sea eagles capturing water serpents. Although there is sometimes an attempt by the carvers to relate the motifs to traditional stories (Tickle, 1987) the production made by artists from throughout the Pacific (from Kiribati to Tahiti) is commissioned to order for export and is little seen in shops or hotels. It is difficult to gauge the impact on this craft work of design consultants from Europe sponsored by UNESCO or other regional aid agencies, but, since it is exported, the tourist is rarely tested in the purchase of such souvenirs.

Graburn (1979, p. 106) distinguished between three kinds of what he calls 'the arts of acculturation'. The first are those he calls functional fine arts which are intended primarily for members of the maker's own culture. These are in a sense analogous to what I have called indigenous souvenirs. The third type he calls souvenir or 'airport' art whose manufacture is dictated almost exclusively by its saleability. I argue that this type of souvenir (the sea eagle) is difficult to acquire in the South Pacific. Tourists may find to their chagrin that there really are no items for sale that offer them a memento of their stay. To find anything to remind one of Niue one has to seek out the rare tin of tuna canned there. But Graburn's second category offers a partial solution to the frustrated tourist's quandary. In this category Graburn includes what he terms commercial fine arts that appeal to tourists as well as local buyers. What this category provides is the possibility of domestic items coming to have a new life in a foreign setting, and becoming a talisman and memento of the tourist's sojourn. When most tourists are also anthropologists or fellow-travellers this makes for an easy accommodation.

Classic anthropological texts make much of the significance of basket work in the Pacific. This is a topic that is still treated as highly important in the region (O'Hanlon, 1993, pp. 69–74). The consequence is that new arrivals in non-commercially oriented locations come to see the world through their predecessors' material categories. This can be an extremely useful introduction. But it may also have its distinct limitations. I would like to illustrate the point with two objects. The first was a basket on sale in Honiara in 1989 in a shop that sold to tour ships on three or four occasions per year and to locals at other times. The same objects were, and still are available in the town market at the wharf. They combine a number of characteristics that make them satisfying tourist objects for the culturally observant visitor. Firstly, they are made of traditional material (pandanus) and are of a design recognisably that of a couple of Polynesian outlier islands, Rennell and Bellona. This is doubly satisfying – enabling one to locate a particular curiosity: a Polynesian design from deep within Melanesia, and one to be seen in daily use on the streets of Honiara, though less frequently a decade later. But on closer inspection these baskets contain a surprise, the inclusion of a Japanese zip fastener, loosely tacked in but quite serviceable. This reminds the tourist/anthropologist collector of the transience of material culture, and in such a neat and summative manner.

The second basket comes from the same period but appears to breach a number of considerations that would endow it with the status of souvenir. However, this is still quite recognisably within the category of basket. It is a container constructed in the same manner as the Bellona pandanus basket but the material from which it is constructed serves to violate the sense of geographic specificity required to make it a memento. However, as Hitchcock has remarked with regard to Bimanese textiles (Hitchcock, 1983, p. 222) what constitutes a traditional material in a changing world is extremely difficult to decide. Here, the material is Japanese nylon fishing filament on sale in Chinese shops throughout the Pacific. How is one to respond to an item that seems so unaesthetic by comparison with its companion? This is a tricky question and one which may pit the souvenir seeker against the local purchaser. The very indestructibility of the material could be either a desirable quality for its user, or an ecological nightmare in its resistance to decay once abandoned. Furthermore, it is difficult, I would guess for the tourist, whether anthropologically trained or not, to wax lyrical over an item that bears such striking resemblance to despised items of Western manufacture. The fact that it is handmade serves rather to heighten the pathos than to limit our dislike of it. It is not just a question of function versus form. It is a test of the elasticity of our concept of souvenir. Yet what is really at stake is the combination of our aesthetic and ethical values in the context of South Pacific material culture.

What I suspect the nylon basket does is to confront us with the limitation of our visual imagination and the ethical consequences that flow from this. If we can't have pre-contact deity figures, clam shell ornaments, or porpoise-tooth necklaces, if we are denied the mementoes of later invasion in the Second World War, we remain stubbornly unwilling to accept anything that looks everyday and which could have come from our local corner store near home. We refuse to invest mystery in nylon string bags, but, I argue, the loss is entirely ours.

References

Clifford, J. (1988), *The Predicament of Culture*, Cambridge and London: Harvard University Press.

Csikszentmihalyi, M. and Rochberg Halton, E. (1981), *The Meaning of Things*, Cambridge: Cambridge University Press.

Dominguez, V. (1986), 'The Marketing of Heritage', *American Ethnologist*, 13, 3, pp. 546–55.

Graburn, N. (ed.) (1976), *Ethnic and Tourist Arts: Cultural Expression from the Fourth World*, Berkeley and Los Angeles: University of California Press.

Hitchcock, M. (1983), 'Thesis Research and Collecting: A fieldworker's view', *Journal of the Anthropological Society of Oxford*, 14, 2.

Rivers, W.H.R. (1997), 'The Disappearance of Useful Arts', reproduced in R. Slobodin, *W.H.R. Rivers*, Stroud: Sutton Publishing.

Smith, B. (1985), *European Vision and the South Pacific*, New Haven and London: Yale University Press.

Stanley, N. (1994), 'Melanesian Artifacts as Cultural Markers: A micro-anthropological study', in H. Riggins (ed.), *The Socialness of Things: Essays on the Socio-Semiotics of Objects*, Berlin and New York: Mouton de Gruyter.

Stanley, N. (1997), 'Old Collections and New Connections: Innovations in the South Pacific', in K. Schofield (ed.), *Collections and Connections: Museums, Galleries and Education*, University of London: Institute of Education.

Tickle, L. (1987), '"Something Nothing"? Significant Meaning and Cultural Artefacts in the Solomon Islands and England', *Museum Ethnographers Newletter*, 21, pp. 20–21.

White, G. (1995), 'Remembering Guadalcanal: National identity and transnational memory-making', *Public Culture*, 7, pp. 529–55.

White, G. (1996), 'War Remains; The culture of preservation in the Southwest Pacific', *Cultural Resource Management*, 19, 3, pp. 52–6.

Woodford, C. (1894), 'Letter to Charles Read', British Museum [Ethnography Store] Q80 OC 340.

18 *Kente* Connections:[1] The Role of the Internet in Developing an Economic Base for Ghana

MARGARET GRIECO

Introduction: Electronic Culture, Craft Inventories and the Internet

Kente cloth is a traditional narrow loom weave produced in Ghana. Two main types of traditional *Kente* cloth are to be found: Akan *kente* and Ewe *kente*. Akan *kente* is produced by Ashantes and Fantes, primarily matrilineal cultures, and Ewe *kente* is produced by the Ewes, a patrilineal culture. There are great divergences between the social and economic organization of Akan and Ewe cultures and a similarly great divide in the design and symbolism contained within their cloths.

Historically, this audience would have required the help of a specialist to lead it through the design, symbolism and production techniques of *kente* cloth. In the present, no such assistance is needed. In this chapter, I want to call your attention to the opportunity which now exists to investigate Ghanaian culture interactively through the Internet and to the implications of this opportunity for the development of better fair trading practices in the production and sale of craft goods and 'souvenirs'.

The greater part of this chapter will take place when you return to your word processor and call up the following Internet addresses or URLs. There are six main addresses that will set each and every person on a path which will allow them not only to visit the cloths of Ghana, and to explore their history and their meaning but also to witness dance, hear drums, hear language, chose from a range of cultural artefacts and purchase them electronically.

- HasaGhana – an electronic shop for Ghanaian artefacts (http://www.igpnet.com/~zac/).
- The Ghana home page[2] - contains an electronic guide to *kente* cloth and other cultural artefacts (http://www.uta.fi/~csfraw/ghana.html).

246

- The Lakeview Museum of Arts and Sciences electronic exhibition of Ghanaian goldweights (http://www.fa.indiana.edu/conner/akan/shape.html).
- The Midwest Trade Group – an electronic shop of *kente* products for ceremonial occasions (http://www. webusers.anet-chi.com/~midwest).
- Chains – an interactive site of drum, dance and Ghanaian culture (http://www.cat.nyu.edu/chains).
- Davi Lojo home page – a cloth designer's site which provides the user with a guided path through own material and linked sites on Ghanaian cloth, its meaning and its production technology (http://members.aol.com/davilojo/dl.htm).

On the Internet Ghana and Ghanaians, with a little occasional help from some friends, have begun to live their culture through the new electronic form in which outsiders can participate. The diaspora of Ghanaians to the healthier economies of the West has produced the human resources acquainted with the power of the new technology and its new commercial forms. These people also have an active pride in their culture and display that pride in the patterns of cultural knowledge that they make available to us on the Internet.

The *kente* connection already exists: entrepreneurial Ghanaians have started marketing cultural goods through the Internet; leading educational institutions have placed previously specialist knowledge on Ghanaian culture and cultural production on open access web sites; US trading companies have already recognized the mass market for African design goods and have started to place their catalogues of goods on the Net; designers, dancers and musicians have all found the Net a useful tool to bring a wider audience to the appreciation of the forms they create. Art is no longer in the age of mechanical reproduction, it is now in an age of electronic interconnection. The relational patterns of culture can now be disseminated in a form which is cohesive and not fragmented: the boundaries of the book are outdated and the users of new electronic forms have opportunities to describe patterns of cultural relations in a global framework which could only previously have been achieved within an on-site, local framework.

The paradigm has moved: the academic register of its movement has been a little slow in coming. It is no surprise that the leading cultural and educational institutions are now making major use of the electronic forms in the academic exploration of Africa (institutions such as Wellesley College and the Lakeview Museum of Arts and Sciences in the United States) – they follow a path first carved by commercial catalogues of artefacts. But what does it mean for the villagers of rural Africa, the home of the craft culture which is now being so widely disseminated?

Can the Internet assist in ensuring the revenue from artefact, craft and souvenir production returns to Africa and assists in the process of local economic development? We believe it can. What follows charts some of the organizational changes that need to be made in both the social and business environment to enable Africa to display its vibrancy and capture the benefits of that vibrancy in its income levels.

Community Connections, Community Enterprise: A Direction for Development

The leader in the field of electronic marketing and purchasing is HasaGhana (http://www.ipgnet.com/~zac/) which has a high quality catalogue of cultural artefacts on electronic display and has organized its distribution of goods to be serviced from Canada, thus breaking the power hold of the bottlenecks found conventionally at African ports. HasaGhana export their goods to a warehouse in Canada, hold their stock in that location and service the on-line visa card sales from that address. This provides the individual customer with a high level of reliability – the company can guarantee the delivery of goods within a certain window, an impossibility if goods were going directly from Africa to the customer, given the level of corruption at the ports.

Communities wishing to sell their goods without making use of a middle agency would in the present in all probability have to develop a similar structure in order to provide customers with reliability and to grow their market for craft goods. Ghanaian local communities could partner with a development aid agency or a reliable business enterprise on the warehouse storage and dispatchment of goods and even on the electronic display and electronic sale of goods. Through the new technology communities can take a very active part in shaping the catalogues of what they want to sell.

The Internet not only provides communities with the ability to catalogue their traditional crafts and artefacts in a way that will enable the market for these goods to grow, but it also allows communities to have sight of what other uses other locations make of their traditional fabrics and local materials. It provides the opportunity for a vision of an alternative to the traditional arrangements surrounding production. For example, it can open doors to the knowledge that in many locations weaving is woman's and not man's business and thus provide for changes in the social organization of production which help alleviate poverty.

It can provide a vision of trading opportunities open to a village or region which are not self evident within the locality itself. For example, *kente* cloth itself could be harnessed to high quality, high revenue furniture design instead of being converted into small item tourist goods. The Net can allow villagers in location to view the uses to which other communities put their traditional products in the bid for increased revenue. The virtual catalogue not only enables design products to be displayed out to the external world but it also enables design enhancements and alternative uses to be displayed in.

The Net can enable remote villages to find business partners in other locations closer to the final markets for the goods, and permits of a new division of labour and equally importantly a new division of the spoils. Remote villages can produce the fine craft goods which have high value especially when incorporated as a design feature into high value items. Crafting customized designs to meet the needs of wealthy but distant customers is now a possibility: the desired designs can be transmitted electronically (an arrangement which has long held in Western carpet design and the Italian knitwear industry). The technology can coordinate the market for customized goods at low administrative costs and in a way not previously possible: a client seeking a special design would have had to make a physical journey or hired the services of an agent to commission and procure the design for her or him. If customized craft production on a spot market sounds an implausible arrangement between Africa and its overseas market then we should focus our attention on the Mid West Trade Group which is involved in the commissioning of high quality, customized woven goods from Africa on just such a base.

The goods sold in America by Mid West Trade Group are produced in Africa and represent an 'authentic' symbol of African-ness as compared with the mass produced, printed imitation *kente* fabric produced in Pakistan, Hong Kong and Bangladesh. Interestingly this printed *kente* cloth also finds a market in low income Ghana.

The Mid West Trade Group, as with HasaGhana, is growing the market for authentic African products. Their use of electronic catalogues has much the same educative quality as electronic museum exhibitions, with the difference that the browser can purchase the goods. In the case of HasaGhana, the company makes a percentage donation of sales to a children's charity in the struggle to alleviate Africa's poverty. In the case of the Mid West Trade Group there is no such donation system apparent in the information presented on the web site.

The production and use of African goods is not sufficient to ensure a growth in African community level resources – the price which African craftsmen receive for themselves in proportion to the total value the work sells for is clearly significant if craft production is to represent a source of major economic improvement.

The two commercial web sites we have described are not community businesses, but community businesses could adopt the same techniques as these two sites and thrive. And even if community businesses do not set up independently of companies such as HasaGhana and the Mid West Trade Group, they can obtain the information on the final retail prices of goods through web access whether this is directly or indirectly through a development worker or some other professional or technology literate person.

Once again, in case this seems fanciful, it should be noted that there are a number of community web sites set up to serve rural Ghana (Brong Ahafo, Wa, Navrongo) where such market information can be obtained. The transparency of trading through the new technology will over time permit craftsmen and -women to make better bargains – especially where authenticity is highly valued for ethno-symbolic reasons. And such a concern with authenticity is likely to retain its importance for a sizeable section of the Afro-American market.

The transparency of the technology does not only permit craft persons to check out the rate they will receive against what is paid for goods on the external market, but it will also permit Ghanaian community business to monitor the performance and trustworthiness of their external business partners. The Internet not only enables Americans to be local in Africa, it also enables Africans to be local in America. African community businesses could through new technology check the level of orders, the value of payments and the stock remaining in partners' warehouses through electronic administrative and stock control processes. A tradition of trust is now replaceable by the innovation of transparency and this increases the range of trading partners open to African community business. Long distance supervision of profits and sales is now more than possible – it is already a practice in a host of commercial arenas. And it clearly began to happen in the arena of cultural production and within the framework of authenticity.

In this section we have talked to the issues of community connections between cultural production and commercial reward and raised the issue of measures that Ghanaian cloth producers, and other craft producers, can use to develop the structure of community enterprise more fully.

Maintaining Skills, Locating the Craft Tradition

So far we have talked about the role of the Internet in the display, sale and revenue monitoring of cultural products. We have indicated the Internet is also involved in disseminating knowledge about the symbolic meaning of such products, an activity which helps grow the market for the products. We have seen that prestige cultural exhibitions with their electronic catalogue also help in the growing of the market – the electronic cultural catalogues and the commercial craft catalogue share a form which is from many perspectives indistinguishable. But there are yet other levels of authenticity and cultural organization embedded in the activities of the Net.

The Davi Lojo web site devoted primarily to the skills of Ewe *kente* weaving contains instructional material on how to build a narrow loom and weave. It is material designed for the activities of the American school room and not for the African education system. Similarly the Lojo site contains information on how to make contact with authentic African weavers who can visit and provide demonstrations in the American school house not the African school room. The issue of how these crafts can be integrated into the African educational experience has been much neglected leaving us with the irony or paradox that the crafts of Africa receive greater educational acceptance overseas.

Of course such programmes fit with the American market for African authenticity but the bottom line is that Africa has been encouraged to adopt inappropriate education traditions in imitation of the West which is presently beginning to imitate through the new learning technology the techniques of traditional Africa. Escher's hand drawing a hand is the image that comes to mind meanwhile the elders of African society have been displaced from their traditional roles of educating the younger generations and their craft skills begin to be lost in Africa itself.

A Vibrant Culture, a Tale to Sell: Symbolic Life as Economic Good

The moral and practical issues are many in the tale we have tried to sell. And not all can be resolved here. Indeed, African communities and enterprises trading in African goods have a deal of bargaining to do. But the market is not simply for the objects, it is for the tale which is embedded in them. The symbols tell the tale, their market is one of the fabric of existence, symbols woven on the small frame of life and stitched to shape and signal the vibrancy of community. The *kente* connection is a good that can build an economic base transformed by a technology of communication from local meaning into international authenticity.

Notes

1   *Kente* is an Asante ceremonial cloth handwoven on a horizontal treadle loom. Strips measuring about four inches wide are sewn together into larger pieces of cloth. Cloths come in various colours and designs and are worn during very important social and religious occasions' (http://www.erols.com/kemet/*kente*.htm). *Kente* cloth is also produced by the Ewe weavers of the Volta region in Ghana. 'In a society traditionally without a written language, West African cloths tell a lot about the moral values and history of a people' (http://members.aol.com/davilojo/dl.htm). The cloth of the Asante has been widely adopted by the Afro-American community in the United States as a symbol of African-ness.

2   The Ghana home page, which contains a wealth of cultural information and linkages to other sites, was put together by a Ghanaian living in Finland.

19 Dalecarlian Masques: One Souvenir's Many Voices

MONICA HANEFORS AND TOM SELWYN

Prelude

Little do the tourists who pass the souvenir shops in Stockholm Arlanda Airport realize what a rich extramural life the rows of Dalecarlian horses (arguably the best known of all Swedish souvenirs) have when the last plane has taken off and the lights go down at night. Then it is as if two ghostly figures – a Swedish Drosselmayer and little Clara, the old man and the young girl of the *Nutcracker* – emerge from the shadows – and set in motion a 'night performance' – a sort of fantastic masked ball to which, in their dreams, all the people of Sweden are nightly invited to take part. The masque revolves around the Dala horses assuming varieties of different forms – wearing all manner of different masks. It soon becomes apparent that the horses are really bearers of the thoughts, projections, and arguments of the dreaming human participants and that the ball is really a huge debate between Swedes – about the nature of their identity, their relations with others, their politics and economics. The issues addressed in the debate are both, at different levels, topical and also enduring, and we can be certain that it is an event to be staged nightly into the foreseeable future.

Introduction

The overall purpose of this chapter is to track the career of the Dalecarlian Horse, whose shape and provenance we will describe shortly, in the Swedish media over a period of about six years from 1990–96. The aim is to show how this one souvenir is no simple memento (if such ever exists anywhere) but is an object which, in its taking on of multiple identities and meanings, serves the people of Sweden as a point of reference around which the issues of the day may be discussed. The present chapter follows a previous one on the

Horse (Hanefors and Selwyn, 1992) in which we described its background and how it came to occupy its present position as an emblem of Sweden. For the sake of clarity, a little of that background needs recalling here before we commence on the main body of the present chapter: 'part two' of our story.

In the forests of eighteenth century central Swedish province of Dalecarlia, modern Dalarna, horses were important assets to the smallholders of the region who customarily mixed farming and fishing with forestry. Used as means of transportation, they also brought status to their owners.

Carved wooden horses have, since that time, been produced domestically as family mementoes – originally by woodcutters from four villages in the region, notably in the village of Nusnäs. Apart from being exchanged between family members, the horses were also sold as toys at local fairs in Sweden. Occasionally they were taken by traders, as gifts and mementoes, as far afield as Russia.

The process of the wooden horse's transformation from an item of local folk art to a national and international iconic souvenir began in the 1920s when two unemployed brothers, the Olssons of Nusnäs, began to produce 20 horses a day in their grandmother's kitchen for sale to a local shop. For two decades this small scale commercial operation remained a local one and the horse retained its close association in people's minds with the region of Dalecarlia. In 1939, however, it appeared in giant form at the World Fair in New York. From then on it began to emerge as a symbol for Sweden as whole and assumed the status of a popular souvenir sold throughout Scandinavia and beyond (Figure 19.1). Nowadays it is no longer produced exclusively, or even mainly, in Nusnäs or other Dalarna villages. Horses are mass-produced in factories, normally in an organge colour, in Sweden and elsewhere, including China (see e.g. Dalademokraten, 1998), for mass consumption in airports and souvenir shops.

The Icon and its Masks

Within Sweden itself the Dala Horse has become a sign with many significations. It is with the identification of these, together with the thematic threads which connect them, that we are concerned with in this paper. The exercise will reveal the issues framing the debate taking place at our masked ball. To this end we will first describe 19 published appearances of the Horse in Sweden over a six year period.

Figure 19.1   Dalecarlian horses

The Horse and the Lion

In the early 1990s a glossy leaflet made an appearance in Swedish banks and other financial institutions, the front cover of which consisted of a Dala horse painted in white and blue stripes (Figure 19.2). Superimposed on the horse was another image, that of a lion.

The lion image appears in various places in Sweden. Woven into the flag of the Swedish National Bank, for example, are two lions facing each other. Stone lions, rather in the manner of those which sit in Trafalgar Square, guard Göteborg harbour (i.e. on the west coast, second biggest town in Sweden, most important export harbour). Lion images take various forms, some fierce, some more benign. The lion superimposed on the Dala Horse of our glossy leaflet, however, was one of the most dragon-like varieties – a furious version, one might say. Thus adorned, the leaflet, slightly cryptically, but in the style of financial promotional literature generally, proclaimed 'Swedish Bonds Get You Better Revenue in Luxembourg'.

Earrings

In April 1991 an edition of *EX Magazine*, distributed in airports, ran an article, with photographs about two Swedish jewellery designers, Hanna Holtblad and Thomas Sandell, both of whom had made use of the Dala Horse. The former had used the Horse as an earring for young women while the latter, a furniture designer, had decorated 1,200 cupboards with images of the Horse.

Holtblad explained that the rationale behind her earring motif in the following terms:

> On the dance floors of Stockholm's smart clubs it is fashionable for girls wearing black body stockings and liberal amounts of make up to shake to the rhythm of the music, the rattling and jangling necklaces and bracelets of small colourful wooden horses attached to silver beads accompanying them as they do so.

Sandall followed this line of thought by wondering why '… if Swedish hip hoppers can wear African badges around their necks, why cannot other people wear Dala Horses around theirs?'.

He had designed his cupboards, he explained, fired by this thought and the *EX* article pointed out that Sandell's cupboard was the Swedish design object of the year.

When asked by *EX* to comment on these two designs, the Principal of Stockholm's most prestigious school of design commented thus:

Figure 19.2   A Dala horse painted in white and blue stripes

The generation that grew up in the sixties is rediscovering Swedish traditions. When they were young – our generation – they turned their backs on crafts and national costumes. Now their children travel around the world – this is the most globetrotting Swedish generation ever – and when they come back, tired of the ever new impressions they are subject to on their travels, they find themselves looking for things that are typically Swedish. In such moments they no longer find it unfashionable, or awkward, to dwell in the uniqueness of being Swedish.

The Fascist

This concern with the shaping of identity within the twin forces of global cosmopolitanism and Swedish nationalism found a powerful and disturbing echo in an exhibition on utopias put on by 15 students of the Art University of Konsthögskolan in the spring of 1992. Perhaps not surprisingly, since minority Swedish racists, with their shaved heads and army boots, now are accompanied by academics distributing statistics and analyses of the way new organizations and political parties are started.

A review article (*DN*, 22 May 1992) entitled 'Who Manages the Ideals?' drew attention to the inevitable gap between utopian ideas and their pragmatic outcomes. The text reminds readers of the flowering in the 1960s of utopian ideas about the provision of public housing. But now, when these ideas are measured against the black and white photographs of some contemporary housing estates, they seem adrift from any recognizably real world and its essentially mundane economic and political processes.

One of the underlying purposes of this discussion about the relative merits of idealism and realism became clear when placed beside the central image of the piece – a photograph of one of the exhibits (Figure 19.3). This consists of a young blond-haired man gazing into the future against the background of the Dala Horse. The young man, hair streaming in the breeze, is strikingly reminiscent of German romantic portrayals in the 1930s of young 'Aryan' men and women. Here is a youth, with his horse companion, looking into an idealized past/future. The youth reminds us of one of the determining features of fascist art, namely the capacity symbolically to merge past and future within a cognitive landscape from which the present has been expunged. Here, after all, is an imagined past – at once pastoral, deeply local and fundamentally nationalistic – peopled by characters such as woodcutters returning to their families happily carving horses for their wives and children as they do so. It is an image brimming with utopian promises for the future which feeds off an idealized past and necessarily stirs uneasiness about the imperfect present.

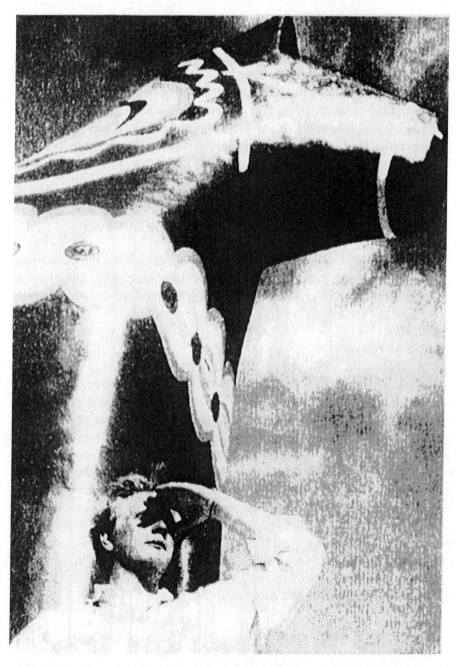

**Figure 19.3   Exhibit from the Art University of Konsthögskolan
exhibition on utopias, 1992**

The Festive Philippino

In the light of the above the next appearance of the horse (Figure 19.4) might, at the time, have appeared surprising.

'Come and celebrate the Philippine Festival of Fashion in August 1992' announced the brochure promoting the event in Sweden in the early part of that year. Under this opening line there was a picture and further text. The picture consisted of a horse printed in a similar way to a Dala horse, surrounded by arrestingly exotic palm trees. The text explained that

> ... it started out as a toy for children ... that soon turned into a show case of artistry: today these hand painted papier mache horses from Paete are much sort after by tourists and locals alike for use as decor.

From a Swedish point of view the resemblances between the Dala Horse and Paete Horse were striking. Not only were the colours of the latter similar to those customarily associated with the former, but the myths were also similar in both cases.[1]

The Seated Horse

In September 1992 an article appeared in the Swedish newspaper, *Expressen*, commenting on an image of a seated Dala Horse which had been produced in the Swedish area of Minneapolis by a former Dalarna resident, then resident in the USA. On her return from America to Sweden, Maud Waters started to produce her 'invention' – the seated horse (Figure 19.5) – for export back to the USA. The *Expressen* article started with the observation that the horse had been on its legs for over a century and now had earned the right to sit down. But the article went on to report that the activities of Maud Waters had been criticized by people living in Dalarna. The basis of this was that for the horse to *sit down* was a potent symbol of Swedish subservience in contemporary world affairs, not only in relation to the USA but also to other political and economic forces and processes. In this vein, the seated horse came to be known as *The EU Horse*.

Kings, Councillors and Capitalists[2]

The World Fair of 1992 was held in the Spanish city of Seville. The symbolism of Seville was rooted in its historical, post-Columbian, role as the centre of

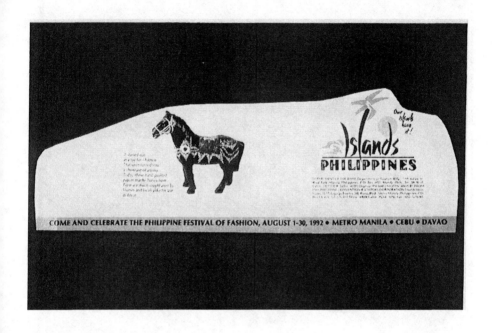

Figure 19.4   The Paete Horse

Figure 19.5   The seated horse

trade between the old and new worlds. After Paris and Naples, Seville was the third largest city in late sixteenth/early seventeenth century and it was to Seville that the South American gold and silver was shipped, giving the city a unique place in the story of the development of capitalism.

World Fairs are, on the face of it, flamboyant events held to glorify nations, rather than serve explicitly commercial functions. Nevertheless, as Hobsbawm (1975) has argued, they have always fundamentally been celebrations of capitalism. In this light they serve legitimating functions – clothing global capitalism with the trappings and decorations of state functionaries, as it were. They are places where royalty, parties of government ministers, managing directors of great national companies, appear all decked out with flags and national fineries. And yes (of course), in the particular case of the Seville World Fair our horse was there (Figure 19.6), splendidly attired, surrounded by Swedish dignitaries (reported in *mtc KONTAKTEN*, 1992/93).

Stuffed Swedes

In the 15 January edition of *Dagens Nyheter* (1993) there appeared a review article of a satirical exhibition on 'Swedishness' by Peter Johansson. Johansson, a native of Dalarna, had assembled models and images which were popularly thought to be 'typically Swedish'. Each of these had then been transformed and represented in such a way that the exhibition became a biting commentary on the state of contemporary Swedishness.

The exhibition was divided into several sections, each marked by an English title. There was 'Red Delicious', 'How to Cook a Souvenir', 'The Souvenir Shop', 'Cultural Occupation' and 'Swedish Attitude'. The review observed how strange it was that so much of what Swedes considered typically 'Swedish' actually came from Dalarna. These included Ekstroms blueberry soup, the Vasaloppet,[3] red Dala Horses, folk dancing, fiddle playing and Falu sausages ... and how ironic it was that the sections of Johansson's exhibition were all in English. Could it be, the reviewer wondered, that contemporary 'Swedishness' was to be found in objects primarily directed at the tourist trade?

The flavour of the exhibition can be savoured by reference to several of the more salient exhibits. In 'How to Cook a Souvenir', for example, there was the Dala Horse, all sliced up and wrapped in aluminium foil, placed side by side with Falu sausages, in the refrigerator, waiting to be consumed. Exhibition patrons could purchase toilet paper inscribed with pictures of the Dala Horse on each leaf, as well as knitted packs of Falu sausages. In the

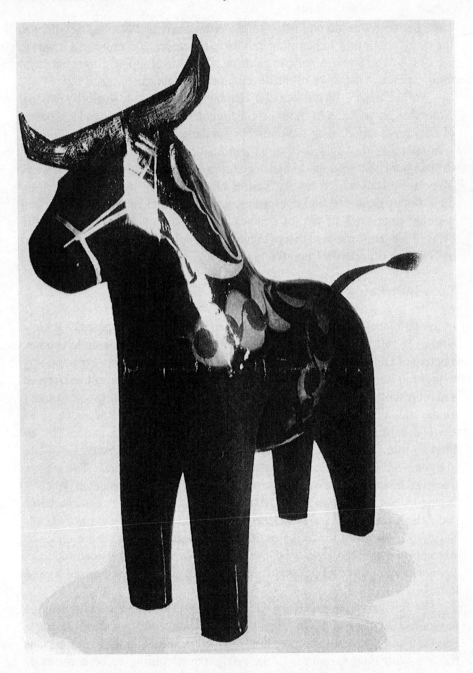

Figure 19.6   The Seville World Fair

'Swedish Attitude' section there was a picture which the reviewer selected as being a particularly brilliant metaphor for the innate provincialism, conservatism and private self-sufficiency of many Swedish people. The picture was of a traditional church pew overflowing with orange stuffed plastic pillows each labelled 'souvenir' (Figure 19.7). Several of the pillows spilled out of one of the openings into the church.

Atlantic Dalarna

On the 14 February 1993 there appeared an article in *Expressen* about the twenty-first anniversary of a 'Vasaloppet Festival' in Mora, USA. The moving spirit behind this festival called himself 'King Gustav', a 63 year-old American with roots in Dalarna who expressed pride in his ancestry in that region and who was well known for taking Swedish snuff. The week-long festival consists of a 'family friendly' party for ex-patriot Swedes (most of whom do not come from Dalarna) and, in the opinion of the article's writer, had more charm than the Swedish version of the Vasaloppet itself. The picture accompanying the article shows 'King Gustav' and Dala horses at the start of the ski race.

The Small and Dynamic Entrepreneur

Clearly sensitive to the feelings about the seated horse and its association in the popular imagination with the EU – with the perceived subordination of Sweden to international forces and processes – the Swedish government came up with a riposte which attempted to play, as it were, a symbolic trump: 'Swedish People Say Yes to the EU: We Have Become Part of the EU' trumpeted a government leaflet explaining the benefits of membership. The leaflet explained that while Sweden paid an annual subscription to the EU of 20 million Kronor, it received much of that money back through the Area 4 Programme. This programme was devoted to the encouragement of small and medium-sized enterprises in Area 4 of the EU – an area defined by the Commission by economic rather than geographical criteria – and the purpose of the leaflet was to explain how its readers might successfully tap these resources. Against a background of global economic uncertainty and change it was suggested that the future for a region such as Dalarna lay in SMEs.

> Everything Goes So Quickly Nowadays … The Future of Dalarna Lies With Small Companies. So:

Figure 19.7   A traditional church pew overflowing with orange stuffed plastic pillows

GET YOURSELF NEW HORSE POWER

exhorted the authors of the leaflet. Standing guard over this energizing text stood our Dala Horse (Figure 19.8), this time with the rings of the EU superimposed on its body. Two sets of images placed in interior pages of the leaflet helped shape readers' interpretations of the horse's signification in this context. The first of these consisted of two photographs opposite each other – an ancient model of a Swedish telephone on one side, a new German BMW car on the other. The second set consisted of a photograph from the 1930s of a factory in the town of Borlänge in Dalarna , with rows of female workers, opposite a recent photograph of a seven year old girl (clearly meant as the symbolic progeny of the factory workers) in front of a computer screen – an essential element of any SME.

The Subsidized Horse

On the 23 May 1993 *Expressen* carried an article using the Horse and its manufacture as a metaphor for the dilemmas of a social democratic government, with Keynesian predilections, in an age of global free trade.

> In the 1980s the government of North (an imaginary country) had a government which subsidised the production of Dala Horses to the tune of many millions of Kronor. The government also regulated the economy to make it difficult for foreign investors to operate effectively. Everyone was happy, everyone – even those not directly employed in Dala Horse production – was employed, no-one took the warnings about impending inflation and economic overheating seriously. But there followed a period of economic slump. Factories were closed, unemployment rose, Dala Horses were no longer in demand, the population protested loudly. Belatedly (according to those hurt by the downturn) politicians got the message and began to pour millions into the Horse industry once again. 'You repair your Dala Horses and we will lower your taxes' ran a government slogan. But this time the employers did not play along and responded by closing the factories and locking their workers out, asking sarcastically how many more tax billions were being prepared to pour into the economy.

The article concluded with describing how the Minister of the Economy was left scratching his head, puzzled at the fact that the industry of North seemed so ungrateful and that it seemed to be cutting the ground from under its feet.

Figure 19.8   Dala Horse with the rings of the EU superimposed on its body

Puppet Sweden

On the 6 September *Expressen* (1993) carried an article by a journalist reflecting on the fact that he had purchased a Dala Horse in Stockholm Old Town – and that the horse had turned out to have been made in Southeast Asia. This led him to reflect on a state of affairs in which the company which baked *wasa* bread was German, that the *JAS* airplane is in fact a good deal less Swedish than a McDonald's hamburger, that *Volvo* was shortly to be manufactured in France under the aegis of the *Renault* car company. While the myths of the great Swedish entrepreneurs such as John Ericsson (of ship propellers), Alfred Nobel (of dynamite), Gustaf Dalén and his lighthouses, Gustaf de Laval with his Separator and the Rausing Brothers (inventors and manufacturers of the tetrapack[4]) hovered around, real economic power was inexorably being leeched out of Sweden towards Paris, Hamburg and the other capitals of the global economy. All that was left seemed to be permutations of Björn Borg, smörgåsbord and schnapps, together with other items of the small change of international leisure, tourism and consumption.

Sweden as Denmark

This sense of the draining of Swedish industrial potency was taken up with a vengeance in an article in *Dagens Nyheter* on the 3 July 1994. Here a writer from Skåne (the Swedish province in the far south of the country which possesses its own flag – a cross between the Danish red and white and Swedish blue and yellow – and whose population feels historically closer to Denmark than Sweden) extolled the virtues of Danes. The author argued that not only were Danes quite simply *nicer* than Swedes, but that Danish birds sang more sweetly than they did in Sweden. For many reasons, not least in their bicycling abilities, Danes were more civilized and continental than Swedes. The accompanying picture (Figure 19.9) consisted of two small piggy banks in the shape of letter boxes and a horse with an exactly similar shape to the Dala Horse but with the white Danish cross emblazoned on its flanks – just like the Danish flag. Furthermore, tourist experience in Denmark can testify that together with this Danish Horse there goes a legend about the old days in the Danish countryside where farmers used to carve horse mementoes for their families.

Tourist experience also tells of American tourists purchasing Danish wooden horses from their hotels in Copenhagen, associating them with

Figure 19.9   Danish Horse

'Scandinavia' rather in the same way that some maps made available by selected American airlines place Copenhagen in Sweden.

The Horse as Alligator

Svenska Dagbladet (25 July 1995) published a short review of an exhibition by the artist Ylva Ekman of her *Rinkeby* horses. These consisted of dinosaurs, alligators, and all manner of others (Figure 19.10) painted in the same style as the traditional Dala Horse, although that horse itself did not figure in the exhibition. For Ekman these horses stood as metaphors for the multicultural population of contemporary Stockholm. The point was, she said, that although people were not shaped as they were before, they were still Swedish. But, unlike the handmade, hand-painted, traditional Dala Horses, Ekman's horses were actually mass-produced children's toys made of plastic – although she had named and hand painted each herself.

The Easy Rider of Hedemora

In the winter brochures of 1995/1996 of summer holidays in Sweden there appeared one directed to Swedish-speaking tourists in search of pastoral relaxation in Sweden itself. Contained within the brochure were the usual compliment of holiday images – trees and lakes, a pretty girl or two, happy milling holidaymakers, a village market, a summer sunset, and so on. On the cover, however, there was a striking, dashing and familiar figure – the Dala Horse in the shape of a motorcycle with rider (Figure 19.11). Hedemora village itself, here shown as the centre of the region into which tourists were being invited by the brochure, is famous in Sweden for holding an annual motor bicycle rally. The Hedemora authorities, sophisticated marketeers as they clearly were that year, aimed to use this notoriety to attract a wide range of holidaymakers. If the rally itself suggested a niche market, the appearance of the Horse proclaimed Hedemora as a suitable and lively destination for holidaymakers of all ages and dispositions.

The Horse as Kangaroo

The 11 February edition of *Dagens Nyheter* (1996) carried further commentary on the Ekman exhibition of *Rinkeby* horses. The author pointed out that Ekman's idea was not a new one. There had been, she observed, a T-shirt worn at the 1986 World Cup in Australia which had on it a kangaroo painted

**Figure 19.10 Dinosaurs, alligators, and others painted in the style of
the traditional Dala Horse**

Figure 19.11 The Dala Horse in the shape of a motorcycle with rider

in exactly the same way as the Dala Horse (Figure 19.12). She goes on to reflect that perhaps the Horse has given way, globally, to an image which has become a universal, commonplace and anonymous icon appearing in different shapes as different animate and/or inanimate species. 'Are all horses *Rinkeby* horses now', she asks half rhetorically.

Copies and Copyists

Interest in the *Rinkeby* horses continued to grow and cause controversy. There was a report in the 16 February 1996 edition of *Borlänge Tidning* of the 'Dalarna Uprising' in which the province's governor, Gunnar Björk, led a verbal revolt against the *Rinkeby* horses and the ideas associated with them by their artist creator. The revolt was built on several different but interlinked grounds. First of all, the governor argued that Ekman could not claim the *Rinkeby* horses were her own idea since they were patently just copies (although appearing in different form) of the Dala Horses. She was, he complained, a plagiarist. Secondly, it was in exceedingly bad taste for the artist to take mass produced toys and confuse them with genuine folk art – with all its special history of the countryside, the huge forests, woodcutters, and so on. Thirdly, when Ekman argued that she was neither plagiarist nor disrespectful of Dalarna history – after all, not only had she *not* included a horse in her collection but her 'horses' were metaphors for people who had come to Sweden from abroad (and who thus had nothing to do with Dalarna history) – manufacturers of the Horse in Nusnäs retorted that, in fact, the Nusnäs factories had long produced painted chickens, elephants and pigs as well as horses. She was, the charge went, indeed a copyist.

By now, the article explained, matters had become even more confused. Shortly after the appearance of the *Rinkeby* horses a petrol company approached one of the Nusnäs factories and asked them to produce a giraffe – to be painted in the *Kirbitz* fashion (i.e. the traditional Dala Horse style). No sooner had the factory responded to this order and the giraffe become the company logo/mascot than Ylva Ekman complained that *she* had become the victim of plagiarism, the idea of the giraffe being rightfully hers.

The Ambassador

In Figure 19.13 the Horse appears as medieval knight gladiator riding into South America bearing ideas, values and associations from Sweden – 'that mysterious northern country which is now part of the EU'. In this disguise

Figure 19.12 Kangaroo painted in the same way as the Dala Horse

Figure 19.13 The Horse as medieval knight gladiator

our horse was the invention of a South American author, writing on the 3 June 1996 in *Svenska Dagbladet*. Writing of the need for the horse as the blue and white liveried ambassador for Sweden in South America, she reported that Swedish books were now being translated from Swedish into Spanish and that Swedish culture was becoming more accessible to Spanish speakers as a result.

Captors and Captives

On the 4 June 1996 there was a report, again in *Svenska Dagbladet*, of an exhibition mounted by French and half-French pupils at Stockholm's French school. The task set them was to design an exhibition entitled 'Horses in Freedom' in which they interpreted the Swedish Dala Horse tradition. Once more Horses appeared in various transformations. There was, for example, a bird, an angel whose body had been pierced by nails, and a horse enclosed by fences (Figure 19.14).

The Trojan Horse: Enemies Within?

The final image (Figure 19.15) is of our Dala Horse as a Trojan Horse inside the gates of Stockholm, pictured in *Dagens Nyheter* of the 28 August 1996. This is an article reviewing an exhibition by Jörgen Platzer on horses and bridges. Both, he is reported as saying, are carriers. The Trojan Horse, he reminded readers, carried the enemies of Troy into the heart of the capital. Could the modern Dala Horse in some of its manifestations also turn out to be a Trojan Horse? Whether as carrier of *Rinkeby*, European financiers, or both is left to the imagination of the reader.

Debates and Disguises

What are we to make of all these disguises? What are the terms of the debate they engender?

One way of approaching an answer is to pick out a set of propositions and counter-propositions which seem to inhere in the string of different appearances of our Horse as we have described them. It is a method having the advantage of following normal debating procedures. Furthermore, as with the best debates, the danger of simplification, which is sometimes encountered when working with binary distinctions, will be overcome in both the flow and texture

**Figure 19.14 Dala Horse as a bird, an angel whose body had been
pierced by nails, and enclosed by fences**

Figure 19.15 Dala Horse as a Trojan Horse inside the gates of Stockholm

of the argument and this develops and becomes more nuanced.

There is clearly a preoccupation, apparent in several of its disguises, with the Horse as a symbol of either strength or weakness. Thus, for example, in its manifestation as Guardian of the National Bank or its appearance in the World Fair in Seville it embodies power and confidence. By contrast, people interpreted the horse in its seated form as a metaphor for weakness and the decline of Swedish influence in the world.

We should notice that the Horse's strength and weakness is related to questions of national pride. In its emergence from the land and work of central Sweden, it appears as the source of national pride – a representation of all that is solid, real and dependable. On the other hand, what is suggested by its seated form – or (even worse) by its form as slices of meat in a refrigerator – suggest not pride but national humiliation in the face of exterior forces. In these contexts these appear to be a combination of the EU and/or the tourist industry.

Anxiety about the capacity of Sweden to retain its own strength and independence in the face of the international forces which seem to threaten both pervades most, if not all, the Horse's manifestations. Thus, when a journalist discovered the Southeast Asian provenance of a Dala Horse purchased in Stockholm Old Town, he used it to demonstrate some sad and uncomfortable facts. These included the Swedish loss of Volvo to Renault, about the (ignoble) transition from being a country widely associated with great engineering and technological projects to one which is best known, if known at all, for its schnapps and smörgåsbord. Furthermore, in this particular article, there is surely a further sub-text. This concerns whether or not the old centre of the capital city itself retains any credibility as the heart of Sweden or whether, like other places and objects, it has simply become an urban decoration – a splendid folly – to provide a backdrop for the undiscriminating eyes and sensibilities of tourists. McDonalds, the Old City, mass produced Southeast Asian Dala Horses – all are good fun, all stimulating, none greatly different from each other. It is, after all, only the appearance that counts.

In this context the debate concerns two ideas. The first is of Sweden as an independent country, holding its own in the world and legitimated by its royal family, its inventions, and its self-sufficiency. This is what was on display at the World Fair. The second is the idea of the people and products of Sweden as increasingly subject to, and dependent upon, international political and economic forces. One dimension of this debate has to do specifically with ideas and values. 'What', the different costumes of our Horse seem to ask, 'should Swedish people really care about? What should they really value?'.

Here, like elsewhere, the answer is not a simple one. Indeed, in the asking of the question and the thinking about possible answers to it, the symbolic complexity of the part played by the Horse becomes apparent – for it represents (according to the disguise of the moment) a wide spectrum of values.

At one end of the spectrum stands the fascist horse with it's connotations of the necessary links between blond features, visionary eyes, work on the land, merry workers and their families – an essential (and, implicitly, endangered) Sweden. At the other end, however, cluster the *Rinkeby* horses: immigrants of all shapes, sizes and colours without – precisely – any link to the soil of Sweden. The facts that these *Rinkeby* horses can be so different both from one another and from the 'real' Dala Horse, and that they can be 'mass-produced' – and yet *still* be Swedish, and honourably so, makes a powerful counter-proposition to the doom laden certainties of fascism and overbearing nationalism.

In amongst and underlying these arguments is another. This concerns the extent to which 'the economy' has come to dominate and determine ideas and values which, in some more distant and imagined past, were rooted in the social relations of villages, woods and 'real' geographical locations. This particular argument sheds light on the nature of souvenirs more generally. They have a Janus-faced character. On the one hand they stand for 'the old days', the authentic – when families were families, when people were measured by the quality of their social personae, when a person's value was calculated accorded to the success or failure with which they fulfilled their social obligations, and so on. On the other hand, souvenirs are quintessentially, part of the flotsam and jetsam of the market place. In this sense they tease us with their irony and ambiguity.

One of questions raised by the subsidizing in the 1980s of the Dala Horse production concerned the extent to which the Swedish people, through the agency of the Swedish state, could control their own economy. The saliency of this question derived from a global economic context in which the power to control domestic economies appears increasingly to have been lost. The Swedish economy of the time was viewed from further West in Europe undergoing at that time the rigours of Thatcherism or it's continental equivalent, as being a beacon of enlightened social democracy and Keynesian economics. Sweden's own politicians, as we know from the newspaper article about the country called *North*, believed in economic interventionism too. Indeed the general sense of well-being amongst the population of Sweden at the time of that article must have provoked some of the British visitors passing through Arlanda to fill their cases to the brim with Dala Horses to remind them that even the bitterest winters come to an end. How truly chilling in the early 1990s it must have seemed, therefore, when the factory owners locked the Dala Horse factory workers out and the Swedish people were faced with the nightmare that globalization had arrived to stay – and that there was little they could do about it.

The coming of globalization, as several disguises (the Philippine and Danish Horses, the cast of *Rinkeby* horses, the Horse as kangaroo, for example) indicated, raised many kinds of interrelated questions about national identity. What does globalization do to countries, their myths, legends, and the identities of their populations? Does 'Sweden' become 'Denmark' (and vice versa) if willed that way by American tourists? Does a Swede in Australia become Australian? Are Philippine ritual artefacts as transient as the Dala Horse itself seems to be? How can a Gambian or Columbian immigrant become Swedish? And so on.

Such reflections inevitably lead on to the Trojan Horse and its connotations. Who are the enemies? Global financiers or the immigrants their operations sweep over the national drawbridge into the heart of the citadel? And such thoughts as *these* lead backwards (and forwards) to the young blond man and his hair blowing in the wind.

In the end there is a theme which effectively links each of the disguises to each other. This has to do with the contradictions inherent in the contemporary global political economy. On the one hand global capitalism works across frontiers, paying scant respect to national sovereignties or sensibilities. On the other (or so the story goes) the world's political system is built upon nations and principles of national self-determination. The schoolchildren with French connections, who expressed their feelings of being hemmed in by a symbol of a nation, are children of a world (for them) with few visa restrictions. Most of them may be destined to become global nomads in one way or another. At the other end of the labour market spectrum, immigrant workers arriving in Sweden are faced with many passport restrictions. But the fact that the world's economy increasingly demands mobility of labour just as it does of capital necessarily making them nomadic too. In such a world, asks our Dala Horse, in different ways and in different guises, what happens to our sense of place? Despite the presence of the souvenir shops (providers of nostalgic memories of place) is the overall message which emerges from the symbolic landscape of airports correct in seeming to assert that we all now endlessly on the move from one non-place, to use Auge's (1995) evocative expression, to another?

Notes

1 The similarity of the two horses calls to mind Hitchcock's (1998, p. 132) reporting of a version of a Bavarian castle in the Indonesian village museum of Taman Mini.
2 Acknowledgment to A.M. Hocart's (1936) inspiration for this title.
3 The famous cross-country, 90 kilometres, annual ski walk.
4 The universally-used milk carton.

References

Auge, M. (1995), *Non-Places: Introduction to the Anthropology of Supermodernity*, London: Verso.
Hanefors, M. and Selwyn, T. (1992), 'Mobile Imagery: The Case of the Dalecarlian Horse', in J.P. Jardel (ed.), *International Tourism Between Tradition and Modernity*, Nice: University Press, Laboratoire d'Ethnologie – Universite de Nice, Centre d'Etudes Tourisme et Civilisation.
Hitchcock, M. (1998), 'Tourism, Taman Mini and National Identity', *Indonesia and the Malay World*, 26, 75, pp. 124–35.
Hobsbawm, E.J. (1975), *The Age of Capital: 1848–1875*, New York: Schribners.
Hocart, A.M. (1936), *Kings and Councillors*, Cairo.

Newspapers

Borlänge Tidning (BT) (1996), 'Konflikter runt Dalahästen', 16 February.
Dagens Nyheter (DN) (1992), 'Vem förvaltar idealen? Konsthögskolans elever undersöker utopierna', 22 May.
Dagens Nyheter (1993), 'Satiren som vapen', 15 January.
Dagens Nyheter (1994), 'Danskar är helt enkelt trevligare', 3 July.
Dagens Nyheter (1996), 'Nytt om Rinkebyhästens ursprung', 11 February.
Dagens Nyheter (1996), 'Gåtfull kompanjon', 28 August.
Dalademokraten (DD) (1998), '"Made in China". I Borlänge säljs importerade dalahästar mycket billigare än äkta', 30 September.
EX Magazine (1991), April.
Expressen (1992), 'Nu har hästen satt sig', 19 September.
Expressen (1993), 'Välkommen till Vasaloppet', 14 February.
Expressen (1993), 'Sagan om Dalahästen', 23 May.
Expressen (1993), '… och så var det Volvos tur', 6 September.
mtcKONTAKTEN (1992/93), 'Expo '92 i Sevilla och världutställningarnas ekonomiska rationalitet', (22), pp. 20–22.
Svenska Dagbladet (SvD) (1995), 'Rinkebys djur liknar inget annat', 25 July.
Svenska Dagbladet (1996), '150 Dalahästar tolkade av 150 elever i Franska skolan Saint Louis på Stora Essingen', 4 June.
Svenska Dagbladet (1996), 'Sanna gladiatorer för blågul litteratur', 3 July.

20 The 'Whimsey': A Part of American and Canadian Victoriana

IAN WEST

In 1985 the notable scholar and collector June Bedford staged an exhibition in Canada House featuring Micmac, Mohawk and Malliseet Indian souvenir art from her own personal collection, the whole of which was subsequently acquired by the National Museum of Man in Ottowa. The exhibition included moosehair and porcupine quillwork on birch bark, silk embroidery and beadwork on bags, hats, containers, moccasins and a few so-called Whimsies, and it is these latter objects that have interested me and are the subject of this short chapter. Although of no great ethnographic importance, they do have a place and are fascinating as a unique type of tourist art, apart from which they are beautiful artefacts in their own right.

Before I go further perhaps I should explain Whimsies for those who have not encountered them. The Oxford English Dictionary defines whimsey as 'a capricious idea or notion, light or fanciful, quaint and unusual' and it is thus that Whimsey is an appropriate name for these unique and rather exotic articles. The name came into general use in about 1950 when there was a resurgence of interest in these much-neglected artefacts. So Whimsies take the form of overstuffed, lavishly beaded pincushions, small shoes and boots highly decorated with the so-called 'raised' beadwork technique, hair tidies, whisk broom holders, match holders, picture and mirror frames and beaded model canoes.

These objects were produced in vast quantities and countless numbers of them were brought back to this country by travellers as souvenirs. Even today, they appear occasionally on stalls selling old beadwork and clothing at antique fairs and markets. They were made mostly by the Tuscarora and Mohawk people – tribes of what was once the renowned Iroquois Confederacy. Other tribes such as the Cayuga and Onandaga were also involved in the same trade. The Iroquois generally were also known for their manufacture of similarly decorated tourist items such as flat purses, moccasins and Glengarry hats, a vast array of which graced June Bedford's exhibition, as mentioned before.

All these were produced solely for the tourist trade and were made of commercially tanned leather and used cotton cloth, velvet, paper patters and commercial sewing thread in their manufacture. As opposed to the Whimsey, however, these objects were virtually direct descendants of pre-contact objects – all Native Americans wore moccasins and used pouches of various kinds, as their clothing had no pockets. These things would originally have been decorated with paint, porcupine and bird quills. Beads and trade cloth would have been used later, when they became available.

The Whimsey, however, was wholly an adoption from the dominant white Victorian culture, such fancy objects being quite foreign to Native American usage. It is certain that Native American women were influenced by articles in Victorian ladies' magazines, many of which encouraged their readers to take up such genteel arts as embroidery, particularly beadwork. An interesting point here is that the Native American-made items, bought as souvenirs, often became incorporated into Victorian interior house decoration, both in America and Europe and can still be seen, even today, in many old mansions and country houses as part of the Victorian decorative scheme.

Those who attended June Bedford's exhibition will have seen the room decorated in Victorian splendour, incorporating several Canadian First Nation souvenir items. The catalogue accompanying the exhibition featured a photograph of a room in a house in Manchester in 1890 showing two Huron fans with moosehair embroidered handles.

No doubt these souvenirs were sold wherever a Native American woman could find a spot to set up a sales stall, but the main outlets were the larger tourist centres such as Niagara Falls, Saratoga Springs, summer fairs and trade exhibitions. Niagara Falls was the most prolific of these sales outlets.

One might well ask why visitors to the Falls would want to buy souvenirs made by Native Americans – there must have been a hundred other mementoes of this incredible sight in the visitor centres and local shops. In the East at this time, the vision of the Noble Savage, who was also supposedly vanishing, was prevalent. The 'Indian' as wild and untamed somehow matched the Falls, and as the Falls became a symbol of America, so the 'Indian' became a symbol of the Falls. In the early nineteenth century the story of the Maid of the Mist became popular. This was the sweet Indian maiden who was supposed to have sacrificed herself for the good of her people by going over the Falls in a canoe. Hence the names of the boats that today take tourists on river trips to the Falls. This image of the noble 'Redman' became closely associated with the Falls and, as they were supposed to be a vanishing race, they posed no threat and there developed a nostalgic interest in Native American art. Add to this the fact that the area had been an important trade centre *before* the coming of white people, and that there are references in the literature to this neutral area being a place of trade for many of the local warring tribes. So it is not, perhaps, surprising that such a huge market developed in this area for Native American work in all its variations.

Such business was at its height from about 1860 to the 1920s, after which it began to die out, with a mild resurgence in the 1940s, albeit in a debased form, and it is thus produced today.

Basically, embroidery of all sorts, including beading, was a woman's preserve, but to keep pace with the demand for such things as flat purses and small pouches, men and children were called upon to use their skills in this trade and certainly children and young girls of the Tuscarora played their part in the craft of beading small purses for this tourist trade.

As has been said, Whimsies came in many shapes and forms. They were made of materials such as cotton, wool, velvet and velveteen with heavy decorative beadwork sewn with the unique, so-called 'raised' or 'embossed' stitch, whereby the sewing thread was strung with more beads than the number that would lie flat in the given distance so that the beads bunched up, forming arches on the surface. This method often reached ridiculous excesses, mainly on mirror and picture frames, when some floral work was raised half to three-quarters of an inch from the base surface. Bead sizes varied from the quite small seed beads to the larger, so-called pony beads. In fringing, and often as the central motif on most Whimsies, 'bugle' beads were also used. These were simply cut from cylindrical glass tubes and were produced in limited colours. Sequins were used scattered among the patterns, when available. Whilst similar items made by white women employed scraps and fancy backings, Native American work can most often be recognized by the use of shiny waxed cotton cambric as a backing. Cardboard was used as a stiffener and, on the flat objects, was done over a paper pattern.

Exact dating can sometimes be decided by the type and colour of beads and cloth used. Identifying the makers of particular items is more difficult, but tribal likes and dislikes can be discerned.

Shapes such as the use of scalloped edging can be seen on many examples. Motifs took ingenious forms such as birds, animals such as beavers, bowls of flowers and flags – English, Canadian and American – as well as a vast array of stylized floral patterns. Bead looping was present on many pieces as decorative hangings at the base and sometimes as handles.

Like many objects made especially for the tourist trade, these Whimsies could now be classed as bad taste – the word 'kitsch' comes to mind. They were also quite useless and had no practical purpose except as decorative memorabilia. But in spite of their sometimes bizarre appearance, their merit lies in the skill and time-consuming effort that went into their manufacture, together with the fact that of the thousands that were made, each one was a 'one-off': there were no duplicates.

The market in Native American-made souvenirs was nationwide. Records quoted by Ruth Holmes Whitehead of the Nova Scotia Museum (1978) lists 'boxes' (indicating crates rather than individual boxes) sent to Great Britain as five in 1935, nine in 1836, six in 1837, five in 1838, etc. These would be birchbark boxes with porcupine quillwork. Once the middleman took over the market expanded, and one of the first newspaper advertisements by such a one appeared in 1837, offering 'Indian porcupine quillwork consisting of boxes in nests, canoes, cigar cases and lady's (sic) reticule foundations, for sale in Halifax bazaar. April 6th, W. Carrit'.

The Abnaki (Pelletier, 1982) of Quebec had a flourishing market in basketry, model canoes, miniature snowshoes, bows and arrows, moccasins and pouches of all sorts. Most of this material was sold through middlemen calling themselves 'direct Indian agents', who also issued catalogues illustrating these various wares.

Such selling was not confined to the east. Southern Plains indigenous peoples incarcerated in Florida found a large market for pictographic drawings – the so-called Ledger drawings – and in other Plains areas, beadwork and stone-headed clubs provided the impoverished people with a small income. In the southwest dealers and traders were telling Navaho weavers what patterns and colours to use in their blankets and rugs in order to please their white souvenir hunters.

So, to sum up – and to return to Whimsies – they were just one small part of a particular market that flourished for about 60 years and, although they may never command the interest or study of ethnologists, they were a fascinating part of the souvenir business.

References

Pelletier, G. (1982), *Abnaki Basketry*, Ottowa: Canadian Ethnology Service Paper No. 85.
Whitehead, R.H. (1978), *Micmac Porcupine Quillwork 1759–1950*, Ottowa: Canadian Ethnology Service Paper No. 40.